THE
WEDDING
PAGES ®

_____

Bride

_____

Groom

_____

Date

_____

Maid of Honor

_____

Best Man

Copyright 1983, 1986, 1988 by Wedding Information Network, Inc.

Congratulations!

On behalf of all of us at Wedding Information Network, Inc., publishers of **The Wedding Pages**, *it is my pleasure to extend our best wishes to you and your fiance. Our goal is to provide the two of you with all the valuable information you need to plan the unique wedding day of your dreams.*

The Wedding Pages *has been designed to serve as your personal wedding consultant. Newlyweds all across the nation have praised* **The Wedding Pages** *for its experienced, expert advice, for its comprehensive approach to wedding planning, and for its functional workbook practicality.*

This new and expanded edition of **The Wedding Pages** *contains several additional sections not included in earlier editions, plus the most up-to-date directory of wedding professionals in your area.*

I personally encourage you to contact these professionals early in your wedding planning process. They can help you make exactly the right choices . . . choices you and your spouse will remember and cherish for the rest of your lives.

Sincerely,

Sanford L. Friedman
President

Published by

T H E

WEDDING PAGES

U.S. $19.95, Canada $26.95

11128 John Galt Blvd.
Omaha, NE 68137
(402) 331-7755
1-800-843-4983

Chairman:
Douglas A. Newman

President:
Sanford L. Friedman

Author:
Monica McFarland Foster

Editor:
Kenneth L. Nanfito

Art Director:
Frank Dolphens

Advertising Director:
Dale Ellen Solov

(402) 331-7755
1-800-843-4983

ISBN 0-929879-00-7

Copyright© 1983, 1986, 1988 by Wedding Information Network, Inc. All rights reserved. Reproduction or use without permission of editorial or graphic content in any manner is strictly prohibited.

Our Cover Bride depicts new formality with captivative elegance. A stunning array of soft satin and french alencon lace iced over with pearls and sequin clusters.

The split satin sleeves reveal more beaded lace with sheered bridal points.

The sheering on the bodice hosts a victorian lace yoke with a split mandarian collar.

The basque waist is shaped by a bubble peplum with more alencon bordering the hem and cathedral train.

J.P. Originals, Ltd., P.O. Box 724, Fremont, NE 68025.
402-721-6166 or 800-228-6135.

Cover Model: Suzie MacKenzie from American Models

Photography: Jacques Malignon

Veil: Maries Bridal Millenary

Hair: James Weigland for Dan Brennan

Makeup: Nadiya Nottingham for Timothy Priano, Inc.

Flower Arrangement: Richard Des Jardins

The information in this planning book is believed to be accurate; however, Wedding Information Network, Inc. cannot and does not guarantee its accuracy. Wedding Information Network, Inc. cannot and will not be held liable for the quality or performance of goods or services provided by advertisers listed in the directory of advertisers or any other portion of this planner.

We have helped over 1,000,000
brides and grooms plan their weddings.

Here's what they say . . .

"The Wedding Pages is like having a bridal consultant at your fingertips."

Maria A. and George B.
Danville, California

*"Our hats off to you all! In May of this year, we were married. Had we not had 'The Wedding Pages' to refer to, we are sure that our preparations would have been much more difficult. Even **two** months later, we are still using it as a reference for all the follow-up information. The emphasis on enjoying the planning and doing it 'our own way' is great!"*

Grant B. and Sandy C.
Tacoma, Washington

"I was at a local store and saw your brochure, so I sent in, thinking any little thing can help me. Little did I know I would soon receive the book that took care of everything all under one cover, helping make my dream be just the way I wanted it."

Brianna S.
New York, New York

"A word of THANKS to all involved in the making of 'The Wedding Pages'. I am getting married November 19th of this year. I cannot tell you how much this book has helped me in my preparations for my wedding. It is very informative, well put together, and is VERY, VERY HELPFUL! The section for notetaking is great! I have all the necessary information I need in this wonderful book!"

Susan H.
Chicago, Illinois

*"I was just married in June of this year and used your book, 'The Wedding Pages', as a guide to help me out. I want to thank you because it was **very helpful**! I'm a very organized person (especially in the case of my own wedding) and it was very nice to be able to find something that was already in order for me so that I couldn't forget a thing."*

Sherry S.
Houston, Texas

"I have received your wonderful book, 'The Wedding Pages', and am thrilled with it! I have also received your follow-up material helping and suggesting photographers, places for the reception, etc., etc. and I think all of this is great!"

Lisa C.
Atlanta, Georgia

How To Use This Book

1

Review the Wedding Planner section of the book. It is made up of the first 176 pages of text. This planner will provide you with all of the information you need to plan the perfect wedding.

2

The second half of the book is a directory of Wedding Professionals that desire to serve you and make your wedding day a perfect day. This directory will save you hours of time in locating those specialized Wedding Professionals truly interested in your wedding. Use the directory as a tool in selecting each category of service you will need. Remember, it is the Professionals listed in this book that support THE WEDDING PAGES and make it available to you FREE! Give them your business to show your appreciation. Be sure to mention you saw them in THE WEDDING PAGES!

3

Keep your records and schedules within the book. It provides you with budgeting records, wedding and shower gift records and calendars to keep track of appointments and other necessary tasks. Take the book with you to the various Wedding Professionals you will be contracting with in order to keep all your important records and notes in one place.

Contents

CHAPTER

I

Your Engagement

Announcements

Telling Your Families

An engagement is one occasion that you'll want everyone to know about. First, you'll want to let both your parents know. This is best done in a personal visit. If they live out of town, try to plan a trip to tell them in person.

In many cases, the parents have never met. If this is the case, plan for the families to meet. They will all want to play a role in the wedding.

A short personal note or a phone call is a good way to tell close friends or relatives about the big decision the two of you have made.

The Engagement Announcement

Next, you will want to let everyone else know. The best way is through an announcement in your hometown newspaper. These must be received at least one month before the wedding. Most papers do not take the information over the phone, but they will provide you with a form to complete.

If your paper does not have a form, there is certain information they will need from you. Call the life-style or society editor to find out what they need from you. A sample form is included showing basic information requested.

Type or print clearly to avoid mistakes. Include the name, address and daytime telephone number of someone who can verify the information you have provided. A release date should be placed at the top of the announcement.

If you would like to include a photograph with your announcement, it should be a black and white glossy, either wallet size or larger. Call your local paper for their preference. The pose should be a head and shoulder photo of the bride-to-be or the engaged couple.

Be sure to attach some kind of identification to your photo and sandwich it between stiff pieces of cardboard for protection. Follow up with a call to the newspaper to confirm the receipt of your announcement.

The Wedding Announcement

As soon as you have set the date and reserved the church, you should think about announcing your wedding. The newspaper must receive it at least one week before the wedding. The wedding announcement covers the same information as the engagement, but will also include such things as your occupations, schooling, parents, and the time and place of the wedding.

You might also want to include the officiator's name, the names of the honor attendant and the best man, the location of the reception and honeymoon, and where you plan to live.

The photograph should also be a black and white shot of the head and shoulders, but of the bride only. Remember, only one photograph will be used, however, both the engagement and wedding announcements will appear. Again, be certain to follow up with a call to the newspaper to confirm the receipt of your announcement.

Changing Your Mind

The stress of arranging your wedding can create a lot of tension for you. If a conflict develops, take time out to sort out your thoughts and feelings.

If you find you are having problems making this final commitment, you should first talk about it openly to your intended. You might also want to discuss it with your clergyman or a counselor.

If the problems are irreconcilable, you will want to postpone or cancel the wedding. In either case, act as quickly as possible.

Engagement/Wedding Information Form

Release Date: _____

BRIDE-TO-BE

Name: _____ Phone No: _____

Address: _____

_____

Occupation: _____

Employer: _____

Education: _____

BRIDE-TO-BE'S PARENTS

Name: _____ Phone No: _____

Address: _____

_____

Mother's Occupation: _____

Father's Occupation: _____

FIANCE

Name: _____ Phone No: _____

Address: _____

_____

Occupation: _____

Employer: _____

Education: _____

FIANCE'S PARENTS

Name: _____ Phone No: _____

Address: _____

_____

Mother's Occupation: _____

Father's Occupation: _____

CEREMONY

Date: _____ Time: _____ Church: _____

City: _____ Officiator's Name: _____

Engagement/Wedding Information Form

MAID OR MATRON OF HONOR

Name: _____ Relationship: _____

Address: _____

_____

BEST MAN

Name: _____ Relationship: _____

Address: _____

_____

VERIFIED BY: _____ Phone No: _____

SIGNATURE: _____

Rings

Purchasing Information

One major wedding expense that will endure and appreciate in value is your ring. Shopping together will assure that both of you will be pleased with your choice. It will also help you to stay within your budget.

Before shopping, decide on a price range. Keep in mind that jewelry prices are set according to the purity and type of metal, the quality of the gem and the workmanship of the setting. Consulting a reputable jeweler will assure you the most for your money.

There are four criteria to keep in mind when purchasing a diamond ring. The first is the cut. Although many confuse cut with the shape, most diamonds are cut with a full 58 facets. The work of a master cutter permits the maximum amount of light to be reflected through the diamond. This gives it more scintillation and sparkle. The shape of the diamond is a matter of personal preference and does not affect the value per se. The most common shape is round, but rectangular, pear shaped, heart shaped or marquise (oval) designs are also seen.

The best color for a diamond is no color. This is because a totally colorless diamond acts as a prism, allowing light to pass effortlessly through the diamond and be transformed into rainbows of color.

> ### "The best color for a diamond is no color."

Diamonds have the capability to produce the maximum amount of brilliance. A diamond that is virtually free of interior or exterior inclusions, or flaws, is of the highest quality. Nothing interferes with the passage of light through the diamond. The diamond's clarity is determined by viewing it under a 10-power magnification by a trained eye. Minute inclusions neither mar its beauty nor endanger its durability, however, the clearer the diamond, the higher its value.

The number of carats is a measure of the weight of the diamond. One carat is divided into 100 points. Size is the most obvious factor in determining the value of a diamond. This does not mean the bigger diamond is necessarily better. The value depends on the quality. Diamonds of high quality can be found in all size ranges.

Some brides may choose a gem other than a diamond for their engagement ring. If you do, remember you will most likely be wearing this ring every day. Talk to your jeweler to find out the characteristics of the stone you choose.

Once you have decided on the stone, select the metal. Gold and platinum are the most popular. Gold is usually yellow or white in color. Most rings are either 14K or 18K alloys. Pure gold, 24K, is too soft for rings.

Platinum, a white metal, is the strongest ring metal available. It is also the most expensive. Usually, it is used for prongs in gold rings.

Matching Ring Sets

The popular choice of many brides is to have a matching engagement ring and wedding band. This is not a must. Just make sure the styles you choose complement each other. You may also choose a wedding band that matches your groom's. Because more grooms are wearing wedding rings, make sure he is happy with the selection too. Diamonds aren't just a girl's best friend. Diamonds can add just the right touch to your groom's wedding band. Consult your jeweler for a wide variety of styles, gems and metals.

Custom Designs

Many jewelers will do custom design work for you to make the rings uniquely yours. This allows your creativity to become a permanent part of your life together.

Insurance

Protect your investment by insuring your new rings as soon as possible. Discuss this with your jeweler.

Caring for Your Rings

Daily wear can leave soap, lotion or skin oil film on the stone and mounting of your ring. Regular cleaning brings back the brilliance. There are several ways to do this.

Let the ring stand in a solution of mild household detergent for a few minutes. Then clean with a small soft brush. Rinse under warm water and pat dry with a soft cloth.

Allow your ring to soak for about 30 minutes in a solution of half water and half ammonia. Loosen the dirt with a brush. Let your ring dry. This should not be done with pearls or opals.

Also available are liquid cleaners that are specially formulated for jewelry. Usually stocked by jewelers, all it takes is a dip to clean your ring. This should not be done with pearls or opals.

Guidelines

To avoid damage or loss of your rings it is important to keep the following in mind.

1. Have your jeweler check the prongs once a year to make sure they are not loose or worn.
2. Don't let your ring come in contact with bleach or other harsh chemicals. It may pit or discolor the mounting.
3. Don't wear your rings when you are doing rough work. Hard blows can chip your gem and damage the prongs.
4. When removing your ring for cleaning or laundry, don't leave it on the sink. It could fall down the drain or you might forget it. Put it in your ring box or in your purse.
5. Store your diamond in its own compartment. It can scratch other gems.

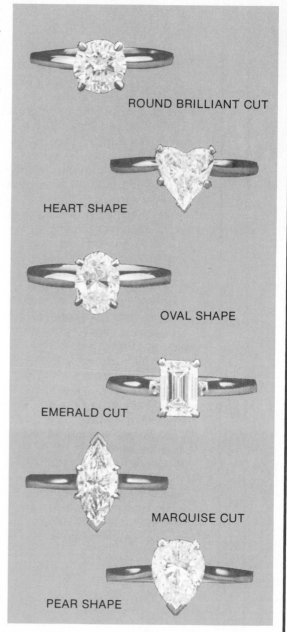

ROUND BRILLIANT CUT

HEART SHAPE

OVAL SHAPE

EMERALD CUT

MARQUISE CUT

PEAR SHAPE

CHAPTER

II

Expenses and Budget

Expenses and Budget

THE EXPENSES

In the past, the bride and her family have assumed the majority of the wedding expenses. But, as so many traditions have changed, so too has the financial responsibility. Many couples are choosing to divide the cost between the couple and both sets of parents. Below are some traditional guidelines you may want to follow.

Bride and Her Family

- Wedding dress, headpiece and accessories.
- Trousseau of clothes and lingerie.
- Wedding stationery, personal notes and mailing costs.
- Cost of reception . . . hall rental, caterer, food, music, flowers and decorations.
- Cost of ceremony . . . rental fees, decorations and musicians.
- Groom's wedding ring.
- Physical exam and blood test.
- Gifts for bride's attendants.
- Photographs at the wedding and reception.
- Video of wedding.
- Transportation for bridal party.
- Attendants' bouquets.
- Groom's gift.
- Wedding guest book.
- Wedding consultant's fee.

They might also pay for

- Accommodations for out-of-town bride's attendants and guests.

Groom and His Family

- Bride's rings.
- Marriage license.
- Honeymoon.
- Wedding gift for bride.
- Gifts for best man, groomsmen and ushers.
- Flowers . . . bride's bouquet, corsages for mothers and grandmothers.
- Boutonnieres for groom's attendants.
- Fee for clergyman.
- Physical exam and blood test.

- Rehearsal dinner.
- Formal wear rental.

They might also pay for

- Accommodations for out-of-town groomsmen, ushers and guests.
- Liquor at the reception.

Attendants and Ushers

- Travel expenses.
- Wedding attire.
- Parties or entertainment for the bridal couple.
- Wedding gift for couple.

THE BUDGET

Because this is a day you have dreamed of for a long time, you will no doubt want the best of everything. This is not an impossibility, but first you must consider your budget.

Traditionally, the bride's parents paid for everything, but it has become increasingly popular for the groom's parents and the couple to share the expenses. It is best for all involved to sit down and discuss the type of wedding the two of you would like and estimate the costs.

Included in this book are budget worksheets. There is a section for each major expense with room for any additions you need to make. At the end is a section recap to tie everything together. Using the budget worksheets will keep everything in one place, thus making it easier to keep track of the expenses.

In order to avoid any last minute misunderstandings which might frustrate this very memorable occasion, it is advisable to sign contracts for all goods and services needed in the wedding. The contract should list the services to be performed, the dates and times at which they are to be performed, and the charges to be paid for the services. This contract does not necessarily have to be formal, but at the minimum a document spelling out all of the details and signed by both parties. It is also important for you to get receipts for all deposits you have made.

The Rings Budget

	ESTIMATED COST	ACTUAL COST
Bride's engagement ring	_____	_____
Bride's wedding ring	_____	_____
Groom's wedding ring	_____	_____
TOTALS	_____	_____

The Ceremony Budget

	ESTIMATED COST	ACTUAL COST
Church or ceremony site	_____	_____
Officiator	_____	_____
Organist	_____	_____
Musicians	_____	_____
Soloist	_____	_____
Aisle runner	_____	_____
Candles	_____	_____
Canopy	_____	_____
Decorations (other than flowers)	_____	_____
Miscellaneous		
_____	_____	_____
_____	_____	_____
_____	_____	_____
_____	_____	_____
_____	_____	_____
TOTALS	_____	_____

The Reception Budget

	ESTIMATED COST	ACTUAL COST
Room/hall rental	_____	_____
Cakes & Mints	_____	_____
Food	_____	_____
Entertainment	_____	_____
Beverages	_____	_____
Decorations (other than flowers)	_____	_____
Additional Services (servers, bartenders, parking valets)	_____	_____
Rental Equipment (linens, china, tables, chairs, etc.)	_____	_____
Wedding Consultant	_____	_____
Miscellaneous		
_____	_____	_____
_____	_____	_____
_____	_____	_____
_____	_____	_____
_____	_____	_____
TOTALS	_____	_____

The Wedding Attire Budget

	ESTIMATED COST	ACTUAL COST
Bride's dress	_____	_____
Headpiece/Veil	_____	_____
Alterations	_____	_____
Shoes	_____	_____
Lingerie	_____	_____
Jewelry	_____	_____
Accessories	_____	_____
Formal Wear rental	_____	_____
Bridal gown preservation	_____	_____
Miscellaneous		
_____	_____	_____
_____	_____	_____
_____	_____	_____
_____	_____	_____
_____	_____	_____
_____	_____	_____
_____	_____	_____
_____	_____	_____
_____	_____	_____
TOTALS	_____	_____

The Photographer Budget

	ESTIMATED COST	ACTUAL COST
Formal engagement		
Glossy (engagement)		
Formal wedding		
Glossy (wedding)		
Album		
Proofs		
Candids		
Parents' sets		
Photographer Fee		
Miscellaneous		
TOTALS		

The Videographer Budget

	ESTIMATED COST	ACTUAL COST
Ceremony		
Reception		
Miscellaneous		
TOTALS		

The Floral Budget

	ESTIMATED COST	ACTUAL COST
CEREMONY SITE		
Altar or chuppah	_____	_____
Pew markers	_____	_____
Bride's bouquet	_____	_____
Attendants' bouquets	_____	_____
Boutonnieres	_____	_____
Corsages	_____	_____
RECEPTION SITE		
Room/hall	_____	_____
Cake table	_____	_____
Buffet table	_____	_____
Head table(s)	_____	_____
Guest tables	_____	_____
Miscellaneous		
_____	_____	_____
_____	_____	_____
_____	_____	_____
_____	_____	_____
TOTALS	_____	_____

The Balloon Budget

	ESTIMATED COST	ACTUAL COST
CEREMONY SITE		
Altar or chuppah	_____	_____
Pew markers	_____	_____
RECEPTION SITE		
Room/hall	_____	_____
Cake table	_____	_____
Buffet table	_____	_____
Head table(s)	_____	_____
Guest tables	_____	_____
Miscellaneous		
_____	_____	_____
_____	_____	_____
_____	_____	_____
_____	_____	_____
TOTALS	_____	_____

The Stationery Budget

	ESTIMATED COST	ACTUAL COST
Invitations	_____	_____
Announcements	_____	_____
At home cards	_____	_____
Thank you notes	_____	_____
Personal stationery	_____	_____
Printed napkins	_____	_____
Matches	_____	_____
Cake Boxes	_____	_____
Guest Book	_____	_____
Plumed Pen	_____	_____
Ceremony programs	_____	_____
Reception favors (place cards, wedding scrolls or ribbons)	_____	_____
Marriage certificate holder	_____	_____
Miscellaneous		
_____	_____	_____
_____	_____	_____
_____	_____	_____
_____	_____	_____
TOTALS	_____	_____

The Gifts Budget

	ESTIMATED COST	ACTUAL COST
Bride	_____	_____
Groom	_____	_____
Bride's attendants	_____	_____
Groomsmen & ushers	_____	_____
Hostess	_____	_____
Host	_____	_____
Guest book attendant	_____	_____
Miscellaneous		
_____	_____	_____
_____	_____	_____
_____	_____	_____
_____	_____	_____
_____	_____	_____
_____	_____	_____
_____	_____	_____
_____	_____	_____
_____	_____	_____
TOTALS	_____	_____

The Transportation Budget

	ESTIMATED COST	ACTUAL COST
Transportation	_____	_____
Parking	_____	_____
Miscellaneous		
_____	_____	_____
_____	_____	_____
_____	_____	_____
_____	_____	_____
TOTALS	_____	_____

Miscellaneous Expenses

	ESTIMATED COST	ACTUAL COST
_____	_____	_____
_____	_____	_____
_____	_____	_____
_____	_____	_____
_____	_____	_____
_____	_____	_____
_____	_____	_____
TOTALS	_____	_____

Wedding Expense Record

DESCRIPTION	AMOUNT BILLED	DEPOSIT PAID	BALANCE DUE	DATE DUE	EXPENSE OF BRIDE/FAMILY	EXPENSE OF GROOM/FAMILY
Ceremony						
Flowers						
Balloons						
Gifts						
Photographer						
Videographer						
Reception						
Rings						
Stationery						
Transportation						
Wedding Attire						
Miscellaneous						
Total						

Notes _____

_____

_____

_____

_____

_____

_____

_____

_____

_____

_____

_____

CHAPTER

III

Timetables

Timetables

Checklist Calendar

Nine to Twelve Months Before

- ☐ Determine the type of wedding you want, size, degree of formality, setting.
- ☐ Select a wedding date and time.
- ☐ Notify your clergymember and reserve date and time for wedding and rehearsal.
- ☐ Set a tentative budget.
- ☐ Decide how expenses will be shared.
- ☐ Shop together for wedding rings.
- ☐ Determine the size of the guest list.
- ☐ Plan reception and book reception location. (Note: This should be booked as soon as the wedding date is set to assure availability.)
- ☐ Select and book caterer.
- ☐ Select and book photographer.
- ☐ Select and book videographer.
- ☐ Select and book entertainment.
- ☐ Select and book transportation for wedding day.
- ☐ Compile names and addresses of your guests.
- ☐ Decide on your color scheme.
- ☐ Select wedding attendants, yours and his.
- ☐ Determine sizes for all attendants.
- ☐ Choose your dress and headpiece.
- ☐ Schedule fittings and delivery date.
- ☐ Choose bridesmaids' dresses and accessories.
- ☐ Start planning for your honeymoon.
- ☐ Discuss where you will live after the wedding.
- ☐ Choose music and musicians/soloists for the ceremony and reception.

Six to Nine Months Before

- ☐ Announce your engagement in the newspaper.
- ☐ Register your preferences at the bridal registries of your choice.
- ☐ Maintain records of all gifts received and send thank you notes immediately upon receipt of your gifts.
- ☐ Select florist and/or balloonist and discuss color schemes.
- ☐ Begin shopping for men's wedding attire.

Four to Six Months Before

- ☐ Start health and fitness program.
- ☐ Order invitations and other related stationery needs.
- ☐ Complete your guest list.
- ☐ Help both mothers coordinate and select their dresses.
- ☐ Ensure that all bridal attire has been ordered.
- ☐ Begin shopping for trousseau.
- ☐ Check blood test and marriage license requirements.
- ☐ Experiment with hair style and cut.
- ☐ Select baker and order wedding cake, groom's cake, and mints.

Two to Three Months Before

- ☐ Choose the men's wedding attire and reserve the right sizes.
- ☐ Start addressing invitations and announcements.
- ☐ Purchase accessories such as toasting goblets, ring pillow, garter, candles, etc.
- ☐ Confirm all details with your hired professionals.
- ☐ Confirm ceremony details with your officiant.
- ☐ Arrange rehearsal details.
- ☐ Plan rehearsal dinner.
- ☐ Plan attendants' parties.
- ☐ Choose responsible person to attend your guest book.
- ☐ Make appointment with your hairdresser.
- ☐ Arrange accommodations for out-of-town attendants and guests.
- ☐ Finalize honeymoon plans.

One Month Before

- ☐ Finish addressing invitations and mail them four weeks before the wedding.
- ☐ Get blood test and marriage license.
- ☐ Have your final dress fitting.
- ☐ Have formal bridal portrait done.
- ☐ Have final fitting for wedding attendants.
- ☐ Purchase gifts for wedding participants.

- [ ] Purchase gift for fiance.
- [ ] Complete shopping for your trousseau.
- [ ] Have attendants' parties.
- [ ] Purchase going-away outfit.
- [ ] Ensure that your accessories are in order—toasting goblets, garter, candles, ring pillow, etc.
- [ ] Finalize rehearsal dinner details.
- [ ] Make a calendar of events for your wedding day.
- [ ] Draw a map to direct guests to the ceremony and reception sites if necessary.

Two Weeks Before
- [ ] Finish addressing announcements to be mailed on your wedding day.
- [ ] Contact guests who have not responded.
- [ ] Pick up the wedding rings and make sure they fit properly and that engraved inscriptions are correct.
- [ ] Meet with your photographer and give him/her a list of special pictures you want taken.
- [ ] Meet with videographer and give him/her a list of special events or people you want in the videotape.
- [ ] Meet with entertainer and give him/her a list of the music to be played during special events such as bouquet tossing, garter tossing, dollar dance, etc.
- [ ] Continue writing thank you notes for gifts received.

One Week Before
- [ ] Provide the caterer with the total guest count and confirm all details.
- [ ] Provide your wedding party and out-of-town guests with timetables and maps if necessary for the rehearsal dinner, ceremony and reception.
- [ ] Review details on last minute arrangements and timetables with all service companies.
- [ ] Plan seating arrangements, if used.
- [ ] Confirm all honeymoon reservations and accommodations, pick up tickets and travelers checks.
- [ ] Discuss the details of the reception with your host and hostess.
- [ ] Assign tasks to be done on the wedding day to your wedding party.
- [ ] Practice applying makeup and styling your hair and determine the amount of time needed to do this on your wedding day.
- [ ] Make sure you have your marriage license.
- [ ] Pick up wedding attire and make sure everything fits properly.
- [ ] Keep writing thank you notes for gifts received.
- [ ] Pack your suitcase for your honeymoon.
- [ ] Rehearse wedding ceremony with all participants in attendance.
- [ ] Attend rehearsal dinner.
- [ ] Give the best man the officiator's fee and instruct him to deliver it on the day of the wedding.
- [ ] Get a good night's sleep the night before your wedding day.

On the Wedding Day
- [ ] Remain calm and try to relax.
- [ ] Don't forget to bring the wedding rings and your marriage license.
- [ ] Check with florist to ensure that flowers will be delivered on time.
- [ ] Apply makeup and style your hair slowly.
- [ ] Start dressing 1½ hours before the ceremony.
- [ ] If pictures will be taken before the ceremony, the entire wedding party should be dressed and ready about two hours before the ceremony.
- [ ] Mail the wedding announcements.
- [ ] Have music start thirty minutes before the ceremony begins.
- [ ] Have guests seated as they arrive.
- [ ] Groom's parents should be seated five minutes before the ceremony begins.
- [ ] The bride's mother should be seated immediately before the processional, and before the aisle runner is rolled out.

After the Wedding
- [ ] Write and mail all thank you notes as soon as possible.
- [ ] Take care of business and legal affairs (change name if necessary on records and legal documents) as soon as possible.

Calendars

For the Month of _____

For the Month of _____

For the Month of _____

Calendars

☐	☐	☐	☐	☐	☐	☐	☐
☐	☐	☐	☐	☐	☐	☐	☐
☐	☐	☐	☐	☐	☐	☐	☐
☐	☐	☐	☐	☐	☐	☐	☐

For the Month of _____

☐	☐	☐	☐	☐	☐	☐	☐
☐	☐	☐	☐	☐	☐	☐	☐
☐	☐	☐	☐	☐	☐	☐	☐
☐	☐	☐	☐	☐	☐	☐	☐

For the Month of _____

☐	☐	☐	☐	☐	☐	☐	☐
☐	☐	☐	☐	☐	☐	☐	☐
☐	☐	☐	☐	☐	☐	☐	☐
☐	☐	☐	☐	☐	☐	☐	☐

Calendars

For the Month of _____

For the Month of _____

For the Month of _____

Calendars

For the Month of _____

For the Month of _____

Calendars

For the Month of ______________________

☐	☐	☐	☐	☐	☐	☐	☐
☐	☐	☐	☐	☐	☐	☐	☐
☐	☐	☐	☐	☐	☐	☐	☐
☐	☐	☐	☐	☐	☐	☐	☐

For the Month of ______________________

☐	☐	☐	☐	☐	☐	☐	☐
☐	☐	☐	☐	☐	☐	☐	☐
☐	☐	☐	☐	☐	☐	☐	☐
☐	☐	☐	☐	☐	☐	☐	☐

For the Month of ______________________

☐	☐	☐	☐	☐	☐	☐	☐
☐	☐	☐	☐	☐	☐	☐	☐
☐	☐	☐	☐	☐	☐	☐	☐
☐	☐	☐	☐	☐	☐	☐	☐

CHAPTER

IV

Arrangements

There are so many things to think about when planning your wedding. Don't worry. The following sections will tell you everything you need to know about planning your wedding. There is a section for every major division in your wedding. Following each section is a list of pertinent questions to ask the professional who will assist you. There are also checklists, examples and illustrations to make things easier for you.

SECOND MARRIAGE

Brides who have been married before often worry that their second wedding should be smaller or more subdued than their first. Since there are no longer any strict "rules" regarding second marriages, your choice of wedding style and size is entirely up to you, your fiance, and your families. Your second wedding may be just as big, or bigger, than the first. This is a time for celebration.

Another concern for these brides is the color of their wedding gowns. White is still considered an appropriate color, for it is not a question of purity, but rather a time of joy.

Families

If you or your groom have children, it is appropriate to make them a part of the ceremony. You may even have a daughter or son act as attendant if they are of suitable age. Make sure your children have a desire to be a part of the wedding.

Often, former in-laws are close to the bride or groom. They may be invited, but first consult them to make sure they would like to participate. You should also be sure your future spouse feels comfortable having them at the wedding.

Friends that were introduced through your prior marriage, and are now your friends, should be treated as such. They, too, are interested in sharing your happiness.

YOUR CEREMONY

Location

The location of your wedding will often depend on the religious affiliation of you and your groom. Although the ceremonies of all creeds are similar in several respects, some denominations have distinctive features. To find out what is required of you and your groom, the first person you should contact is your clergyman.

He can tell you what his preferences are as well as the details of the wedding ceremony itself. Meeting with him a minimum of nine to twelve months in advance will enable you to integrate your special touches with the requirements of the rite.

The clergymember should also be contacted to explain the details of traditional ceremonies. If you and your groom are of different faiths, this meeting is especially important. Often, you will have to make arrangements for a ceremony involving clergy from both denominations. Some religions also require pre-marital counseling sessions.

If you wish to have your wedding in his church or synagogue, you will also need to ask about the rules for photographers, videographers, ceremony music, decorations and special equipment such as aisle carpets, extra chairs, candles and live or recorded music. You will also need to ask about the rules for throwing rice or bird seed. Many, if not most, churches and reception locations will no longer allow rice to be thrown because it kills birds if they eat it and people may slip on it. However, the throwing of bird seed is generally accepted at these locations since no clean-up is necessary. It may be purchased in decorative individual packages for convenience in distributing to your guests. A checklist is provided to assist you with these important considerations.

> ## "Some religions require pre-marital counseling sessions."

Make sure the site you choose has enough parking for your guests and secure dressing rooms with good lighting and mirrors.

If you are using a commercial site or wedding chapel, you should first indicate your religious preferences and inquire what types of officiants, ceremonies, and other assistance they can make available to you. In some cases, you may still need to provide your own clergy, but they can assist with many of the other matters. You may still need to cover most of the points mentioned above however.

Most clergymembers charge a fee or request a donation. It will vary, so be sure to ask. Some fees will cover everything, but others only include the use of the facility. Extra charges may be required for such things as candles, the organist, custodial and other services.

Wedding Styles

The formality of your wedding will determine where it will be held and how it should be put together. It will also depend on custom, budget and personal preference.

A very formal wedding is usually held in a church, synagogue, temple or hotel. Engraved stationery, formal portraits, a large reception dinner, many floral displays, an orchestra and a limousine are normally included. There are between four and twelve attendants including one usher for every fifty guests, a maid or matron of honor, best man, bridesmaids, groomsmen, a flower girl and a ringbearer. A wedding consultant can be helpful in arranging the wedding for the full effect.

A formal wedding includes many of the same elements as the very formal, but it may be held in a hotel, restaurant, banquet room, private club, wedding chapel or someone's home, in addition to a religious setting. Engraved invitations with separate reception cards should be used. The large reception and other areas may be arranged by a wedding consultant. The number of attendants is the same.

The location for a semi-formal wedding is the same, except the reception is often held in the same place as the ceremony. A single engraved or handwritten invitation is satisfactory for both. Many of the formalities may be eliminated, but there should still be one usher for every fifty guests, as well as two to six attendants.

The rules of good taste govern the informal wedding. Handwritten or telephone invitations are the rule. It may take place in a home or even outdoors.

The Rehearsal

Except in the case of an informal wedding, there should be a rehearsal to insure the ceremony will run smoothly. You will want to have it at the wedding site if that is possible. Be sure to make the arrangements with your clergymember well in advance.

The rehearsal should be held a few days before the wedding, although it is common to have it the night before if there are out-of-town participants. All members of the wedding party, the organist/musician, and the soloist should be present as decisions made at this time will affect them. Your clergymember will be able to assist you with such things as what kind of step you will use walking down the aisle, the order of the wedding party in the processional and recessional, and who stands where at the altar.

Take this time to let him hear any special music you have chosen. He may be able to offer recommendations about any changes you might want. Make sure you are prompt!

If your wedding is being handled by a wedding consultant, many of the details can be prearranged, easing the burden on your clergymember.

The Rehearsal Dinner or Party

The rehearsal dinner party is usually given by the groom's parents, but it can be given by someone else if the parents are some distance away. The dinner itself can be an elaborate formal dinner, a casual dinner, or even a barbecue. It can be held at a restaurant, a hall, or in someone's home.

The dinner guests should include both sets of parents and stepparents, if appropriate, all the adult attendants of the bridal party with their spouses or dates and the parents of the child attendants. Many also include the clergymember presiding over the ceremony, relatives and out-of-town guests.

Because the dinner is often the night before the ceremony, a few recommendations are in order. First, do not try to plan the affair yourself. Professional party planners, your wedding consultant, caterers, or friends and relatives can take on that responsibility. Secondly, try to have the dinner end at a reasonable hour. You are going to want to be well rested for the next day's ceremony.

A casual note or phone call is considered a proper invitation. Double check transportation arrangements for all attendants during the dinner.

The Processional

The bride's family and friends should be seated on the left side of the altar and the groom's family and friends should be seated on the right side of the altar. The seating is just the reverse in a Jewish wedding. Just before the processional begins, the groom's mother is escorted by the best man or one of the ushers, followed by his father. The bride's mother is the last to be seated according to traditional Christian order. She is escorted by the head usher to the front and seated on the left. In Jewish ceremonies, both parents escort the bride and groom.

If the aisle runner has not previously been rolled out, then two ushers will roll it out. As the music begins, the bride's mother gives the cue to stand. The procession begins with the groomsmen, paired according to height. They are followed by the bridesmaids, either singly or paired. Next comes the maid or matron of honor, the ringbearer and flower girl. At the end of the procession is the bride with her father (or male relative if the father is deceased).

> *"The bride's mother gives the cue to stand."*

During this time, the clergymember, followed by the groom and his best man, will make their way to the altar.

Once at the altar, the groom and his best man stand to the right in front of his parents. The bride's father, standing on her right, will then "give his daughter away" by offering her hand to the groom. At that time, the clergymember will precede them to the altar. The maid of honor stands to the bride's left, holding her bouquet and the groom's ring. The best man stands to the groom's right holding the bride's ring.

As with many aspects of your wedding, the processional is flexible and can be done many different ways.

The Recessional

The bride and groom lead the recessional arm in arm. The bride should be on her groom's right. They are followed by the maid of honor with the best man, then the bridesmaids paired with the groomsmen. The bride's and groom's parents will follow. The bridal party may also leave according to religious custom, or in the order you choose.

Ushers should then remove ribbons from reserved sections and escort honored guests up the aisle.

The Receiving Line

It is your responsibility to greet and thank each of your guests. It is the custom to have a receiving line at the church immediately after the ceremony, as not all guests will attend the reception. If your party is large, however, you may wish to have the receiving line at the reception.

As the wedding hostess, the first person in the receiving line should be the bride's mother, standing next to her the groom's father, then the groom's mother and the bride's father. Next should come the bride and groom, the maid of honor and then the bridesmaids. The best man and ushers do not take part in the receiving line. This will be an excellent opportunity for them to get the transportation in order for the bridal party.

An alternative to the receiving line is for the bride and groom to re-enter the church after the recessional. Beginning on the bride's side, at the row closest to the altar, the couple releases the aisles and greets every guest as they leave. The couple continues this, alternating between the bride's and groom's sides until all guests have been greeted. This method is especially helpful if parents are divorced or just don't wish to participate in the receiving line.

Traditional Ceremony Formations

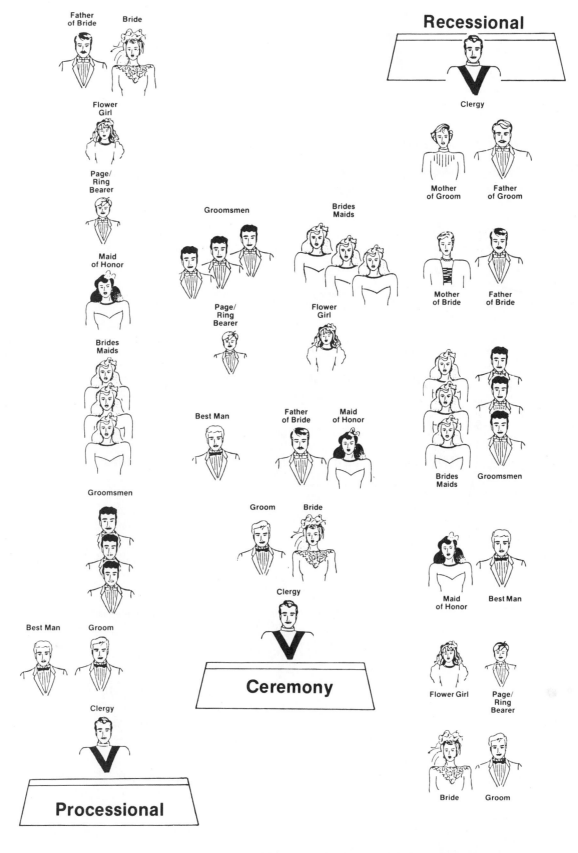

Recessional

Clergy

Mother of Groom — Father of Groom

Mother of Bride — Father of Bride

Brides Maids — Groomsmen

Maid of Honor — Best Man

Flower Girl — Page/Ring Bearer

Bride — Groom

Father of Bride — Bride

Flower Girl

Page/Ring Bearer

Maid of Honor

Brides Maids

Groomsmen

Best Man — Groom

Clergy

Processional

Groomsmen — Brides Maids

Page/Ring Bearer — Flower Girl

Best Man — Father of Bride — Maid of Honor

Groom — Bride

Clergy

Ceremony

Receiving Line Formation

Mother of Bride — Father of Groom — Mother of Groom — Father of Bride — Bride — Groom — Maid of Honor — Brides Maid — Brides Maid — Brides Maid

Reception Seating Arrangements

Head Table with the Bridal Party

Brides Maid — Groomsman — Brides Maid — Best Man — Bride — Groom — Maid of Honor — Groomsman — Brides Maid — Groomsman

Best Man — Bride — Groom — Maid of Honor

Bridal Party Table

Brides Maid

Groomsman

Groomsman — Brides Maid — Groomsman — Brides Maid

Grand-mother — Father of Groom — Mother of Bride — Clergy

Parents Table

Father of Bride — Mother of Groom — Grand-father

Best Man — Bride — Groom — Maid of Honor

Bridal & Parents Table

Father of Bride

Mother of Bride

Father of Groom — Mother of Groom — Clergy

Jewish Ceremony Formations

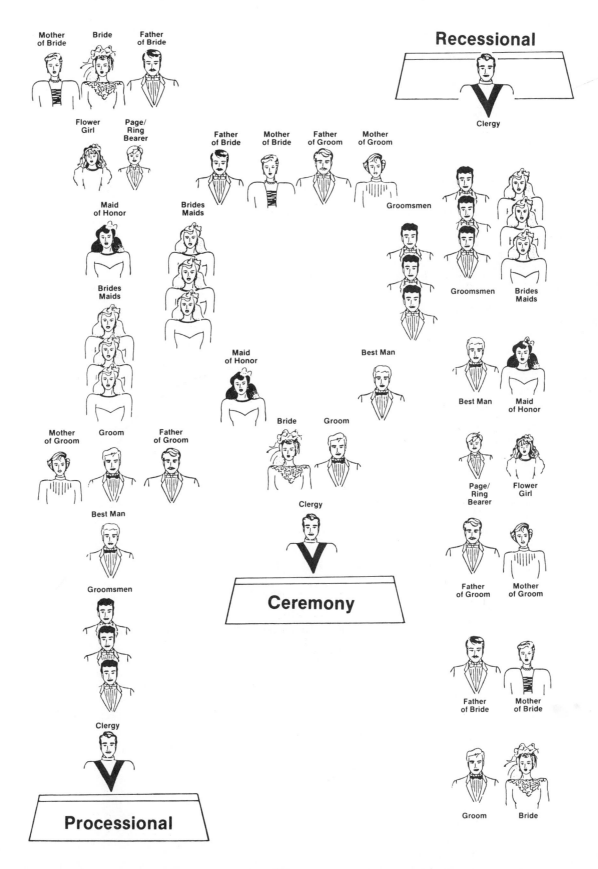

Mother of Bride   Bride   Father of Bride

Recessional

Clergy

Flower Girl   Page/Ring Bearer

Father of Bride   Mother of Bride   Father of Groom   Mother of Groom

Groomsmen

Maid of Honor

Brides Maids

Groomsmen   Brides Maids

Brides Maids

Maid of Honor   Best Man

Best Man   Maid of Honor

Mother of Groom   Groom   Father of Groom

Bride   Groom

Page/Ring Bearer   Flower Girl

Best Man

Clergy

Ceremony

Father of Groom   Mother of Groom

Groomsmen

Father of Bride   Mother of Bride

Clergy

Processional

Groom   Bride

Church/Synagogue Ceremony Checklist

Date and time of wedding: _____

Location of ceremony: _____

Clergymember or officiator: _____

    Address: _____ Phone: _____

Date and time of rehearsal: _____

Dressing facilities for bridal party: _____

Church/Synagogue requirements concerning:

    Attire: _____

    Flowers or decorations: _____

    Photographer: _____

    Videographer: _____

    Type of music: _____

    Type of readings: _____

    Throwing of bird seed or rice: _____

    Composing own vows: _____

    Aisle runner: _____

Does the church/synagogue provide:

    Aisle runner: _____ Knee cushion: _____ Canopy: _____

Officiator fees: _____ Church/synagogue use fee: _____

Organist fee: _____ Soloist fee: _____

Miscellaneous: _____

Ceremony Music

The music is an important aspect of your wedding. It sets the tone of the ceremony and expresses so much emotion. While your guests are being seated, the prelude music, beginning thirty minutes prior, should be playing.

The processional march will introduce you and your attendants. The recessional will be joyous in expressing the celebration of your marriage.

Options

This music can range from organ to harp and anything in between. Some churches require you to use their organist and have certain requirements concerning secular music. The ultimate decision of what selections are played, however, is up to you.

One or more soloists are often hired to provide that special music. Be sure to contact the soloists you desire as early as possible to assure they have the date open.

You might also consider a string or woodwind quartet, harpist or pianist. They can give just the right feeling of intimacy and formality. If you are marrying in a home or garden and space doesn't allow musicians, you might want to use recorded music of your favorite selections.

> *"You might consider a string or woodwind quartet, harpist or pianist."*

Musicians and soloists performing in your wedding should be included in the rehearsal and invited to the rehearsal dinner. Remember to ask the amount of their fee. If you are using a close friend or relative, a gift is appropriate.

Rather than leave the decision to the last minute, the music should be selected as soon as the location of your wedding has been determined. In case any problems arise, this will give you time to come up with alternatives.

The time each selection is to be played should be set. During rehearsal, make sure the musicians and soloists know their cues.

Music Selections

Bridal Chorus - Lohengrin's (Here Comes the Bride)

Wedding March - Mendelssohn's (Midsummer Night's Dream)

Wedding March - Alexander Guilmant

The Lord's Prayer - Malotte

The Wedding Song - Peter, Paul and Mary

Evergreen - Barbra Streisand

The Hawaiian Wedding Song - Andy Williams

Three Times a Lady - Commodores

Lady - Kenny Rogers

First Time Ever I Saw Your Face - Roberta Flack

Loving You - Minnie Ripperton

Sunrise Sunset - from Fiddler on the Roof soundtrack

Feelings - Morris Albert

Longer - Dan Fogelberg

Truly - Lionel Richie

Beautiful - Gordon Lightfoot

Misty - Johnny Mathis

Chances Are - Johnny Mathis

That's All - Johnny Mathis

Endless Love - Diana Ross and Lionel Richie

I Only Have Eyes for You - Art Garfunkle

Unforgettable - Nat King Cole

I Love You So - McDonald and Chevalier

Waiting For A Girl Like You - Foreigner

Up Where We Belong - Joe Cocker

In the Mood - Glenn Miller

New York, New York - Frank Sinatra

Theme from Ice Castles - Melissa Manchester

Because of You - Tony Bennett

Love Theme from The Godfather - Andy Williams

Arthur's Theme - Christopher Cross

Could Have Danced All Night - Anne Murray

When I Fall in Love - Lettermen

You Are the Sunshine of My Life -
Stevie Wonder

On the Wings of Love - Jeffry Osborne

Can't Help Falling in Love - Elvis Presley

Try to Remember - Harry Belafonte

Only You - The Platters

Colour My World - Chicago

You Light Up My Life - Debby Boone

Love You Just the Way You Are - Billy Joel

And I Love You So - McLean

The Hands of Time (Brian's Song) -
Michel LeGrand

Hopelessly Devoted To You -
Olivia Newton John

More - Ortolani and Oliviero

Love Song - Anne Murray

Our Love - Carpenters

I Just Want to be Your Everything -
Andy Gibb

What Are You Doing the Rest of Your Life -
Michel LeGrand

Annie's Song - John Denver

Top of the World - Carpenters

The Song Is Love - Peter, Paul and Mary

I Won't Last A Day Without You -
Andy Williams

A Love Song - Kenny Loggins

Time In A Bottle - Jim Croce

Till There Was You - Beatles

In My Life - Beatles

A Time For Us - Snyder

Sunshine On My Shoulders - John Denver

Sound of Music -
Rodgers and Hammerstein

Sometimes - Henry Mancini

People - Barbra Streisand

Love Is A Many Splendored Thing -
Percy Faith

This Is The Day - Brown

Through the Eyes of Love - Sager/Hamlisch

Celebration - Cool And The Gang

Something - Beatles

You Are So Beautiful to Me - Joe Cocker

You've Made Me So Very Happy -
Blood, Sweat and Tears

We've Only Just Begun - Carpenters

Beginnings - Chicago

Ceremony Music Checklist

PRELUDE

Time/Cue: _____ Selection: _____

Time/Cue: _____ Selection: _____

Time/Cue: _____ Selection: _____

FIRST SOLO

Time/Cue: _____ Selection: _____

PROCESSIONAL

Time/Cue: _____ Selection: _____

BRIDE'S ENTRANCE

Time/Cue: _____ Selection: _____

SECOND SOLO

Time/Cue: _____ Selection: _____

THIRD SOLO

Time/Cue: _____ Selection: _____

RECESSIONAL

Time/Cue: _____ Selection: _____

POSTLUDE

Time/Cue: _____ Selection: _____

MUSICIANS

_____ Cost: _____

_____ Cost: _____

SOLOISTS

_____ Cost: _____

_____ Cost: _____

TOTAL COST: _____

Reception

Now that you're married, it's time for everyone to share in the celebration. The reception should reflect and complement the tone and style of your wedding. By planning ahead with some important professionals, your reception will be a fun and joyous occasion. They can help you make sure it is well organized, alleviating any worry. There are a few things you should keep in mind while planning your reception.

Guidelines

1. Plan at least nine to twelve months in advance, especially if you are getting married during the popular wedding months (summer). The best idea is to book the location as soon as the wedding date is set. You may have to set the wedding date based on reception facility availability.
2. Let the hour of the ceremony offer the approximate guide to the appropriate reception.
3. If possible, invite all your guests to both the ceremony and the reception.
4. The reception should immediately follow the ceremony.

> **"Plan at least nine to twelve months in advance."**

The Site

The location you choose for your reception will depend on your date, its availability, the price and the number of people that will be attending. There are many types of facilities available.

The most common locations are hotels, restaurants, private clubs or halls. They normally have the facilities and complete food services available for the reception.

Churches or temples are also possibilities. If you choose to use this type of facility, be sure you know the policy regarding alcoholic beverages and any music restrictions they may have. It is also important for you to know what the fee will be and if they will allow you to use your own caterer.

Homes or gardens are often the location of the reception. If you are planning the reception in a garden, be sure to have a site that will allow you to move inside if the weather does not cooperate.

In many areas of the country, yachts or other ships and boats are available for receptions. They will take the reception party on a short cruise and provide all the food and alcoholic beverages. Mansions, too, are available for rent. They may be used for the ceremony, the reception or both.

The grounds of a winery can be a beautiful site for the reception and the ceremony as well. Many wineries will rent out their grounds for a ceremony and help make your reception one to remember.

Historical and public sites are available in some places. There are many beautiful homes and old mansions that have been donated to local governments that can be rented for your wedding ceremony or as a reception location.

To find a site that suits your needs, first phone and ask for a description of the facility and what type of services they provide — catering, waiters and waitresses, bartenders, parking valets, and checkroom attendants. If it seems to fit your needs, make an appointment for a tour.

While on the tour, make sure there is enough room to accommodate all your guests. See that there are enough electrical outlets, in the right places, for the entertainment. If you are going to decorate the room or hall, see if there are any restrictions.

Your reception location may be the perfect choice for other wedding-related functions as well — such as wedding showers, engagement parties or the rehearsal dinner.

During this meeting you will want to ask about the fee. How long will you have the hall? Are you the only party to use the facility for that day, allowing you to go beyond the time contracted for? Who is your contact person? Can you deal exclusively with them? Can you set up the night before or must you wait until the morning of the ceremony? Will they provide the clean-up services or must you provide them yourself? Are tables and chairs provided? Is there a dance floor available? What is its capacity?

Because this will be a busy time for you, you may want to ask them if there is anything else you should know. This way there will be no misunderstandings.

The management of some halls and banquet rooms can also provide catering and liquor. The following sections will assist you with these decisions.

It is important to let them know where the fire exits and telephones are located at the reception in case of an emergency. You may wish to have your wedding consultant perform this function to alleviate any stress on those in attendance at the wedding reception.

Host and Hostess

To allow you to enjoy the party and alleviate any worry on your part, you may want to invite several of your relatives or close friends to act as hosts and hostesses at your reception. They will greet your guests, assist them in finding their seats if seating is assigned, instruct your guests at the buffet table and mingle to be sure everyone is enjoying themselves.

Reception Location Questions

When selecting your reception location, ask these questions:

1) Will it accommodate all of my guests comfortably?
2) Does it have adequate parking? Handicapped parking?
3) Are there adequate restroom facilities?
4) Is the dance floor large enough?
5) Is there a public address system?
6) Will you provide extras such as valet parking, serving attendants or bartenders?
7) Is security necessary? If so, will you provide it?
8) Are there enough electrical outlets for the entertainment?
9) Am I required to use your food and beverages?
10) Are there enough tables and chairs?
11) How early can I get in to set up?
12) By what time must I be out?
13) Will I be responsible for clean-up?
14) Will someone be on hand to let the caterer, florist, baker, etc. in?
15) How much will it cost?
16) How much are all the extras?
17) How soon must it be reserved?
18) How much is the deposit? When is it due? When is the balance due?
19) What is the cancellation policy?
20) Are the guests permitted to throw bird seed or rice?
21) What measures are taken for liquor liability?

Reception Location Checklist

TYPE OF RECEPTION

☐ Sit-Down   ☐ Buffet   ☐ Cocktails/Hors d'oeuvres

☐ Cake/Punch   ☐ Garden   ☐ Other: _____

WHEN AND WHERE

Wedding Date: _____ Time: _____ Place: _____

Reception Time: From _____ To _____ Location: _____

Manager: _____ Phone No: _____

CONTRACT INFORMATION

Guaranteed Rate? _____ Deposit? _____ Amount? _____

When is deposit due? _____ Balance due? _____

Cancellation terms? _____

FACILITIES

Catering service? _____ If not, are there kitchen facilities? _____

Who provides & serves liquor? _____

Are tables & chairs provided? _____ Bar facilities? _____

Decoration limitations? _____ If so, what? _____

Is room accessible early for decorating? _____ Time: _____

Only party to use facility for that day? _____

Dance floor available? _____ Ample power outlets? _____

Room capacity? _____ Dance floor capacity? _____

Will there be a representative available during reception? _____

Clean up requirements? _____

Are there ample parking facilities? _____ Restroom facilities? _____

Host and Hostess Checklist

HOST

Name: _____ Phone No:_____

Address:_____

Relationship to couple: _____

HOSTESS

Name: _____ Phone No:_____

Address:_____

Relationship to couple: _____

INFORMATION FOR HOST & HOSTESS

Time to be at reception:_____

Introduce to master of ceremonies: _____

Introduce to manager or caterer: _____

Schedule of events during reception: _____

Location of telephones and fire exits: _____

Professional Planners

Wedding Consultant

There are so many details to attend to when planning a wedding. If you are already busy with work responsibilities or if you are planning your wedding out-of-town, the professional services of a wedding consultant are invaluable.

A wedding consultant can offer expert wedding advice and guidance. The professional locates the florist, caterer, photographer, musicians and other wedding retailers and services that will create the special atmosphere you desire. Using a wedding consultant does not mean you give up control of your own wedding. Instead, you add a very competent facilitator to your wedding staff. In fact, there are many advantages to using a consultant.

You probably have many ideas for your special day. A wedding consultant has the skill and knowledge necessary to incorporate these details into your wedding plans. The consultant can also warn you of any pitfalls in your plans and provide acceptable alternatives.

Although the wedding day is supposed to be for you and your groom, many times well-meaning family and friends may pressure you in your planning. A consultant can act as a buffer between the bride and her family, enforcing the bride's wishes.

Not only does a wedding consultant ease your mind by seeing to details, she can also save you time and money. It takes hours to research and locate wedding services and retailers. The consultant's experience and expertise enables her to find the right merchant who will provide exactly what you are looking for.

> ## "A wedding consultant can save you time and money."

A wedding consultant knows the most cost effective ways to plan a wedding while staying within your budget. The planner maximizes the bride's buying power. Wedding service retailers know the consultant will continue using their products and services only as long as they provide quality at a fair price.

It is also possible to use the consultant's services for the rehearsal dinner. This is just another way of delegating the responsibilities during this very busy time.

Party Planners

Party planners can help to create the exact setting and atmosphere you are looking for at your reception. A professional party planner will help you select a theme, coordinate music, food, flowers and proper decor. All of the necessary tools will be right at their fingertips.

By communicating what you are looking for in the reception and with the help of the planner's ideas, you can have a reception that will be as unique and impressive as you want.

It is also possible to use a party planner's services for the rehearsal dinner.

Wedding Chapel

Some wedding chapels offer services similar to that of wedding consultants. They can plan the wedding and reception, provide the site, and even arrange for the clergy.

This service can be especially helpful if you and your spouse-to-be are of different religious affiliations.

Baker

The picture-perfect wedding is not complete without the wedding cake. Whatever flavor, filling, icing, topping, size, shape, or decoration you select, it is sure to make an impression on your guests.

At least four months in advance, shop around for a quality baker. Ask to see pictures or models of their cakes. Compare cost and workmanship.

When deciding on your cake, don't let yourself be limited by tradition. Although chocolate, yellow and white cakes are delicious, lemon, spice, rum, carrot and pound flavors can provide a unique taste. You might want to try combining your cake flavor with a custard, lemon, chocolate, strawberry, mocha or coconut filling.

Now, how would you like your cake to look? The elegance of a tiered cake has made it the favorite. Usually frosted white, the flower or border decorations are usually pastel. You may want two, three, or even four tiers. This is often determined by the number of guests. Whatever the size, the shape can be heart-shaped, round or square.

Top your cake with the traditional bride and groom or an arrangement of fresh flowers, sugar wedding bells, or glass top.

Be sure to get the detailed instructions on how the cake should be cut, taken apart, and what decorative pieces need to be returned.

When ordering your cake, you may also wish to order a groom's cake and wedding mints. There are many flavors, colors and styles available for each.

At the Reception

The cake should have its own table, perhaps decorated with flowers and ferns.

When it is time to cut the cake, standing on his left, you and your new husband will cut the first slice together and share it. This insures future happiness.

Ask the baker if the cake knife is included in the package. If you wish to have a family member cut the rest of the cake, ask that a waitress be near for any assistance.

The top layer should be kept and frozen for your first wedding anniversary.

Need a checklist to work with your planning? Take a look on the next pages.

Baker Questions

When selecting your baker, ask these questions:

1) Do you specialize in wedding cakes?

2) What types of wedding and grooms cakes do you make?

3) Do you specialize in any flavor, style or size?

4) May I have a taste test of the cake and frosting?

5) When will you deliver and set up the cake?

6) Do you supply a cake knife? What is the best way to cut the cake?

7) When do I need to return the support pieces?

8) Do you make mints? If so, what colors and shapes are available?

9) What are the payment terms?

10) How far in advance should I order my cake?

Baker Checklist

WEDDING CAKE

Cake Shape   □ Two Tier   □ Three Tier   □ Four Tier   □ Flat

Other _____

Cake Flavor   □ Yellow   □ White   □ Chocolate   □ Lemon   □ Spice

Other _____

Filling Flavor   □ Lemon   □ Chocolate   □ Strawberry   □ Mocha

Other _____

Icing Flavor   □ Lemon   □ Vanilla   □ Butter Cream   □ Chocolate

Other _____

Topping   □ Flowers   □ Bells   □ Bride & Groom   □ Love Birds

Other _____

Other Decorations   □ Fountain   □ Stairsteps to side tiers   □ Figurines

Other _____

GROOM'S CAKE

Flavor: _____ Size: _____

Cake boxes provided? _____ No. of packages needed: _____

MINTS

Type: _____ Shape: _____ Color: _____

Quantity: _____ Cost: _____

EXTRAS

Is cake knife provided with wedding cake? _____

Extra sheet cakes available? _____ Cost: _____

Will instructions be provided for cake cutting? _____

COST

Guaranteed Rate? _____ Deposit? _____ Amount: _____

Written Contract? _____ Balance Due: _____

Cancellation terms: _____

Caterer

When it's time to plan your reception, choosing the right caterer is most important. An experienced one should be able to deal with everything from soup to nuts. Because the catering is such an integral part of your reception, you should interview prospective caterers at least nine to twelve months in advance. The details concerning the menu selections should be confirmed three months before the date.

Food

The food served is determined by the time of day. Ask to see a number of menus and rely on your caterer's experienced advice. Menus should include such items as hors d'oeuvres, canapes and a variety of buffet and main dishes. You might also provide special foods for those guests with dietary or health concerns.

Generally, the caterer will supply all dishware, flatware, glasses, cups, saucers and table linens. If they do not provide all you need, chances are they work closely with suppliers that do.

Services

Decide what services you will need. Can the caterer provide servers, waiters, bartenders and valet parking? Is this cost included or is it a separate charge? When does everything go into effect and how much extra is it? Does the labor charge include clean-up?

Bar

Most caterers supply mixers, garnishes, ice, glasses, napkins and perhaps a bartender. Although most state and local laws prohibit them from providing liquor, their expertise in party-giving will prove very useful to you. Don't forget to check on facilities for ice with the person in charge at your reception.

Reception Planning

The caterer can be a great benefit to you in many areas. He can help you decide where and how to set up tables, what to serve and also give you ideas for table decorations, such as ice sculptures.

Cost

The cost of catering will depend on the services and food provided. Some caterers charge a flat rate or on an all-inclusive per head basis. Before you sign anything, make sure you know what's included and what your responsibilities are. Check to see if the gratuities are automatically added to the final bill. Your contract should specify the food and beverages to be served plus the number of people to serve the food and beverages. All estimates should be in writing.

A deposit is usually required when signing the contract. In case there are any problems at a later date, ask about postponement and cancellation policies and charges.

Caterer Questions

When selecting your caterer, ask these questions:

1) What equipment is provided?
2) For what services are there additional charges?
3) Are labor charges additional? For how many and how much?
4) When does overtime go into effect?
5) Are taxes and gratuities extra?
6) Does the cost cover set-up and clean-up?
7) How much is the deposit? When is it due? When is the balance due?
8) When is the deadline for notifying you regarding menu selection?
9) What are the postponement and cancellation policies?
10) Will you cut the cake and supply plates and forks?
11) Will you serve the buffet or is it self-serve?
12) If self-serve, will you provide waiters/waitresses to collect dishes after guests have finished eating?
13) Will you provide references or a portfolio?
14) What are the sizes of the portions?
15) Do you use disposable china and flatware?
16) Will you serve the punch and coffee?
17) How do you determine the head count?
18) Will you set up the room?
19) Can you provide colored linen and ice sculptures?
20) How much will the extras cost?

Caterer Checklist

TYPE OF RECEPTION

☐ Formal   ☐ Buffet   ☐ Hors D'oeuvres   ☐ Cake and Punch

COST

Per Person Rate: _____ Estimated Guests: _____ Cost: _____

Flat Rate: _____ Estimated Guests: _____ Cost: _____

Deposit: _____ When is balance due? _____

Cancellation Terms: _____

_____

SERVICES

If buffet, will bridal party be served? _____

Is representative available on site? _____

Name: _____ Phone No: _____

When is final guest estimate needed? _____

Is a diagram of the table and seating arrangements provided? _____

Is there a minimum charge? _____ If so, how much? _____

How many waiters and waitresses will be provided? _____

How long will they serve at the reception? _____

What type of equipment does the caterer provide? _____

_____

_____

_____

_____

_____

_____

_____

_____

_____

Wedding Reception Menu Worksheet

Hors d'oeuvres:_____

_____

Appetizers: _____

_____

Soup/Salad: _____

_____

Beverages: _____

_____

Breads/Rolls: _____

_____

Main Course:_____

_____

_____

Side Dishes:_____

_____

Desserts: _____

_____

Nuts:_____

Wedding Cake: _____

Groom's Cake: _____

Mints: _____

_____

Miscellaneous: _____

_____

_____

_____

Beverages

The location of your reception will determine the decisions you make about the liquor and service that will be provided for your guests. If it is to be held in a hotel or restaurant, you will most likely not be allowed to provide your own liquor. You will either want to limit the open bar during the cocktail hour followed by a cash bar or provide your guests with an unlimited open bar. Be sure to find out how the cost of drinks is determined and get an estimate based on the number of guests you expect to attend.

You may have to supply the liquor if the reception is held in a hall or private home. A liquor dealer will be able to assist you in determining the types of liquor and the quantities needed. The liquor dealer may also provide bartenders and set up the bar at the reception site. Since this is such a busy day for you, be sure to utilize these services available to you. Don't forget to ask about returning the unopened bottles.

Types of Liquor and Mixes

White wines, scotch, bourbon, blended whiskies, vodka, gin, rum, and beer are the popular liquor choices. The preferences of your friends and relatives will also be a factor in your final selection.

In addition to the liquor, you will also want a good stock of mixes. Tonic water, bitters, lemon, club soda and ginger ale are the standard choices. In addition, lemon, lime and orange juice or sections are used in the preparation of many cocktails. You will also want to have tomato juice and spices on hand for those who prefer Bloody Marys.

Alcohol Alternatives

Not all of your guests will want to consume alcoholic beverages. Be sure to include a stock of carbonated beverages, juices, carbonated waters, coffee, and fruit punch.

Champagne

What wedding reception would be complete without champagne? You should have enough on hand for the toasts. (A case will allow 50-60 guests one drink apiece.) Extra cases are necessary for those who prefer to stay with champagne.

An enchanting addition to any reception is a champagne fountain. This dazzling spectacle will insure lifetime memories for you and your guests.

Beverage Questions

When selecting your beverage dealer, ask these questions:

1) Do you offer a volume discount?

2) How much liquor and other beverages should I order?

3) What alcohol alternatives would you suggest?

4) Do you supply ice?

5) Do you supply bartenders?

6) Do you supply bar supplies and equipment?

7) Do you deliver the beverages and equipment?

8) Will you pick up the equipment?

9) Is a deposit required for the equipment?

10) Can we return unopened bottles?

Beverage Checklist

SUPPLIED BY WHOM

Liquor:_____ Mixers:_____ Garnishes:_____

Ice:_____ Bartenders:_____ Equipment:_____

BARTENDERS

Name:_____ Phone:_____

Name:_____ Phone:_____

Name:_____ Phone:_____

Name:_____ Phone:_____

OPEN BAR COST

Bar open from: _____ to: _____ Estimated No. of Guests: _____

How charged? _____ Estimated cost: _____

CASH BAR COST

Bar open from: _____ to: _____ Estimated No. of Guests: _____

How charged? _____ Estimated cost: _____

DINNER

Is bar to be closed during meal? _____

Beverages served during dinner?_____

FOUNTAINS

Kind of champagne: _____ Quantity:_____

Kind of punch:_____ Quantity:_____

Beverage Checklist

LIQUOR

Kind: _____ Source: _____ Quantity: _____

Kind: _____ Source: _____ Quantity: _____

Kind: _____ Source: _____ Quantity: _____

Kind: _____ Source: _____ Quantity: _____

Kind: _____ Source: _____ Quantity: _____

Kind: _____ Source: _____ Quantity: _____

MIXERS

Kind: _____ Source: _____ Quantity: _____

Kind: _____ Source: _____ Quantity: _____

Kind: _____ Source: _____ Quantity: _____

Kind: _____ Source: _____ Quantity: _____

Kind: _____ Source: _____ Quantity: _____

Kind: _____ Source: _____ Quantity: _____

GARNISHES

Kind: _____ Source: _____ Quantity: _____

Kind: _____ Source: _____ Quantity: _____

Kind: _____ Source: _____ Quantity: _____

Kind: _____ Source: _____ Quantity: _____

EQUIPMENT

Type: _____ Source: _____

Type: _____ Source: _____

Type: _____ Source: _____

ALCOHOL ALTERNATIVES

Kind: _____ Source: _____ Quantity: _____

Kind: _____ Source: _____ Quantity: _____

Kind: _____ Source: _____ Quantity: _____

Kind: _____ Source: _____ Quantity: _____

Favor Favorites

In addition to the fond memories your guests will have of your wedding day, you may also wish to allow them some special remembrances. Bomboniere, Italian for favors, can provide a special touch to your wedding and bridal showers. What types of favors are available? The list is nearly endless.

If reasonably priced favors are what you are interested in, provide a candy tray for each reception table, purchase or make individual packets of candies such as mints, Jordan almonds or other assorted candies. Long-stemmed chocolate roses in a variety of wrappings can also add a unique touch.

Individual miniature bottles of liquor, liqueur or sparkling wines from Spain, Italy or the United States are another idea. They can be purchased by the case.

Poems, scrolls, imprinted napkins or matchbooks are special. Or, fill long-stemmed satin rosebuds with rice or birdseed and personalize them with a stamped ribbon. These can become keepsakes for your guests.

If your style is more elaborate, you may be interested in porcelain items or assorted ceramics. Have them custom-fired with you and your groom's names and the wedding date in gold. You may also etch the information in glassware, brass, pewter, sterling or silver-plated items.

Shops and stores handling such favors will have a selection of items and ideas for you. Their ideas and your imagination can make your wedding one to remember.

Reception Entertainment

Because your guests will be made up of people from all age groups, you will want to select your reception music carefully. If you prefer to have live music, there are many groups to choose from. Your choice of entertainment should be made as soon as possible, since entertainers book up to a year in advance. If you are not sure of the type of entertainment you want or the groups available in your area, an entertainment agency or company that specializes in weddings can assist in selecting both the type of music and group best suited to your needs. Using an entertainment agency relieves you of the responsibility of seeing that the band is at the reception on time.

An orchestra, a small combo, a band, or an individual can set the mood you want. Whatever you decide, find out how many people are involved, what they will wear, how many breaks they will take and how long they will play. Union rules mandate one 15 minute break every hour for musicians. The entertainers should provide recorded music during their breaks.

Be sure to find out if their rate is computed on an hourly basis or if they charge a flat fee. If you think your reception will go past the time you have hired them for, ask how much they charge for additional time.

If you want the leader to act as master of ceremonies, be sure to let him know when you will cut the cake and toss the bouquet and garter. Also, let him know what special tunes you would like played for special dances and what music you do not want. You may want to ask them for suggestions, since these individuals and groups provide music for many weddings.

"Be sure to ask for references."

Mobile recorded music is a popular alternative to live music. It can allow you more versatility in the music that is played. It can range from big band, rock, country and western, to ethnic music such as the hora or the polka. The disc jockey who manages the show can provide the professional sound systems and special lighting effects.

Before you hire the entertainer, be sure to ask for references and ask to listen to them perform. It is often possible to see them perform on videotape. For the protection of both parties, you should request a written contractual agreement. It should be drawn up immediately upon making your decision.

You should select the entertainment as soon as you know the site. Book your entertainment at least six to twelve months before the wedding. Make sure there are enough electrical outlets and decide where they will be positioned. If the reception will be outside, decide where they will go if it rains. Also be sure to provide the entertainer with the reception facility contact person, so he/she can coordinate a set-up time and space requirements.

To assist you in making the right choices, a convenient checklist has been provided for your use. Following this page you will find a complete checklist for your final musical selections.

Reception Entertainment Questions

When selecting your reception entertainment, ask these questions:

1) Can I see a video recording or live performance of the individual or group that will appear at my wedding?

2) Can you play a variety of music? For example: dance music, specialty songs for polkas, horas, tangos, big band or jazz?

3) Will you act as master of ceremonies?

4) Are you affiliated with a union? If so, what rules apply?

5) Will you dress appropriately?

6) How long will you play? How many breaks will you take?

7) Will you provide music during the breaks?

8) When is the deadline for notifying you?

9) How much will it cost?

10) How do you handle overtime?

11) Will you supply special effects lighting? For example: mirror ball, strobe or spotlight?

12) How long will it take to set up equipment? Will you do it before the guests are scheduled to arrive?

13) What is your policy regarding cancellations and postponements?

14) Will you accept special requests?

15) Will you be available to play longer if the reception time is extended?

16) Will you allow us to control the volume of your music?

Reception Entertainment Checklist

TYPE OF MUSIC

Live or recorded music? _____

Name of group: _____ Leader: _____

Number of musicians: _____ Phone No: _____

Name of disc jockey: _____ Phone No: _____

Type of attire: _____

COST

Guaranteed Rate? _____ Deposit Required? _____ Amount? _____

When is deposit due? _____ When is balance due? _____

Flat fee? _____ Hourly rate? _____ Overtime rate? _____

Cancellation terms: _____

GENERAL INFORMATION

Hours of Music: _____ From: _____ To: _____

Continuous music? _____ Background music during dinner? _____

If breaks, how often? _____ How long are the breaks? _____

Will leader act as master of ceremonies? _____

Take special requests? _____ Equipment requirements? _____

Will same members & leader play at wedding? _____

Need early set-up time? _____ When? _____

REFERRALS

_____

_____

_____

_____

Reception Entertainment Special Requests

RECEIVING LINE

Time/Cue: _____ Selection: _____

ARRIVAL OF BRIDE & GROOM

Time/Cue: _____ Selection: _____

BACKGROUND MUSIC

Time/Cue: _____ Selection: _____

Selection: _____

Selection: _____

Selection: _____

Selection: _____

Selection: _____

Selection: _____

DURING DINNER

Time/Cue: _____ Selection: _____

Selection: _____

Selection: _____

Selection: _____

Selection: _____

Selection: _____

Selection: _____

FIRST DANCE

Time/Cue: _____ Selection: _____

DOLLAR DANCE

Time/Cue: _____ Selection: _____

Reception Entertainment Special Requests

SPECIAL REQUESTS

Time/Cue: _____ Selection: _____

Time/Cue: _____ Selection: _____

Time/Cue: _____ Selection: _____

Time/Cue: _____ Selection: _____

Time/Cue: _____ Selection: _____

Time/Cue: _____ Selection: _____

Time/Cue: _____ Selection: _____

Time/Cue: _____ Selection: _____

CAKE CUTTING

Time/Cue: _____ Selection: _____

THROWING OF BOUQUET

Time/Cue: _____ Selection: _____

THROWING OF GARTER

Time/Cue: _____ Selection: _____

LAST DANCE

Time/Cue: _____ Selection: _____

Decorations and Rental Equipment

DECORATIONS

The color scheme you choose for your attendants' dresses and flowers should prevail through to the linens and other decorations at your reception.

If you decide the reception hall needs a few extra touches, you might want to use floral arrangements on every guest table, candelabras for soft lighting or tall vases filled with seasonable flowers. Ice sculptures, fountains, candles, balloons and colored lighting can also provide decorating ideas. (See Florist and Balloonist Sections.)

Ask the manager what he may be able to provide for you or ask for any recommendations. Depending on the time of the year or holiday season, you can make it all very festive without spending a lot of money. Don't forget, you can always rent!

RENTAL EQUIPMENT

Why buy when you can rent it! What you rent will of course depend on what type of ceremony and reception you have chosen, the location, your budget and your needs. Looking into the types of items rented can give you ideas for your wedding.

If your dreams have always included an outdoor wedding or reception, a party canopy might solve your worries about rain or extreme heat. There are a variety of tent styles and sizes available.

Rental Equipment Questions

When selecting rental equipment, ask these questions:

1) What items are available for rent?
2) Will you deliver the rental items?
3) When can the items be picked up? Delivered?
4) When must they be returned? Picked up?
5) How much is the rental fee?
6) Is there a deposit? How much is it? When must it be paid? When is the balance due?
7) When must the items be reserved?

Other examples of rental items are:
- Tables and chairs
- Coat racks
- Linens
- Serving pieces
- Dishware
- Glasses
- Flatware
- Punch bowl
- Tents, canopies, awnings
- Aisle runner
- Candelabras
- Portable bars
- Dance floors
- Fountains
- Decorations

To add a special touch, rent unique items like mirrored tabletops and placemats, glass napkin rings, an illuminated dance floor, a marquee, or even live trees. Be creative!

For a better idea of what you can rent, contact your rental agent. We have also provided a worklist for you. Keep these concerns in mind when dealing with rental agencies. Remember, many times these agencies can save you money.

Rental Equipment Checklist

COST

Rental agency: _____

Deposit required? _____ Amount: _____

Rates guaranteed? _____ Balance due: _____

Cancellation terms: _____

_____

GENERAL INFORMATION

Delivery provided? _____ Pickup provided? _____

Representative available in case of problem? _____

Representative name: _____ Phone No. _____

ITEMS RENTED FOR CEREMONY

Item: _____ Cost: _____ Pickup/return date: _____

Item: _____ Cost: _____ Pickup/return date: _____

Item: _____ Cost: _____ Pickup/return date: _____

Item: _____ Cost: _____ Pickup/return date: _____

Item: _____ Cost: _____ Pickup/return date: _____

ITEMS RENTED FOR RECEPTION

Item: _____ Cost: _____ Pickup/return date: _____

Item: _____ Cost: _____ Pickup/return date: _____

Item: _____ Cost: _____ Pickup/return date: _____

Item: _____ Cost: _____ Pickup/return date: _____

Item: _____ Cost: _____ Pickup/return date: _____

TOTAL COST _____

Attire

Bridal Gown

A favorite experience for most brides is shopping for the wedding gown. Although there are many styles, fabrics and colors to choose from, there is one gown that is right for you. This gown should suit your height, weight, body shape and the type of wedding you are planning.

To get an idea of what is available, look through bridal shops and department stores.

There may be several dresses that you like. To narrow down the choices, try them on while shopping with someone whose opinion you trust.

If you have an antique gown in your family, it may be possible to restore it to its original beauty. A restoration expert can look at it and tell you what the possibilities are.

In most areas, local merchants sponsor bridal shows. Attending these allows you to see current as well as traditional styles. You will also get many ideas for just the right accessories that will complement that special dress you have chosen.

While shopping, there are several things to keep in mind. First, be sure to stay within your budget. It is often helpful to budget a little extra money for your gown as an allowance for unforeseen expenses, such as alterations and undergarments.

If you find the perfect gown is not available and choose to customize your own wedding gown and/or that of your attendants, there are many reputable custom tailors and designers that you may contract to do this. If you choose to make the dresses yourself, consult a fabric store that specializes in bridal fabrics and accessories. Keep in mind, however, that making your own wedding attire will take a considerable amount of time.

Second, shop at least nine months before your wedding if possible. This will give you plenty of time to find the perfect dress for you and to have it ordered and altered if necessary.

Finally, make sure the style of gown matches the type of wedding you plan to have: very formal, formal, semi-formal or informal.

Very formal wedding gowns are usually made of satin, lace or Peau de Soie and are floor length. They are worn with a long train, either cathedral or chapel length. Veils are full length and decorated with lace, beading or silk flowers. The bride carries an elaborate bouquet of flowers or a flower-trimmed prayer book. Shoes may be adorned with lace or pearls and may be purchased from bridal shops or better shoe stores. If the gown is short-sleeved or sleeveless, long gloves can be worn to enhance the formality.

The **formal wedding** gown has a chapel or sweep train and is a little less elaborate. The white gown is usually worn with hem-length veil or mantilla, but a shoulder or fingertip-length veil or hat may also be worn. Shorter sleeved dresses may be worn with white kid, lace or matching fabric gloves. The bouquet is simpler, but the shoes and accessories are the same style as in a very formal wedding.

The bride in a **semi-formal wedding** should wear an elegant short dress or a simple floor-length dress without a train. Accessories and flowers are simpler than those in a formal wedding. A short veil is worn with a street-length dress; a longer veil may be worn if the dress is a floor-length dress. A hat or flowers in the hair are also seen.

A street-length silk suit or jacketed dress is appropriate for an **informal wedding**. These are usually white, but may be any other color except black. If you would like to include flowers, they should be worn, not carried.

The Veil

The veil should complement the bride's height, facial contours, hair style and gown. It is usually made of nylon or silk illusion, but old lace is also popular. Many have several layers with the piece closest to the face called the 'blusher'. It is worn over the bride's face during the ceremony and turned back by the maid of honor before the bride is kissed by the groom.

There is a wide variety of headpieces. Your selection should be chosen with the same consideration used in selecting a veil.

Accessories

Jewelry, if worn, should be simple. Small earrings and a delicate chain or pearl necklace may be worn. Because the jewelry selection is so important, rely on a jewelry store professional to assist you in matching your style and that of your dress. Your engagement ring is worn on your right hand until after the ceremony when it may be moved back to the left.

Many shops specialize in shoes and accessories for the bride and her attendants. They can assist you in matching colors and making sure your shoes are comfortable.

Lingerie shoud be as elaborate as the wedding gown you choose. Not only will it enhance the fit of your gown, but it will also make you feel as beautiful as you look. Petticoats should be the same length as your gown. They should be white if your gown is white, nude if your gown is pastel. Your bra should not show above the lines of the bodice. Plain, patterned or embroidered stockings can be worn, but choose a shade the color of your gown.

The bride's garter is an optional accessory. If worn, it should be made of lace, satin or ribbon and placed just above your knee. Tradition calls for the groom to remove the garter during the reception. It is tossed by the groom after the bride has thrown her bouquet.

Bridal Gown Preservation

While your wedding is a time of great joy, it is also a big investment. One of the most beautiful and costly items is your wedding gown. A good understanding of the care your gown requires will preserve its beauty for generations to come.

Before you bring your gown home, be sure you understand the care procedures completely. Knowing the variety of fabric, lace and other decorations that make up your gown will assist your professional dry cleaner to properly clean the garment after the wedding.

No matter how careful you are on your wedding day, your gown will be soiled to some extent. All gowns will absorb perspiration and body oils. It is also likely to sport food and beverage stains. If a long train is part of your gown, it will pick up soil on the hem and train.

To make sure this does not ruin your gown, do your best to keep food and beverages off the gown. Also, it is best to have the gown professionally dry cleaned within a few days or weeks of your wedding. Remember, the longer the stains are on the dress, the more likely they are to become permanent.

Storage

To preserve your gown, it should be wrapped in proper storage materials or in a hermetically sealed box. It should then be stored in a cool, dry, dark place. A hot attic or damp basement are not good locations.

A periodic check of the gown is a good idea. This will allow you to locate any stains that may be developing. If they are caught in time, a professional cleaner may be able to remove them. After the cleaning, repack the gown carefully for continued storage.

Bride's Attendants

Once you have selected your gown, it is time to select the dresses that your attendants will wear. Their dresses should be of the same length and formality to complement your own. Shop with your honor attendant and choose her dress first. Then narrow the selection to about three dresses you find appropriate for your attendants. Allow them to make the final decision, since they usually assume the cost of their own dresses.

Make sure the dresses you select are simple enough to flatter a variety of figures. Because the attendants will have their backs partially toward the guests during the ceremony, the backs of their dresses are important. Bows, inserted panels and a graceful line are desirable.

The color is usually chosen according to season. The dresses can all be the same color or graduated. In many cases, the honor attendant wears a different color or a deeper tone of the same color. Her style of dress, however, should be the same. Your attendants may wear white, but their dresses should be trimmed with color or colorful accessories. Keep in mind that a white dress will take away from the effect of the bride.

The accessories for the attendants should be understated. A soft hat or a wreath of flowers in the hair looks becoming. They may carry bouquets, a single flower or, with an old-fashioned dress, a basket of flowers. Shoes and stockings should match the dresses and, if not identical, should be carefully coordinated. Bridal shops and better shoe stores can dye the shoes to match the dresses. When dying, take a fabric sample so the shoes match the dresses perfectly.

If you are having children in your wedding, keep in mind that they will perform better if they are wearing clothes they are comfortable in.

and groom are on display as much as other members of the wedding party, their dresses should be selected carefully.

Because they too should harmonize with the style and formality of the wedding and yet be flattering to the figure and coloring of the mothers, it is helpful for both mothers to shop together with the bride.

Mothers of the Bride and Groom

Because the mothers of the bride

Bridal Gown Questions

When selecting your bridal gown, ask these questions:

1) How long will it take to special order my size?
2) How much is the deposit?
3) When must the deposit and balance be paid?
4) What are the exchange and cancellation policies?
5) When should I schedule the appointment for my final fitting?
6) How much are alterations?
7) Can I have formal portraits taken at the salon?
8) What is the cost for extra size and extra length?
9) Can I bring the dress back to the shop to be pressed?
10) Is there a charge for pressing?

Bridal Gown Preservation Questions

When selecting your bridal gown preservationist, ask these questions:

1) Will you dry clean my gown before you preserve it?
2) If not, can you recommend someone who can?
3) How soon after the wedding should this be done?
4) How much will it cost?
5) How should I care for my preserved gown?
6) Will my gown be vacuum sealed and all oxygen removed?
7) What type of warranty or guarantee do you offer in case of discoloration or rot?

Questions for the Wedding Party

When selecting your wedding party's attire, ask these questions:

1) How much is the deposit?
2) When must the deposit and balance be paid?
3) When should the order be placed?
4) What are the exchange and cancellation policies?
5) What is the cost for extra size and length?
6) When should they schedule the appointment for their final fitting?
7) How much are the alterations?
8) Can they bring the dress back to the shop to be pressed?
9) Is there a charge for pressing?

Attire Checklist

Bridal Shop: _____

Address: _____

Phone Number: _____

Bridal Shop Representative: _____

BRIDE

Dress — Style: _____

_____

_____

_____

Color: _____ Size: _____

Headpiece — Style: _____

_____

_____

Color: _____

Accessories — Undergarments: _____

_____

_____

Shoe — Style: _____

Color: _____ Size: _____

Fitting Dates: _____ Times: _____

_____ _____

Pick-up Date: _____

Attire Checklist

MAID OF HONOR: _____ Phone No: _____

Dress — Style: _____

_____

Color: _____ Size: _____

Headpiece — Style: _____

Color: _____

Accessories: _____

_____

Shoe — Style: _____

Color: _____ Size: _____

Fitting Date: _____ Time: _____

Pick-up Date: _____

MAID: _____ Phone No: _____

Dress — Style: _____

_____

Color: _____ Size: _____

Headpiece — Style: _____

Color: _____

Accessories: _____

_____

Shoe — Style: _____

Color: _____ Size: _____

Fitting Date: _____ Time: _____

Pick-up Date: _____

Attire Checklist

MAID: _____ Phone No: _____

Dress — Style: _____

_____

Color: _____ Size: _____

Headpiece — Style: _____

Color: _____

Accessories: _____

_____

Shoe — Style: _____

Color: _____ Size: _____

Fitting Date: _____ Time: _____

Pick-up Date: _____

MAID: _____ Phone No: _____

Dress — Style: _____

_____

Color: _____ Size: _____

Headpiece — Style: _____

Color: _____

Accessories: _____

_____

Shoe — Style: _____

Color: _____ Size: _____

Fitting Date: _____ Time: _____

Pick-up Date: _____

Attire Checklist

MAID:_____ Phone No: _____

Dress — Style: _____

_____

Color: _____ Size:_____

Headpiece — Style: _____

Color:_____

Accessories: _____

_____

Shoe — Style: _____

Color: _____ Size:_____

Fitting Date: _____ Time:_____

Pick-up Date: _____

MAID:_____ Phone No: _____

Dress — Style: _____

_____

Color: _____ Size:_____

Headpiece — Style: _____

Color:_____

Accessories: _____

_____

Shoe — Style: _____

Color: _____ Size:_____

Fitting Date: _____ Time:_____

Pick-up Date: _____

Attire Checklist

MOTHER OF THE BRIDE:

Dress — Style: _____

_____

Color: _____ Size: _____

Fitting Date: _____ Time: _____

Pick-up Date: _____

MOTHER OF THE GROOM:

Dress — Style: _____

_____

Color: _____ Size: _____

Fitting Date: _____ Time: _____

Pick-up Date: _____

Health and Beauty

Your wedding day is a time that you have probably dreamed of for a long time. Gliding down the aisle with all eyes on you, you will want to look and feel your best. What better way than by pampering yourself?

Hair Styles

Is there something you have always wanted to do with your hair, but could never justify? Now is the time. Get it cut or vary the style. You may even want to change the color. Most of today's hair coloring will not damage your hair. If a complete change in hair color is too drastic, why not enhance your natural color with a rinse or henna, or just highlight the layers. Get a permanent wave to either create curls or to provide fullness and body.

Hairstylists and beauticians can help you decide. Let them show you pictures of a variety of styles and then create a look that suits your life-style, features, and personal taste. You may want to experiment with different styles.

About a month before your wedding, take your headpiece with you to a beautician. She can assist you in choosing the style that would be most becoming. While there, make an appointment for a shampoo and set. If you are going to get a permanent wave, make sure you get it at least a month in advance of the wedding.

Some salons will offer a complete hair, makeup, nail and massage package. In many cases, they will come to the wedding to do the bride's hair and makeup and that of the entire wedding party.

Manicures/Pedicures

Give yourself a real treat . . . you deserve it. Get a manicure, pedicure and facial the week of your wedding or any time you need to relieve the tension by spoiling yourself. This would also be an excellent gift for your attendants. They, too, will want to look and feel their best.

These services are often offered through specialty salons. There are also professionals who will come to your home to provide the services and allow you to purchase the necessary supplies to do them yourself.

Cosmetics

Would you like a new way to care for your skin and makeup your face? You can get these services through a wide range of professionals — cosmetic salons, department stores or in-home consultants. All can help select skin care products and makeup that provide a new look or enhance the old.

The wide range of product lines will allow you to select soaps, moisturizers, foundation, powder, blush, eye shadows, eye liners, mascara and lip colors that are suitable to your skin type, coloring and life-style.

Experiment with a variety of looks for work, play or an evening out. Their expertise will help them to show you how to use the products on your own.

Toiletries

Maybe a new fragrance is what you need to make you feel special. These same professionals can also provide this service. Fragrances can range from a flowery perfume to a heavy musk. Select from colognes, lotions, powders and perfumes. Spray or dab it on. Perhaps you should choose several to match a variety of your moods.

When making your selection, be sure to apply the scent directly on your skin. Often, your body chemistry can change the smell.

Do not be too concerned with expense. Many more expensive perfumes require you to use less because the scent lasts longer. Besides, you are the bride. Live it up.

Image Consultants

Instead of shopping around trying to unify all the different parts that make up your look, why not meet with an image consultant. A consultant can perfect your hair, makeup, poise and overall wardrobe. This individual can give you expert advice on the look you want for your wedding day and help you develop an ongoing style for your personal and professional life.

A variety of services are available to you. A color analysis can help you select the correct colors that look best on you and say what you want to say about yourself. Brighten your skin; intensify the color of your eyes; or add a glow to your face. Whether soft, bold, bright or delicate, the look will be right for you.

The right haircut, eyeglasses, make-up and application techniques will enable you to maximize your positives and minimize the negatives. When you feel good about yourself, you project self-confidence and assurance.

Closet evaluation and wardrobe planning and selection will allow the image consultant to work with you to either enhance your current wardrobe or assemble a new wardrobe. This way you can organize your existing clothing and plan for future purchases. Again, this will be compatible with your physical features, suit your life-style and make you comfortable with the image you wish to present.

An image consultant is not just for women. Men can also benefit regardless of their vocation. A positive image can be created based on good grooming, correct and flattering colors and an effective combination of clothing.

The fees vary with the number of services you require of the consultant.

Muscle Toning/Weight Loss

You want your appearance to be picture-perfect. Why not exercise to lose weight, increase muscle tone, or just to become physically fit? There are many health clubs and diet centers available to you.

Health clubs offer a variety of programs such as swimming, weight lifting, running, aerobic exercise or simple stretching and toning activities. A monthly or yearly fee will usually allow you unlimited use of the facility.

The professionals at these centers can assist you with a varied regimen that concentrates on problem areas or provides for overall fitness.

Be sure to alert them to any medical limitations and consult your physician.

If a health club is not your style, consider purchasing exercise equipment for home use. The equipment will always be accessible to you. If you buy quality, you can use it for years.

The professionals at weight-loss centers can help you to lose weight and inches through diet and exercise. These programs will not only help you to lose the initial pounds, but can also help you to form new eating habits which will discourage future weight gain.

Before these professionals make recommendations, they should be informed of any medical condition you may have. You will also want to visit with your physician.

Tanning Centers

If you feel you look better with a tan or if you are honeymooning in a warm weather zone, you may want to use a tanning center's services. The representatives in the tanning or beauty salons can recommend the number of sessions right for you based on your skin type.

Artificial tanning processes can eliminate some of the results of sun bathing, such as sunburn. Be sure to listen to the salon representative and do not try to receive additional tanning time. It can be harmful to you.

> *"Relaxation is the key to reducing stress."*

Stress

Wedding planning and stress often go hand-in-hand. Often you do not have the time to take care of yourself the way you should. You and your future spouse will need to use some preventive tactics to limit stress.

Relaxation is the key to reducing stress. Reserve some time for yourself. Read, take a luxurious bubble bath or participate in some light exercise.

Exercise is a good way to release tension. Aerobic exercise performed three times a week is recommended. It can consist of fitness center activities, aerobic dance, swimming, bike riding, walking, jogging, etc.

Diet is also important. Make sure your diet includes plenty of vitamins and iron. A lack of iron can limit your endurance.

Watch your caffeine and alcohol intake. Caffeine after 5:00 p.m. can cause insomnia. Alcohol before bed can disturb deep sleep patterns making good rest impossible.

It is not unusual for conflicts to break out amongst family members involved in the planning. Remember, this is your day so be open with those involved in your planning. Do not lose your sense of humor. It will go a long way towards keeping stress down.

Take care of yourself during this time and your body will respond splendidly.

Birth Control

Birth control is a personal choice and an issue that should be discussed early on. Whether you have children and when can be a sensitive issue, as can the choice of birth control methods.

Some religions place strict restrictions on the types of birth control which are acceptable. In some cases, no method is acceptable. It is important you and your future spouse know where you stand on this issue. This is especially true if you come from different backgrounds or religions. If religion is a factor in your decision, it is wise to consult an official of your church and ask what type of counseling is available.

There are many types of birth control available today. Some of them have health risks associated with them and some are more effective than others. The more common methods are Birth Control Pills (The Pill), Diaphragm, Foam, Intra-uterine Device (IUD), Contraceptive Sponge, Condom, Vaginal Inserts, The Rhythm Method and Sterilization.

A decision on what method is right for you should be made only after consultation with a health care professional such as your family doctor or gynecologist. These individuals can offer the proper recommendations based on their knowledge of the effectiveness of the method and their knowledge of your medical history.

After receiving their recommendation, be sure to discuss it with your future spouse to assure a proper comfort factor. This way, you both can be a part of the decision.

Should you and your spouse have a difference in opinion on what method or whether any birth control should be used, be sure to seek counseling within your church or go to an outside counselor for advice. This could become a major issue after the wedding, so it's best to be prepared and have the answers beforehand.

Health Care

Newlyweds today enjoy more choices in medical and dental care than any generation in history. But the changes in American health care which created so many choices have, at the same time, made it harder for you as a "health care consumer," to understand all of your options and to make intelligent decisions.

> ## *"It pays to carefully compare health insurance plans."*

Health Insurance. Picking the right health insurance plan for you and your spouse is a major financial decision. Even if both you and your spouse are employed and your employers provide health insurance benefits, it pays to carefully compare the plans. Some of the important questions you should ask include:

— Do either of you have a "pre-existing health condition" which would not be covered if you changed health insurance plans? How long must you wait before a health condition is covered?

— Which policy or plan covers the broadest range of medical, dental and optical services that you are likely to use in the future? At what cost?

— Does either employer pay for health coverage of the employee's spouse? For additional family members? Some progressive employers offer a wide range of employee benefits "buffet style" and encourage employees to pick from a list. Would you receive more benefits for your new family at a lower cost if the spouse without the choice carried the health policy and the spouse with the choices picked additional benefits?

— And, on the subject of choices, does either plan limit your choice of physicians, dentists, clinics or hospitals? If so, are the limitations acceptable to both you and your spouse?

— Does either plan encourage or require a "second opinion" before major medical procedures are covered? Even though studies have shown "second opinions" seldom vary from the "first," it can be very important for your peace of mind to know that two experts agree.

Do not be discouraged if you find that comparing policies is a confusing process. The technical and legal language of most policies sometimes confuses even experts in the field! If you work for a company that has insurance specialists in the personnel office, they can be good sources of information. Another possible source of objective information is an agent who has worked with either your parents or your spouse's parents for many years and who would have no financial interest in the health plan you are reviewing.

Doctors, Dentists and Other Health Professionals. Not very long ago, people did not give much thought to picking a doctor or dentist because there simply was not much choice. Newly married couples often grew up in the same city or neighborhood and planned to stay there. Americans grew up with a "family doctor" and a "family dentist." When the doctor retired, his or her practice was sold to a younger doctor or dentist.

There was even less choice for hospitals. People went where their doctor sent them. Most doctors then admitted patients to only one or two hospitals. If the family doctor sought support from a specialist, it was almost always a specialist from the hospital where the family doctor practiced.

Today, the only major restrictions are limits within health insurance plans and the patient's ability to pay. Group medical and dental practices are now common in most communities. In some cases, these group practices charge on a "fee-for-service" basis. In others, you pay a specified amount each month for health care.

> ## "Medical and dental care have become increasingly competitive."

Urban hospitals, too, have become more involved in medical care by establishing clinics — often in suburban neighborhoods miles away from the main hospital buildings — where the doctors receive support from the hospital in exchange for referring patients to that hospital. Individual doctors may be in "private practice," working independently for themselves, or they may be employees of a large medical center working for a salary.

No matter what arrangement the doctor works within, your most impor-

tant consideration is the quality of care provided for you and your family.

Quality care begins with respect for the patient as an individual. Is the office staff friendly and helpful? Can you see a doctor without unreasonable waiting? Do the doctor and staff communicate openly and completely with you? Does the doctor treat you like a fellow human being, or are you treated as though you are just another disease to be cured or injury to be healed?

Medical and dental care have become increasingly competitive in recent years. It is no longer enough just to complete formal education, residencies, and then hang the diplomas on the wall. Good doctors and dentists constantly strive to improve their knowledge and skills through additional training. At the same time, they work hard to provide genuine, caring attention to every patient.

If you are new to a city or have never had the need to seek medical help before, one way to pick a doctor is to call the hospital nearest your home and ask for the hospital's physician referral service. The office should be able to provide you with several choices convenient to where you live or work. You also should talk to your friends and co-workers to see whom they recommend.

The important thing to remember is that you have a choice. If you are dissatisfied with the medical or dental service you receive at the first visit, do not be reluctant to speak up. Find out if the care you received is typical for that office or clinic, or if your situation was unusual. Doctors and dentists are human beings, of course, and no person is perfect, but a good health care professional will try to correct whatever problem you may have encountered. If you do not receive a satisfactory response to your questions, do not hesitate to try another professional. It is, after all, your health.

Cosmetic Surgery/Dentistry

Cosmetic surgery is a way to change or improve appearance. It includes procedures such as rhinoplasty (nose surgery), otoplasty (ear surgery), genioplasty (chin augmentation), and suction-assisted lipoectomy (redefining body contours through fat reduction). In addition, cosmetic surgery can be used to restore disfigurements or scarring resulting from accidents, diseases, tumors or birth defects.

This type of surgery may help you to feel better about yourself and the way you look.

Cosmetic dentistry might include caps, crowns, laminates or plastic bonding. The purpose is to make your teeth look uniform.

Cosmetic dentistry can repair chipped and broken teeth and make discolored teeth look white again. These simple procedures will make you feel and look your best on your wedding day.

THE WEDDING PAGES ®

Washington Metropolitan Edition ™

The Yellow Pages of the Bridal Industry

Publishers
BILL & MICHELLE VANDERBILT

Art Director
FRANK DOLPHENS

Production
QUALITY GRAPHICS
ANSON BOWLES GRAPHICS

FOR MORE INFORMATION CONCERNING THIS PUBLICATION PLEASE CALL

(703) 356-7586

INDEX

Index Continued

Bridal Registry

Loving Expressions

THE PERFECT UNION OF EXPERT SERVICE AND COMPUTER CONVENIENCE

Woodward & Lothrop's Bridal & Gift Registry. Our professional consultants personally guide you in making those important choices. Purchases are recorded in our computer to help avoid duplication. The Wedding Guest and Gift Organizer is our gift to brides who register, and guests receive complimentary gift wrap. Plus, our experts will assist you with invitations, photography, formalwear, gown selection and more. The service is complimentary, so call for your appointment today.

Metro Center...................... 202-347-7275	Columbia Mall ....301-730-3500 ext 341
Tysons Corner.................... 703-893-6400 ext 341	Montgomery Mall................. 301-365-4700 ext 277
Wheaton Plaza ....301-949-4700 ext 341	Landover Mall .... 301-341-5300 ext 341
Iverson Mall.......................301-423-4500 ext 341	Lakeforest Mall ....301-840-5800 ext 341
Chevy Chase .... 301-654-7600 ext 344	Fair Oaks Mall ....703-385-1800 ext 341
Seven Corners .... 703-532-4200 ext 341	Parole Plaza ....301-224-3300 ext 341
Landmark Mall....................703-354-1700 ext 341	White Marsh Mall................. 301-256-7800 ext 343

Prince Georges Plaza .... 301-559-7100 ext 341

THE BRIDAL GIFT REGISTRY

WOODWARD & LOTHROP

IN FIRST PLACE

A bridal registry that will astonish you with its selection, service and special attention

★ 800 Service Nationwide

★ Worldwide shipping and free gift wrap

★ 600 patterns *on display* at special prices

★ The only store in the area with Christian Dior, Rosenthal, Pickard, Hutschenreuther, Spode, Wedgewood, Fitz and Floyd, Royal Doulton, Royal Copenhagen, Noritake, Lenox, Mikasa, and more.

Baycraft china crystal

We Set The Most Beautiful Tables in Washington

301-258-0520
1-800-822-1155

Lakeforest Mall
Gaithersburg, Maryland 20877

You Could Be Macy's Couple of the Year

Each couple has a personal style composed of the special traits that first drew them together. At Macy's we have a varied and distinguished collection of wedding gifts to suit the special style of every couple starting their new life together.

Macy's complimentary, computerized Bridal Registry is the most convenient way to get your special choices to family and friends, avoid guesswork and minimize duplication. Best of all, when you register at any Macy's Northeast store you'll become eligible for our Couple of the Year event and drawing†.

One lucky couple will receive all of the following impressive prizes: • Towle sterling silver for four • Waterford goblets for eight • Royal Doulton fine bone china for eight • Lenox Imperial Bar Crystal Collection • Set of Calphalon professional cookware • Diamond wedding ring • Tosca, Jessica Lynn and Val Mode lingerie collection • Fieldcrest bed and bath collection • Honeymoon trip 🖤

BRIDAL REGISTRY

For more information on our Couple of the Year event just call. In New York: (212)560-3800. Connecticut: (203)731-3500, ext. 262. New Jersey. (201)843-9100, ext. 527 in Paramus; (201)725-1400, ext. 475 in Bridgewater. Delaware: (302) 366-5800, ext. 223. Pennsylvania: (215)337-9350, ext. 307. Maryland: (301)363-7400, ext. 475. Virginia: (703)556-0000, ext. 274. †Macy's employees and their families not eligible. No purchase necessary. Details and restrictions in store.

macy's

WEDDING SERVICE

You take care of the ceremony. I'll take care of the service—in china, crystal or silver—at up to 60% less than department or specialty stores.

Visit my full-service shop and choose from hundreds of popular patterns on display. Then enter yours in the area's fastest, most comprehensive computerized bridal registry. I'll simplify the ordering. Send out announcements of your selected patterns. Even keep a convenient list of who buys what for you.

It's a high-tech touch that allows me time for more personal attention to your needs. You see, even though your best service is through my computer, your best man is still Michael Round.

Telephone: 703/550-7880, toll free 800/752-6622. Open 7 days a week.
Take Exit 56 (Fort Belvoir/Newington) off I-95 (S). Go right, toward Ft. Belvoir, to 8241 Backlick Rd.

MICHAEL ROUND
Fine China & Crystal, Inc.

WATERFORD TO GO

Waterford
A SIX PACK TO GO

whether it be red wine
glasses, sherries,
cordials, 9-ounce
old fashions
or water...Tiara
has them by
the thousands!
Not to mention
decanters and
all other manner
of the sparkling
Irish legend.

TIARA
Tiara Gifts, Wheaton Plaza
Wheaton, MD 20902 (301) 949-0210
Mail and Phone Orders Accepted

AREA'S LARGEST INDEPENDENT WATERFORD DEALER!

TIARA
Tiara Gifts Wheaton Plaza
Wheaton, MD 20902
(301) 949-0210

Banquet & Reception Locations

The Raindancer

"THE BEST OF THE BEST"
At An Affordable Price!

Look no further for the best location for your wedding reception or rehearsal dinner. Our customers consider us the "best of the best" and so do we. We're the best at providing you with a beautiful, spacious private room, the freshest seafood and prime steaks, hors'doeuvres and drinks and friendly attentive service-

ALL AT AN AFFORDABLE PRICE!

Full weddings starting at **$22.00* a person-** including alcohol! We're the best at providing dependable personable attention. High quality food and service has been a Scaggs family tradition for more than 35 years! We're the best at creating a menu to accommodate your individual taste and

WE'RE THE BEST AT MAKING IT ALL AFFORDABLE TO YOU!

THE SCAGGS GROUP

*Tax and gratuity additional

DON'T MISS OUR EXCITING OFFER ENCLOSED IN YOUR WEDDING PAGES PACKET!

12224 Rockville Pike, Rockville, MD 20852

301-468-2300

12A

R O M A N C E
IN AN ELEGANT SETTING

Memorable weddings don't just happen... they require the most elegant setting, a romantic ambience and meticulous planning down to the last important detail. The experts at Westfields can assist you in planning a beautiful wedding or reception including menu selection, flowers, entertainment, photography and arrangements for out of town guests. Our florist, photography studio and travel agency are located on the premises to make coordination of your special event easy and efficient.

Enjoy the romance of your wedding day in this most elegant setting.

WESTFIELDS
INTERNATIONAL CONFERENCE CENTER

14750 Conference Center Drive · Westfields, Virginia 22021
(703) 818-0300
An International Conference Resorts of America Property

A Wedding Reception That Will Make Your Heart Skip A Beat.

How would you feel if your wedding reception was distinctively yours? One that met your every wish? One that was impeccable? One in which every detail was handled for you, right down to the last hors d'oeuvre?

You'd be so delighted, you'd probably want to kiss and hug the maître d. And all the other Marriott people with the experience, creativity and savoir-faire to make your wedding reception almost as beautiful as you.

So call the Washington area Marriott that would be most convenient for your reception.

After all, your new husband isn't the only one who wants to make you happy.

Marriott People know how.

Bethesda Marriott, (301) 897-9400   Crystal City Marriott, (703) 521-5500   Crystal Gateway Marriott, (703) 920-3230   Fairview Park Marriott, (703) 849-9400
Gaithersburg Marriott, (301) 977-8900   Greenbelt Marriott, (301) 441-3700   JW Marriott, (202) 393-2000   Key Bridge Marriott, (703) 524-6400
Tysons Corner Marriott, (703) 734-3200   Washington Marriott, (202) 872-1500   Washington Dulles Marriott, (703) 471-9500

WASHINGTON **Marriott**
HOTELS

A TIME TO DREAM...

You look into his eyes, softly joining crystal glasses . . . a gentle kiss.

Your lives are now forever entwined, and together you enter a Renaissance Age.

Surround yourselves and your honored guests with the intimate European charm of the Ramada Renaissance Hotel. Our dedicated staff, in its commitment to excellence, stands ready to attend to your every detail. From canapes to crepes flambé we will assist you in designing a menu unique to you and this splendid occasion.

So, come to the Ramada Renaissance Hotel, where your dreams of a perfect Wedding will come true.

Call our Catering Manager, Julie Staley at (202) 775-0800 for more details on our Wedding package.

RAMADA RENAISSANCE™ HOTEL

1143 New Hampshire Avenue, N.W.
Washington, D.C. 20037

AT SHERATON LITTLE THINGS MEAN A LOT • AT SHERATON LITTLE

THE WEDDING ON TOP OF THE WORLD

Experience the Galaxy Ballroom high atop the Sheraton National Hotel. Discover the elegant decor, distinctive cuisine, personalized service and mesmerizing view of Washington, DC.

Our experienced staff will design your perfect wedding. Your reception will unfold with great precision and attention to detail while you and your guests relax, enjoy the special occasion and savor the monumental view.

Conveniently located for local and out-of-town guests, the Sheraton National Hotel is minutes from National Airport via complimentary shuttle. Special room rates available.

Contact our Catering Specialists at 703-521-1900.

Sheraton National Hotel
The hospitality people of ITT

COLUMBIA PIKE & WASHINGTON BLVD.
ARLINGTON, VIRGINIA 22204

AT SHERATON LITTLE THINGS MEAN A LOT • AT SHERATON LITTLE

DULLES CORNER PARK

Garden Weddings and Receptions
938-7525

SEQUOIA MANAGEMENT   CHANTILLY, VA

16A

Picture This

Smiling Faces...Tears of Joy...The Bride and Groom...Family and Friends...Your First Dance...Sparkling Champagne...The Toast...Cutting the Cake...Impeccable Service

For ten years, the Tysons Westpark Hotel has professionally hosted memorable wedding receptions and gala affairs. Celebrate with a reception designed to reflect your unique style. We look forward to helping you plan your special day.

Westpark Hotels

Tysons

8401 Westpark Drive
McLean, Virginia 22102
(703) 734-2800

SUCCESSFUL WEDDINGS

FRESHLY CUT FLOWERS,

SPARKLING CRYSTAL,

PERSONALIZED CUISINE,

MAKE IT SIMPLE
MAKE IT AFFORDABLE
MAKE IT AT FLUTES
RESTAURANT AND CHAMPAGNE BAR

PRIVATE CELEBRATIONS AND
PARTIES ON THE MEZZANINE
DINNER FOR UP TO 50
RECEPTIONS FOR UP TO 250

FLUTES
GEORGETOWN

CALL 333-7333 FOR DETAILS
1025 THOMAS JEFFERSON ST N.W.
PARKING ACROSS THE STREET

YOUR SPECIAL DAY
DESERVES A
SPECIAL PLACE

Share with us your special day, and we'll make all your dreams come true. Romantic candlelight and personal service await you and your guests at Days Inn Congressional Park. For an intimate rehearsal dinner or an elegant reception for up to 100, we'll make your day a memory to last a lifetime. Treat your out-of-town guest to the luxury they deserve, and they'll marvel at your good taste! For details on our complete wedding packages, simply contact our Sales Office. Ask about your complimentary suites for the bride and groom.

(301) 881-2300
(800) 255-1775

 CONGRESSIONAL PARK

1775 Rockville Pike, Rockville, MD 20852
Ronald Cohen Investments-Hotel Division

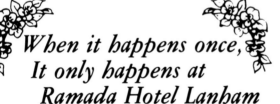

When it happens once, It only happens at Ramada Hotel Lanham

**Bridal Luncheons • Rehearsal Dinners
Wedding Receptions**

459-1000
Ask for the Sales Department

RAMADA® HOTEL
5910 Princess Garden Parkway
Lanham, Maryland

A Coakley & Williams Enterprise

Once upon a wedding...

For a fairy tale wedding, choose the charming ambience of the Old Town Holiday Inn. We offer you the perfect marriage of creative catering, delightful banquet rooms and the personalized attention your special day deserves.

Consider a reception in our courtyard patio. And ask about our delectable menus for groups from 10 to 250. A complimentary Bridal Suite is our gift to the bride and groom. Special room rates are also available for out-of-town guests. Call our Director of Catering to arrange your dream wedding . . . and live happily ever after.

 Alexandria - Old Town

*The Old Town Holiday Inn
480 King Street • Old Town
Alexandria, VA
(703) 549-6080*

The **Gangplank**
RESTAURANT AND MARINA
ELEGANT RECEPTION FACILITIES WITH A
BREATHTAKING VIEW OF THE MONUMENTS
AND THE POTOMAC.
RECEPTIONS UP TO 300 PEOPLE

554-5000

600 WATER ST., S.W. WASH., D.C.-ON THE WATERFRONT-COMPLIMENTARY PARKING

Notes

_____

_____

_____

_____

_____

The most important day of your life
should not be left to chance . . .
Whether a private dinner
for immediate family,
a banquet for 300,
or an intimate rehearsal dinner,
Loews L'enfant Plaza Hotel
celebrates the occasion
with unquestionable
good taste.
Ah! Magnifique.
Call our Director of Catering
484-1000.

LOEWS
L'enfant
PLAZA

480 L'enfant Plaza, S.W. Washington, D.C. 20024

Our Weddings Are Monumental...

Whether it's a cocktail reception or a formal dinner, we have the perfect setting for you.

Enjoy the penthouse facilities with breathtaking views of classic monuments, and our gracious window filled ballrooms.

Let our responsive staff perfect your special moment, For more information, please call or visit.

HOLIDAY INN
CROWNE PLAZA

National Airport
300 Army Navy Dr.
Arlington, Va. 22202
(703) 892-4100 Ext. 1980

Kosher Facilities

Blair Mansion Inn

Wedding Receptions ■ Rehearsal Dinners
Engagement Parties ■ Showers
Private Parties

A country inn offering thoughtful service,
good food, reasonable prices.
Private rooms for groups of 10 to 250.
Free parking. Catering services for your home
or office.

588-1688

7711 Eastern Avenue, Silver Spring

RETURN TO THE TRADITIONAL WEDDING RECEPTION

Rich in Romance

*Say "I DO"
to the
Quality Hotel-Silver Spring*

Accommodations for 5 to 500

**8727 Colesville Road
Silver Spring, MD 20910**

Quality Hotel

(301) 589-5200

Your Special Day Maryland Inn Style

The Maryland Inn specializes in wedding receptions for up to 200 guests in our beautifully decorated Ballroom. Our accommodations include a large dance floor, centerpieces for all guests' tables, champagne toast for the Wedding Party and a room for the evening for the Bride and Groom with champagne on ice. Plus, your own Wedding Coordinator to insure your special day is all you ever dreamed it would be.

Discount rates for out of town guests, rehearsal dinners and bridesmaid luncheons.

Contact Carole Ice, Director of Catering, for details.

BEST WESTERN

Maryland Inn & Fundome

COLLEGE PARK

8601 Baltimore Blvd.   College Park, MD 20740

(301) 474-2800

Conveniently located 1 mile south of the Capitol Beltway.

The Best Weddings are filled with

ROMANCE

…romance of the perfect setting and the perfect function. From the bridal shower to the honeymoon night; the rehearsal dinner, the bachelor party, the wedding, reception, the bridal suite, and special room rates for out-of-town guests, the Old Colony Inn attends to every detail.

Ask about our customized menus for groups from 20 to 500. Enjoy the formal elegance of our ballroom or rooftop gazebo as well as free parking for all your guests.

All you do is provide the wedding party and we add the inspiration. For the most romantic of weddings, call our Director of Catering at **548-6300**.

BEST WESTERN
OLD COLONY INN

OLD COLONY INN
625 FIRST STREET, ALEXANDRIA, VA 22314

Make Your Dreams Come True. . .

Enjoy our complete Wedding Packages which include all those special touches that help make your dreams come true:
- ☐ Champagne toast
- ☐ Large hardwood dance floor
- ☐ Centerpieces on every table
- ☐ Complimentary Guest Room
- ☐ Complementary morning after breakfast

Complete Catering:
- ☐ Menu selection   ☐ Music selection
- ☐ Wedding Cakes   ☐ Flower arrangements
- ☐ Accommodations for up to 250 guests

Memorable pre-wedding festivities:
- ☐ Rehearsal dinners   ☐ Bridal showers
- ☐ Bridesmaid luncheons

Contact Mike Ansara, Catering Director, for details

BEST WESTERN

Maryland Inn & Fundome

LAUREL, MARYLAND

15101 Sweitzer Lane, Laurel, MD 20707

(301) 776-5300

"I'm not going to cry...I'm not going to cry..."

WHEN IT HAPPENS ONLY ONCE, THERE'S ONLY ONE PLACE.

To plan your wedding down
to the last flute of champagne, call
our Catering Department at (202) 429-1700, ext. 1422.
We vow it will be perfection.

VISTA INTERNATIONAL HOTEL WASHINGTON, D.C.

M STREET N.W. BETWEEN 15TH AND VERMONT

Beautiful Beginnings....

Let our professional staff make your special day a memorable one. We're there from beginning to end to assist you with everything from menu selections to entertainment and flower arrangements. We specialize in Wedding Receptions, Rehearsal Dinners and Showers.

We offer complimentary covered parking, cake cutting and airport transportation as well as special rates for your out-of-town guests.

Creative Packages to suit all your needs.
RAMADA SEMINARY PLAZA
I 395 & Seminary Road
Alexandria, VA 22304

703-751-4510

..Lasting Memories

A Wedding Reception as Unique and Special
....as You are

A personal reflection of your own special style, professionally designed to cater to your every wish. Our experienced personal care will take the worry out of your wedding plans and create elegant memories that will last a lifetime. Call our Catering Director at

Fred's Place

Crystal City Holiday Inn
1489 Jeff Davis Highway, Arlington, Va 22202

920-0772

WE'LL HANDLE THE PARTY.

YOU HANDLE THE PRAISE.

CATERING with a concept in Luxury and Elegance . . . by the Pool, under the Stars, or in our Elegant Ballroom.

A discriminating menu created by our Executive Chefs.

The Sheraton at Reston can provide the finishing touches to your *Special Day*.

Sheraton Reston Hotel
The hospitality people of **ITT**

11810 SUNRISE VALLEY DRIVE
RESTON, VIRGINIA 22091

For a tour of our beautiful facility
or more information,
contact our Wedding Specialist at

(703) 620-9000

Authentic Homestyle Cooking

*PERSONALIZED FULL SERVICE
WEDDING ACCOMMODATIONS
TAILORED TO FIT
ALL BUDGETS*

*PRIVATE
BANQUET FACILITY
FOR
25 to 250*

Mama's Italian Restaurant

Celebrating our fifth year in Fairfax	Proudly announcing our newest location
9715 Lee Hwy Fairfax, VA	Countryside Shopping Center Sterling, VA
(703) 385-2646	**(703) 450-5901**

Perfect For Your Wedding...

ᴍᴛ. Vᴇʀɴᴏɴ Sǫᴜᴀʀᴇ Cʟᴜʙʜᴏᴜꜱᴇ

- Charming Accomodations For 200 People
- Kitchen, Fireplace and Dancefloor
- Conveniently Located
- Casual Setting For Intimate Ocassions

768-3232

And Your First Home Together.

ᴍᴛ. Vᴇʀɴᴏɴ Sǫᴜᴀʀᴇ Aᴘᴀʀᴛᴍᴇɴᴛꜱ

A luxury Community featuring one, two and three bedroom apartments.

Mention this ad and receive a special concession on a ONE YEAR LEASE.

768-3200

10 minutes south of Old Town Alexandria   **EHO**

Our Bouquet of Tradition for You

Something Old: A beautifully orchestrated wedding reception, rehearsal dinner and bridal luncheon.

Something New: Contemporary reception planning.

Something Borrowed: Complimentary reception hall for 50 to 300 and a complimentary honeymoon night, too.

Something Blue: One of the many linen choices we offer to you.

Special rates for out-of-town guests

ꜱᴘʀɪɴɢꜰɪᴇʟᴅ ɪɴɴ

For more information call: **703/922-9000**

6550 Loisdale Court, Springfield, Virginia 22150

Discover the Romance Of A Reception On The Waterfront.

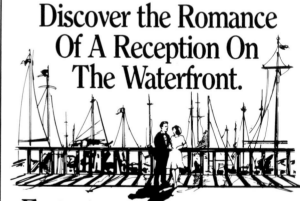

Experience the Victorian splendor of Phillips' ceremony/reception rooms—distinctive facilities for up to 200 overlooking the tranquil beauty of Washington Channel.

Choose our first floor Marble room, with its rich, rose-hued tones and working fireplace. Or the adjoining tented Parkside, reminiscent of a Victorian garden. Sweep up the grand staircase to the romantic Upper Deck, where soft sunlight or sparkling moonlight surrounds your guests at more intimate affairs.

Our varied cuisine may surprise you; its excellence will delight you. Call our Wedding Consultant today for your private tour.

Phillips

900 Water Street, SW
Washington, DC 20024
(202) 488-8515
On-Premise Parking

Large or Small Affair...

Your guide to a perfect wedding is right here at your fingertips.

Take advantage of your local merchants expert ability to help plan for your wedding!

On your wedding day, you want everything to be perfect.

And it will be, when you rely on The Wedding Pages.

THE WEDDING PAGES

Your wedding at our hotel is not expensive, it's *priceless!*

Our specially designed Wedding Packages make it easy for you to plan a complete reception giving you the confidence that once again you've made the perfect choice.

Bride and Groom receive...
- Deluxe Wedding Night accommodations
- Chilled bottle of Champagne
- Complimentary Breakfast

Your Guests receive . . .
- Special room rates
- Free Parking
- Fabulous food, fine service and a great time

Free dinner for two can be yours. Just come and see why our hotel is the perfect choice for your reception. Call 243-9800 to set up your appointment now. Offer excludes alcohol and expires 12/31/90. Limit one per customer.

Holiday Inn
ARLINGTON at BALLSTON

4610 N. Fairfax Drive • Arlington, Virginia 22203

THE WEDDING OF YOUR DREAMS...

Personalized service with impeccable attention to detail in the European tradition. Our experienced staff will create a wedding to remember in our marble garden or elegant ballroom facilities from 20-300. Contact our catering department at:

(202) 232-7000

Radisson Park Terrace Hotel
1515 Rhode Island Ave, N.W.
Off Scott Circle
Washington, D.C. 20005

Notes

Bridal Registry Linens

Walpole's
LINENS ■ SINCE 1766

We are proud to offer our bridal registry of fine linens and fashion accessories. Let our experienced consultants guide you through the shop explaining quality and style to decorate every room of your new home. We specialize in personalized service, hard to find sizes, and a custom program to help create your own special look. All of this and a gift for the bride with our compliments.

Call our bridal consultant, Ilene Burstyn, in our Chevy Chase location.

FALLS CHURCH	**CHEVY CHASE**	**WASHINGTON**
Seven Corners Ctr.	Wisconsin & Western	1722 Connecticut Ave.
6201 Arlington Blvd.	Chevy Chase Center	Near Dupont Metro
237-7993	656-2234	667-2849

Walpole's
Fashions ■ for the Home

Bridal Fabrics

FABRICS & LACES

...for the BRIDE and bridal party...

G Street FABRICS

**11854 Rockville Pike
Rockville, MD 20852
Phone: 231-8998**
White Flint METRO

30A

Bridal Gown
Preservation Service

Preserving Dreams . . .

*Imagine your daughter wearing your Gown. Imagine wearing your mother's Gown. **Imperial Gown Preservation** preserves your dreams and promises you a precious heirloom to be passed down for generations to come. Your Gown is not just another dress!*

***Imperial Gown Preservation** is "The Professional" in the proper handling of your Gown. We gently dryclean and restore it to it's original loveliness with the experience to care for delicate fabrics and trims. Improper storage destroys most Gowns in less than five years.*

*Call **1-800-777-GOWN**, throughout North America, to speak with our Gown Consultant. Our pickup and delivery service is provided at no extra charge. Rely with confidence on **Imperial's** forty years of excellence to protect your heirloom and preserve your dreams. . .*

Imperial Gown Preservation Co.®

1-800-777-GOWN
(1-800-777-4696)
3063 Nutley Street, Fairfax, VA 22031, (703) 573-8989

Balloon Decorations

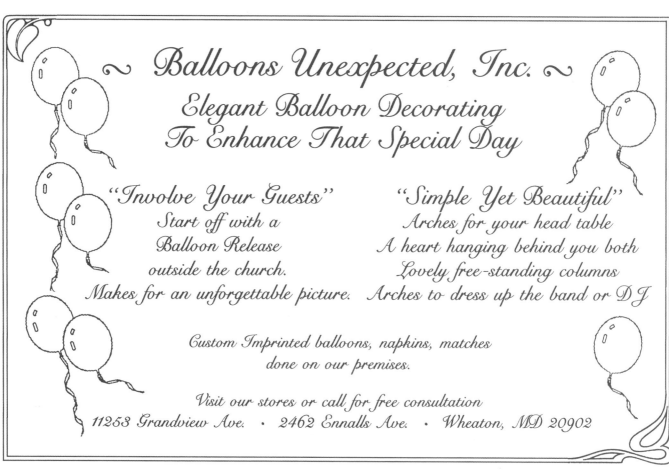

Balloons Unexpected, Inc.
Elegant Balloon Decorating
To Enhance That Special Day

"Involve Your Guests"
Start off with a
Balloon Release
outside the church.
Makes for an unforgettable picture.

"Simple Yet Beautiful"
Arches for your head table
A heart hanging behind you both
Lovely free-standing columns
Arches to dress up the band or DJ

Custom Imprinted balloons, napkins, matches
done on our premises.

Visit our stores or call for free consultation
11253 Grandview Ave. • 2462 Ennalls Ave. • Wheaton, MD 20902

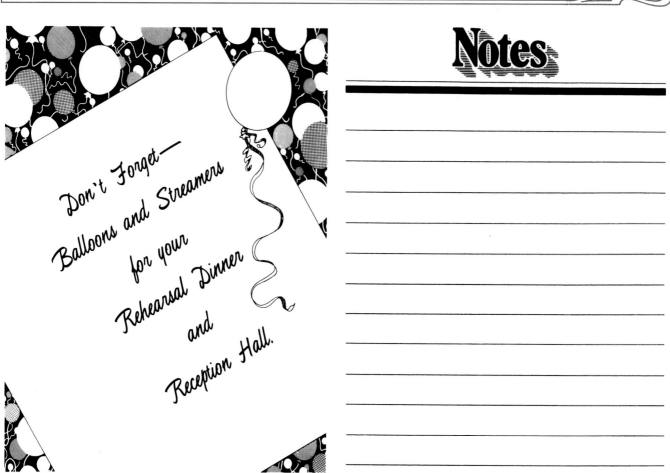

Don't Forget—
Balloons and Streamers
for your
Rehearsal Dinner
and
Reception Hall.

Notes

Balloon Decoration On The Rise
Balloons Gaining Popularity As Wedding Decorations
by Susan Glass

Creative Decorating Concept "Popping" Up at Weddings All over Washington
by Susan Glass

Imagine entering your wedding reception through an elegant canopy of soft pink and white balloons. Watch the reactions on your guests' faces when they first see the ballroom, festive and colorful with its bursts of balloons on the tables and its dramatic arch over the band. This is the way that a party should look.

The balloon decorating industry got its start thirteen years ago in California with a celebration for Disneyland and has been growing steadily ever since. This rapid expansion is due primarily to the versatility and affordability of balloons when compared to other decorating media. Here in the Washington area, one of the top

balloon decorators is Joey Yaffe, a national award-winning designer, and owner of Rockville-based Exquisite Balloon Creations. Says Yaffe "For large scale color and impact in a room, balloons have a size and mass that just can't be matched."

Yaffe, who has designed such impressive pieces as a five-story rainbow and most recently an enormous pantheon sculpture for the Pension Building, is as excited as a wide-eyed child when he talks about his job. He says "I've been doing balloon decorating for over five years now, and every time I get to see the faces of my clients when they walk into their party, I remember all over again why I love what I do."

Phone: 929-1408

Notes

Apartment
Communities

Make a Fresh Start

Wedding Day Special

The coffees on —
I'll be ho
6:00 s
dip
a

The Woode
OF FAIRFAX

703-550-9331
7630 Fairfield Woods Court
Lorton, VA 22079

Gene B Glick

Your Wedding Date Is Your Rent Rate

If you marry in 1990, your first months rent is that date. Example; if you marry on June 1st, your first months rent is **$6.01.**

Enjoy all the amenities that come with top-of-the-line luxury apartment living in an idyllic country setting . . . and still have curbside convenience of Pentagon Metro AND nearby access to I-95 and Route 1.

- Spacious living and dining areas for easy entertaining
- 1, 2 and 3 BR Garden Apts.
- Tropical ceiling fans
- Fashionable miniblinds
- Abundant closet & storage space
- Private patios and balconies

- Fully equipped clubhouse-spa, pools, & lighted tennis courts
- Optional fireplace and carports

EQUAL HOUSING OPPORTUNITY

Bakeries

No Leftovers.
No Leftovers.

Sweet Surrender™

edible
monuments
529-6331

WASHINGTON, D.C.

The Perfect Wedding Cake

Now's the time when every detail counts. Details that can make your wedding a success. Or not.

The centerpiece of the table is the last thing you leave to chance. Nothing short of a culinary work of art will do.

Chef Wolfgang Büchler creates exquisitely tasting originals for every kind and size of wedding. Traditional charm or contemporary elegance. Heidelberg will help you to achieve the right atmosphere.

Come see us about your wedding cake. In one week, you can have a 6" sample of your selection.

♦ Washingtonian Magazine's Best Cakes Award . . . twice!
♦ Sumptuously Delicious
♦ All Natural, Farm-fresh Ingredients
♦ Careful Attention to Every Detail
♦ Competitively Priced (even without a discount!)

Heidelberg

Pastry Shoppe

2150 N. Culpeper Street ♦ 4800 Block of Lee Highway
Arlington, VA ♦ 527-8394

Closed Mondays

Your
Wedding Cake from . . .

Clement's
Pastry Shop, Inc.

A Washington Tradition for over 60 Years!

Clement's Pastry Shop, Inc.
1338 G STREET, N.W.
Washington, D.C. 20005

(202)628-4151

Delivery Service Available Throughout the Metropolitan Area.

*Custom designed wedding cakes
made to your specifications.*

*Personalized service,
including delivery and set-up.*

*Call for an estimate or
an appointment to see my photo album.*

JEANNE JOHNSON ▪ *703/448-7312*
Falls Church, VA

JEANNE'S CAKERY
A Creative Alternative to a Bakery

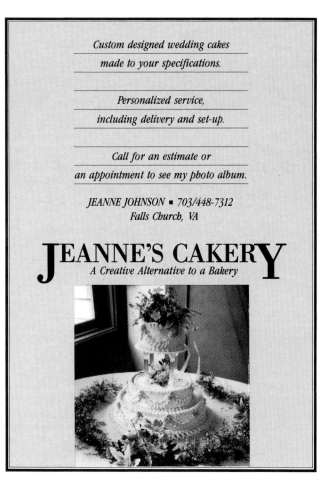

Connie's Cakes

Unique Designs
Created Especially for You

Call for an Appointment
to view the exciting cakes I have on display.
Evening and Weekend consultations available.

Connie M. Moser
Decorator - Designer
13721 Lynhurst Drive
Dale City, Virginia 22193
703-590-8053

DELIVERY, SET-UP and PERSONALIZED SERVICE

"The Wedding Cake Expert"

On Your Wedding Day...

Call a caterer who is equal to your needs and emotions,
one who understands how really important this day is to you.
After all, it is *your* day!
We can decorate a cake with that old world perfection
or create a buffet that will be long remembered.

Lee Bakery Caterers
OF DISTINCTION

*In our 39th year of serving
Washington's finest people, our Customers*
6226 OLD DOMINION DRIVE • McLEAN, VIRGINIA 22101
(703) 538-6574

TIERS
OF
J♥Y®

THE BEST
OU CAN BUY

FREE CONSULTATIONS

TIERS
OF
J♥Y®

(301) 424-7741
ROCKVILLE, MD

Alexandria
Pastry
Shop
and
Cafe

**COMPLETE
CATERING
SERVICE**

*Creative menu planning
to accomodate the size, style
and budget of your wedding
reception.*

*Custom Wedding Cakes
Our specialty using only the
finest ingredients money
can buy.*

*For Weddings we're
the fantasy, the food, and
the frosting on the cake.*

**3690H King Street
Alexandria, Va 22302
703-578-4144**

Notes

_____
_____
_____
_____
_____
_____
_____
_____
_____
_____
_____
_____
_____
_____
_____
_____
_____
_____
_____
_____
_____
_____
_____
_____

Bridal Attire

Personalized Service

◆ *Fabric and style selection*

◆ *Designs from pictures, sketches or any combination*

Bridal Gowns & Veils

Attendant's Dresses

Mother's Gowns

Special Occasion & Prom Dresses

Quintess Designs

Debbie Wise
Greenbelt, Maryland
301-474-8299

The Dreams . . .
The Plans . . .
The Day . . .

The Dress . . .

Gowns by Dawn

For Creation of All Fine Formal Wear

• Bridal Gowns & Headpieces
• Gown Alterations
• Bridesmaid Dresses
• Mother's Dresses

(301) 816-9315   Dawn Brooky

• *Bridal*   • *Special*
• *Bridesmaids   Occasion*
• *Mother's   & Prom*
• *Accessories*   • *Veils*
• *Shoes*

Enjoy personalized service from the first consultation to the final fitting Specializing in the Renaissance Woman

The Bridal Shoppe

7833 Sudley Road K Mart Shopping Center Manassas, Virginia 22110

703-368-0694

Mon-Fri 10-9 p.m.

Sat 10-6 p.m.

Sunday by Appointment

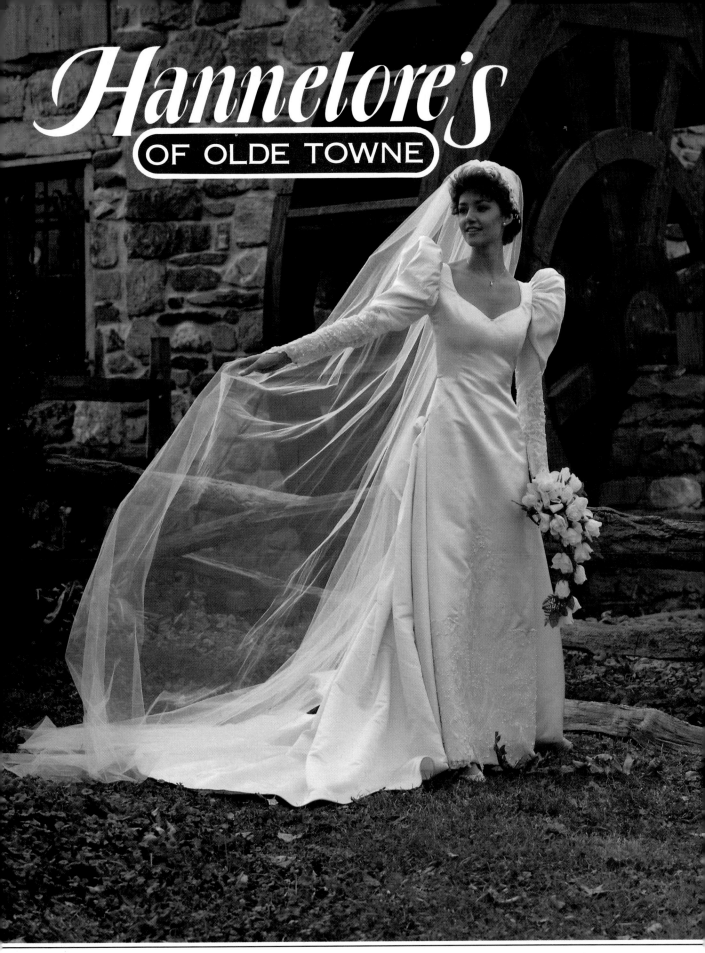

Hannelore's
OF OLDE TOWNE

5 N. PITT STREET • TAVERN SQUARE • ALEXANDRIA, VA   703.549.0387

E, FRI. SAT 10-6   WED, THUR. 10-8   SUN 12-5

Albee's Has Your Dyeable and Evening Shoes...

YEAR ROUND ALBEE'S HAS THE AREA'S LARGEST AND MOST COMPLETE SELECTION OF DYEABLE AND EVENING SHOES. OUR DYEABLE SHOES & HANDBAGS ARE CUSTOM TINTED ON THE PREMISES TO COORDINATE YOUR WEDDING PARTY.

IF THE SHOE FITS IT MUST BE *Albee* SHOES

Please Write Or Phone For Your Free Catalog!

☐ 101 N. Washington St. Rockville, MD 20850 *(301) 762-9380*
☐ Laurel Shopping Center Laurel, MD 20707 *(301) 953-2104 / 725-1298*

Designed for you . . . made for you

CUSTOM DESIGNED HEADPIECES
Unique veils and bridal accessories

LORETTA'S LOVELIES

(301) 946-9300 • (301) 643-1217

Conveniently located in Taramina's - Wheaton, MD

Begin Your Wedding Plans With Us...

A Personal Consultation With Rosalin Will Help You Plan Your Special Day.
We Give Professional Attention To The Finest Detail.

Designer Bridal Gowns
Custom-Designed Gowns
Attendants' Gowns
Mothers' Gowns
Prom & Special Occasion Gowns
Tuxedo Rentals
Shoes & Accessories
Invitations

532-0288

ROSALIN'S
BRIDAL BOUTIQUE

706 S. Washington St. Rt. 29 (Lee Hwy)
Falls Church

Free Ample Parking   All Major Credit Cards

YOU'RE IN GOOD
COMPANY WITH

BETH ROBERTS COLLECTION, INC.

Ilissa

Joelle

SPOSA BELLA

Jena

Bill Levkoff

Alfred Angelo INTERNATIONAL

MORI LEE

REGENCY BRIDAL

St. Pucchi, Inc.

GALINA BOUQUET

Bridal Originals

T&G BRIDAL

Priscilla

the house of Bianchi

private label by G

San-Martin INTERNATIONAL BRIDALS

Fink originals...

Moonlight

Jordan

MISS Elliette

Prashker Flowergirls

Sweetheart G·O·W·N·S

JIM HJELM A PRIVATE COLLECTION

MARY'S P.C. Mary's, Inc.

Visit Them All At...

LAUREL BRIDAL & GOWN SHOP, INC.

LAUREL LAKES SHOPPING CENTRE
14234 BALTIMORE AVENUE
LAUREL, MARYLAND

301-725-4600

*The Finest In Selection, Price
And Service For Your Entire Wedding
Party, From The Bride And Groom To
The Tiniest Flower Girl.*

Designer Boutique

BRIDAL AND FORMALS
(703) 368-8997

**10614 Sudley Manor Drive
Manassas, Virginia**

**Festival At Bull Run
(Next To Chili's)**

Royal Wedding

* *Wedding Consultants are available to help you select your gown, the bridesmaid's dresses, tuxedos for the groom and his groomsmen, and coordinate dresses for your mother and your mother-in-law.*

* *Bridesmaids get a 10% discount on their dresses when the bride purchases her dress from Royal.*

* *Groom's tuxedo rental is free when six or more groomsmen rent tuxedos.*

* *Wedding gowns can be cleaned, treated, and packaged in a special Keepsake Package for easy storage.*

Visit any one of our fourteen Royal Formal & Bridal shops and let us help you make your wedding day everything it should be. The most beautiful day of your life.

We look forward to seeing you soon.

Specialists in women's bridal and men's formal fashions.

1515 Rockville Pike Rockville, MD 770-4477	1328 G Street, N.W. Washington, D.C. 737-7144	Iverson Mall Hillcrest Heights, MD 423-4307	Fashion Center Pentagon City 415-2032
Viers Mill Rd. & Univ. Blvd. Wheaton, MD 933-1512	Springfield Mall Springfield, VA 971-0644	Annapolis Mall Annapolis, MD 266-6535	Laurel Centre Mall Laurel, MD 498-1778
Tyson's Corner Center Tyson's Corner, VA 893-7800	Montgomery Mall at Sears Bethesda, MD 469-4307	The Mall in Columbia Columbia, MD 740-3325	Salisbury Mall Salisbury, MD 546-1032
Capital Plaza Mall Landover Hills, MD 341-5555			Landmark Center at Sears Alexandria, VA 354-1611

Royal
FORMAL & BRIDAL

51A

Martins
Bridal and Formal Shop

Our service shows
we care...
Our prices prove it.

Inquire about our
GUARANTEED
MARK DOWN POLICY

The best bridal buys
in the state
on a year-round basis.

PACE PLAZA
1724 Woodlawn Drive
Baltimore, Maryland 21207
(301) 944-0123

HOURS:
Monday - Thursday 11 a.m. - 8 p.m.
Friday 11 a.m. - 5 p.m.
Saturday 10 a.m. - 5 p.m.

MAKING YOUR WEDDING DREAMS COME TRUE

Formal Occasions

Rossand, Inc.

169 Broadview Avenue
Warrenton, Virginia 22186
On the By-Pass, Next to Liberty Bank

703-347-0513

Monday-Friday 10-7
Saturday 10-5
Evenings by Appointment

Make Your Dreams Come True With The Perfect Wedding Gown...

Order Months In Advance!

The Perfect BRIDAL IMAGE

Bridal and Unforgettable Evening Wear
Men's Formal Wear
BRIGGS CHANEY CENTER
SILVER SPRING 384-6901

ESTHER'S
Bridal Boutique

Wedding Belles...

bridal & formal attire
for the special occasion
where you are expected
to be the "belle of the ball."

Annapolis Formal

is the perfect place
to find that special look
for any occasion.

Stop by our Annapolis
location, or contact us
to make an appointment.

REGISTER NOW for the

Third Annual
CAPITOL CITY BRIDAL SHOW

At The Annapolis Ramada
On January 7th, 1990
For more information and registration, call: 1-800-635-9635.
Vendors participation welcome, call: (301) 267-6797.

Mention this advertisement, and
Save $50.00
on selected purchases of $450.00 or more!

Annapolis Formal
Moments For Life

Bay Forest Shopping Center
954 Bay Ridge Road, Annapolis MD 21403

1-800-635-9635 or (301)267-6797
HOURS: M-F 11-8, S 9-5

Bridal Consultants

Memory Lane, Inc.

Personalized Wedding Coordinating
—from Engagement to Honeymoon—

938-7525

Call today for a **FREE** one hour Consultation

"Let Us Plan Your Special Affair"

Time and money—two essential ingredients for planning the perfect wedding—two ingredients that always seem to be in short supply. We can save you both!

JOYOUS OCCASIONS is a "one-stop" bridal consulting service. We're ready to help you plan it all . . . from the announcement of your engagement to your honeymoon trip. By taking a sensitive approach to budget requirements, we can custom design your wedding to reflect your own unique style. Call today for a Complimentary Consultation.

JOYOUS OCCASIONS
Wedding and Party Planners
(301) 248-8027

WCI
WEDDING CLASSICS INCORPORATED

...BECAUSE CLASSIC NEVER
GOES OUT OF STYLE
COMPLETE WEDDING
PLANNING AND SERVICES

(703) 448-7753
TYSONS CORNER VA

ROSEBUD

ANNIVERSARY / WEDDING
CONSULTING & PLANNING SERVICES
CATHY J. TYER

13361 Glen Taylor Lane
Herndon, Virginia 22071

Bus: (703) 471-1340
Mobile: (703) 850-7675

"BECAUSE SPECIAL TIMES DESERVE A SPECIAL TOUCH"

Once-In-A-Lifetime Events Deserve

A Complete Set, Inc.

WEDDING COORDINATION AND CONSULTATION

♥ *Assistance in Every Aspect of your Wedding Plans or With Just a Few Special Details*

♥ *Guidance on Wedding Etiquette*

♥ *Free Initial Consultation*

301-779-9266

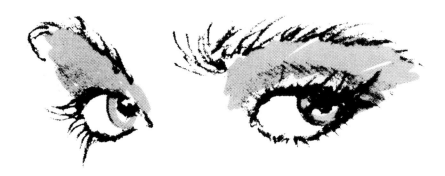

when all eyes are on you

*Isn't it comforting to know
that a professional is taking care of
all the details and those elegant touches
that will make your magical dream come true*

*Let Weddings by Renee be your wedding professional.
Benefit from our experience.
Call today for an in-home complementary consultation*

(703) 548-4924

Member of the Association of Bridal Consultants

57A

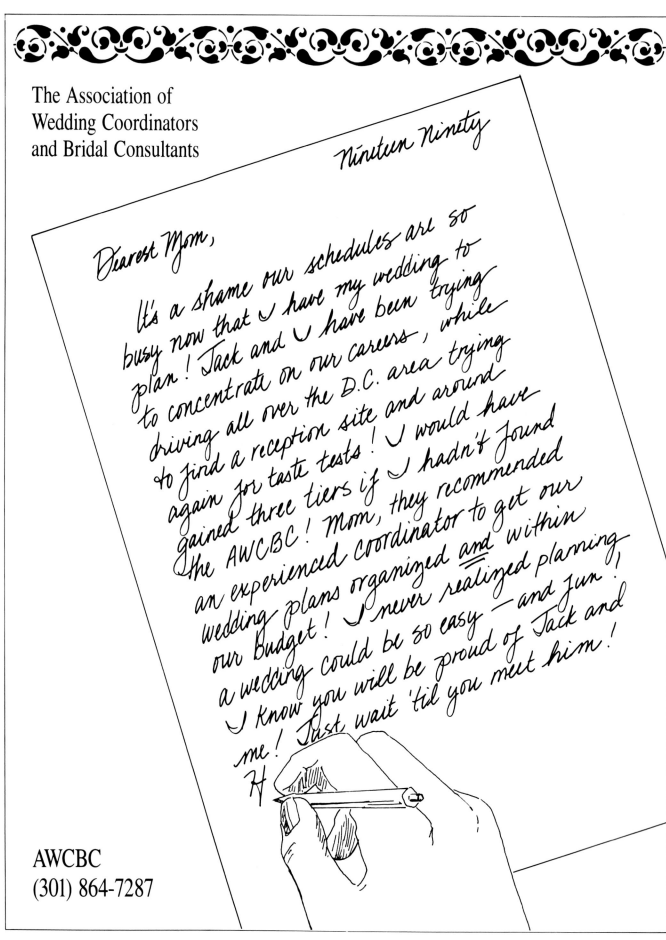

The Association of
Wedding Coordinators
and Bridal Consultants

Nineteen Ninety

Dearest Mom,

It's a shame our schedules are so busy now that I have my wedding to plan! Jack and I have been trying to concentrate on our careers, while driving all over the D.C. area trying to find a reception site and around again for taste tests! I would have gained three tiers if I hadn't found the AWCBC! Mom, they recommended an experienced coordinator to get our wedding plans organized and within our budget! I never realized planning a wedding could be so easy — and fun! I know you will be proud of Jack and me! Just wait 'til you meet him!

H

AWCBC
(301) 864-7287

58A

Unique Weddings

Specialists in Christian Weddings

FOR YOUR SPECIAL DAY

*WEDDINGS * RECEPTIONS *
REHEARSAL DINNERS*

No matter what your budget - our wedding planners will take care of all the details ... Invitations, Florists, Musicians, Video & Photographers, Entertainment, Dressmakers, Tuxedos, Limousines and Honeymoon.

Free Consultation and helpful Wedding Guide

(301) 577-2270

Evening and Weekend Appointments Available

WEDDINGS by LYNNE

Gail Fitzpatrick-Ivey
Wedding Consultant

(202) 635-8584

Weddings • Anniversaries • Parties

_____
_____
_____
_____
_____
_____

WEDDING DREAMS DO COME TRUE WHEN YOU CHOOSE...

"I DO" WEDDINGS
COMPLETE WEDDING PLANNERS
(301) 420-6225

• CONSULTING
• INVITATIONS
• JEWELRY
• SILK FLOWERS

Notes

Caterers

C & H
ATERERS

Finest of Food   Best of Service

ELEGANT, PERSONALIZED FULL SERVICE CATERING

(301) 588-9200

2345 WARREN STREET
SILVER SPRING, MARYLAND

ALL OCCASIONS
CUSTOM MENUS

(301) 384-1123

Orchestrators
of Perfect
Wedding Receptions

Call us
for a copy of our brochure
and a free consultation.

(703) 683-5115

249 South Van Dorn Street, Alexandria, VA

Fresh Seafood Daily

Est. 1973

Open for Lunch & Dinner

Marco Polo Restaurant & Caterers

. . . In Our Location or Yours . . .

Fine Italian, French and Continental Cuisine

Wedding Receptions our Specialty

Catering to all Historic and Private Locations
in the Greater Washington Area

We Are Approved To One Hundred Locations In The D.C. Area
List Furnished Upon Request

Marco Polo Restaurant

Elegant Dining Banquet Facilities for 450 guests in two beautiful rooms

245 Maple Ave. West (Rt. 123), Vienna, Va

VA **(703) 281-3922** • MD **(301) 299-2400**

Contact us for our
Exclusive Bridal Show
Every January.

Private rooms for
Rehearsal Dinners.

When you
want your
wedding reception
to be perfect
depend on...

CREATIVE CATERING CONSULTANTS

Catering*Rehearsal Dinners*Receptions

Creative- Whether your tastes are caviar and champagne, internation cuisines or on the simplier side, we will create a menu to accommodate your individual taste.

Catering- We combine catering expertise with the freshest ingredients and a creative flare that insures your guests enjoyment and your complete satisfaction.

Consultants- Our professional staff will work with you on every detail to provide you with an elegant reception. All with less cost to the bride.

Call for more information on catering menus and reception features.

**CREATIVE CATERING
CONSULTANTS**
12944-D Travilan Road,
Potomac, MD
301-840-2929

NORMANDIE
Caterers
Offering a full line of wedding services

With over 100 years experience, we can assure you of the best day of your life.

Ask about our elegant ballrooms
587-1445

Notes

Have Your
Wedding Occasions
Catered To Your
Special Requests

64A

Beauty

MARY KAY COSMETICS

Free Facials   Glamour Makeovers
Color Awareness Consultation

Discover the radiant glow of Mary Kay
for yourself, your attendants, and your family!

Margaret M. Neill
Senior Sales Director
(703) 750-0929

Janet Kiel
Senior Sales Director
(703) 979-7528

*Let Classic
Image make
you and your
wedding party
beautiful on
your special day!*

*Our full service
salon provides:*
• HAIR STYLING
• FACIALS & MAKE-UP
• MANICURES
• PEDICURES
• TANNING
• COLOR
  COORDINATION

*We offer special wedding
packages for wedding pages
brides - and their grooms too!*

Classic Image

146 Smallwood Village Center
Waldorf, MD
Call for no obligation consultation.
843-8434   932-8090

Choose a veil
that accents you
and your gown—
not overpowers you.

Formalwear

Royal Wedding

* Wedding Consultants are available to help you select your gown, the bridesmaid's dresses, tuxedos for the groom and his groomsmen, and coordinate dresses for your mother and your mother-in-law.

* Bridesmaids get a 10% discount on their dresses when the bride purchases her dress from Royal.

* Groom's tuxedo rental is free when six or more groomsmen rent tuxedos.

* Wedding gowns can be cleaned, treated, and packaged in a special Keepsake Package for easy storage.

Visit any one of our fourteen Royal Formal & Bridal shops and let us help you make your wedding day everything it should be. The most beautiful day of your life.

We look forward to seeing you soon.

Specialists in women's bridal and men's formal fashions.

1515 Rockville Pike Rockville, MD 770-4477	1328 G Street, N.W. Washington, D.C. 737-7144	Iverson Mall Hillcrest Heights, MD 423-4307	Fashion Center Pentagon City 415-2032
Viers Mill Rd. & Univ. Blvd. Wheaton, MD 933-1512	Springfield Mall Springfield, VA 971-0644	Annapolis Mall Annapolis, MD 266-6535	Laurel Centre Mall Laurel, MD 498-1778
Tyson's Corner Center Tyson's Corner, VA 893-7800	Montgomery Mall at Sears Bethesda, MD 469-4307	The Mall in Columbia Columbia, MD 740-3325	Salisbury Mall Salisbury, MD 546-1032
Capital Plaza Mall Landover Hills, MD 341-5555			Landmark Center at Sears Alexandria, VA 354-1611

Royal FORMAL & BRIDAL

FORMAL RENTALS

after Six

pierre cardin   Christian Dior

BILL BLASS

- **Designer Tuxedos**

- **Large Selection of the Latest Styles**

- **Boys' Size 2 to Men's Size 64 in Stock**

FAIRFAX
FAIR CITY MALL
9600J Main Street
(703) 764-1414

SILVER SPRING
8737 COLESVILLE ROAD
at Spring Street
(301) 587-1414

BALTIMORE
MAIN OFFICE
3320 Eastern Avenue
(301) 276-0311
Other Locations
throughout Maryland

Pace Plaza
1724 Woodlawn Drive
(301) 265-1414

North
1903 E. Joppa Road
Joppa & Perring Parkway
(301) 665-1400

Downtown
Baltimore St. at Broadway
(301) 563-1414

Pasadena
Festival at Ritchie Hwy.
(301) 647-7200

Merritt Park Shopping Center
Holabird & Merritt Parkway
(301) 288-1100

6 or more rentals
in your wedding party and the Groom's Tuxedo is **FREE!*￼**
Shoes for Entire Wedding Party at No Charge

*$140 Value
with this coupon

Not just a wedding...A wedding to remember.

Happy Brides . . . Happy Grooms . . . The Best In Formal Wear That's Why *Mitchell's* is Number One!

That's why more brides and grooms call on Mitchell's more than any other formalwear specialist in the Southeast. Your wedding demands the very best and our professionally trained fashion consultants will guarantee you have the perfect style and fit.

With the largest selection on display you'll be sure to find the look you've always dreamed of. Now is not the time to take chances and not all formalwear companies are alike. Over 40 years of commitment have made Mitchell's the number one fashion leader in your area.

With 100 convenient locations, visit the Mitchell's Fashion Consultant nearest you . . .You'll Both Be Happy Ever After.

Ballston Common,
Arlington, VA 22203
703/243-8998

Manassas Mall
Manassas, VA 22110
703/361-4463

gingiss formalwear

World's largest formalwear renter.

Formalwear by:

- Adolfo Couture
- After Six Couture
- Bill Blass
- Chaps-Ralph Lauren
- Charles Jourdan
- Christian Dior
- Francesco Maiolo
- Giorgio Patrino
- Henry Grethel
- Lanvin
- Lord West
- Perry Ellis
- Pierre Cardin
- Kilgour, French & Stanbury
- Polo University Club
  by Ralph Lauren
- Yves Saint Laurent

Rental and Sales

Annapolis Fashion Festival, Annapolis, MD
(301) 224-3772

Lakeforest Mall, Gaithersburg, MD
(301) 258-9350

White Flint Mall, N. Bethesda, MD
(301) 770-1747

Lanham Shopping Center, Lanham, MD
(301) 731-0230

Galleria @ Tysons II, Mclean, Va
(703) 821-8613

Spring Mall Square, Springfield, Va
(703) 971-7303

Christian Dior

Pierre Cardin

LORD WEST
CROWN COLLECTION

BLACK & WHITE

1235
WISCONSIN
AVENUE
WASHINGTON, D.C.

(202)
337-6660

LAUREL TUXEDO

IS FIRST IN . . .

- QUALITY — Newest Suits
- SELECTION — Hundreds of Combinations
- PRICE — Ask about Group Rates
- SERVICE — Fittings and Alterations

SEE US TODAY!

725-4619

Laurel Lakes
US Route #1
Laurel, MD 20707

A Division of Laurel Bridal & Gown Shop

Reserve
the Tuxedos
early
to assure
availability!

In Arlington
"after
hours"
51st Year

TUXEDO RENTAL
WEDDING SPECIALIST

DISCOUNTS TO WEDDINGS

*WE SPECIALIZE IN HARD TO FIND TUXEDOS
SIZES UP TO 72*

*YOUR COMPLETE
TUXEDO CONSULTANTS FOR
WEDDINGS*

522-6455

VISA   MASTERCARD   DISCOVER

2715 Wilson Blvd., Arlington, Virginia

Classic Formal Wear
TUXEDO RENTALS & SALES

Guaranteed lowest
prices on the largest
selection available
on the East Coast

Free groom's rental with
5 additional rentals

"Don't Get Married Without Us!"

Laurel	Clinton
604-4088	**868-1555**

Formal Wear
by FLOWER TOWNE

For those who demand
the ultimate in:
STYLE,
QUALITY & SERVICE

*FREE GROOMS
TUX!*
*Call for details
and information*

COMPARE OUR
PRICES!

FLOWER TOWNE
Indian Head Highway
301-645-6939   301-753-6222
301-743-2220

Notes

Out-of-Town Accommodations

GARFIELD Characters: © 1978, 1980 United Feature Syndicate, Inc.

Your wedding guests can stay in suite luxury.

Make it a suite night to remember at an Embassy Suites® hotel. Look what you'll get:

A luxurious two-room suite complete with living room, private bedroom, and wet bar with refrigerator.
Free, cooked-to-order breakfast served every morning in our beautiful atrium.
Complimentary two-hour manager's reception+ each evening.

And if your wedding party books 20 or more suites, the bride and groom's suite is complimentary.

EMBASSY SUITES HOTELS℠

1-800-EMBASSY

You don't have to be a fat cat to enjoy The Suite Life.℠

WASHINGTON, D.C. DOWNTOWN
1250 22nd Street N.W.
(202) 857-3388

TYSONS CORNER, VA
8517 Leesburg Pike
(703) 883-0707

CRYSTAL CITY, VA
1300 Jefferson Davis Hwy.
(703) 979-9799

*Price is per suite, per night. Price subject to change. +Subject to state and local laws.

Make your wedding a suite affair.

Our luxurious suites are perfect for your out-of-town guests. And when you book 20 or more rooms, the bridal suite is complimentary. We feature:

- Beautifully appointed suites with spacious bedrooms, separate living rooms, and fully equipped kitchens or wet bars

- Champagne, fruit basket, and elegant chocolates for the bride and groom

- Complimentary transportation to the ceremony for your out-of-town guests*

- Complimentary amenities, including full hot buffet breakfast and first-run videos for viewing on your in-suite VCR

- Rehearsal dinner facilities

Extraordinary accommodations at ordinary rates

WOODFIN SUITES

1380 Piccard Drive
Rockville, Maryland 20850

(301) 590-9880 (800) 237-8811

*within 8 miles

Limousine Service

56 Fabergé Eggs
38 DaVinci Paintings
7 Wonders Of The World

But Only 1 Wedding Of Your Lifetime

ANDERSON-LA STRADA
LIMOUSINE SERVICE

"Helping To Create The Wedding Of Your Life"
Call today and ask about our special wedding packages

(703) 761-4CAR   **(703) 761-4227**

Create an "**At Your Service Limousine**" Wedding Package for Your Specific Wedding-Related Transportation Needs or Choose from our **Special**, **Extra Special**, and **Ultimate** Package Combinations.

Special	Extra Special	Ultimate
3 Hours	3 Hours	4 Hours
Unlimited Miles	Unlimited Miles	Unlimited Miles
"Congratulations"	"Congratulations"	Congratulations"
Banner	Banner	Banner
Stretch Limousine	Champagne	Dozen Long Stem Roses
	Rose Bud Vase	Dom Perignon Champagne
	Stretch Limousine	Airport Transfer
		Super Stretch Limousine

Ask About Our Bachelor/Bachelorette Party Limousine Packages

"Our Name Says It All"

• Night on the Town • Weddings • Airport Transfers
• Auto Drive-Away • Sightseeing • Proms

*Ask About Our Concert and Sports Events Packages w/Tickets, Our "Limo Stork",
And Our Atlantic City Express*

Ask About Our
"Wedding Pages Discount"

CORPORATE ACCOUNTS WELCOME
Local & Long Distance • 24 Hours

DC, Maryland, & Virginia

CALL (301) 762-2255

*Embassy
Limousine Service*

Limousine service is one of the best bargains available for your wedding day. And on that very special day, you'll want to choose a limousine service upon whom you can ultimately depend. If you're not familiar with limousines or how to utilize one in conjunction with a wedding, please call and we'll be glad to assist you.

 232-1000
Major Credit Cards Accepted

Two Thousand Weddings!

Elite has driven for over 2,000 weddings in the past 5 years, and we have learned what couples want from a limousine service - prompt courteous chauffeurs, beautiful limousines and affordable prices. Not to mention features like red carpet, **free** airport transportation and, of course, champagne. Call today for our free brochure.

ELITE LIMOUSINE SERVICE
100 W. Jefferson St., # 200 • Falls Church, VA
(703) 533-8764   1-800-673-8188

CINDERELLA

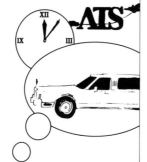

can dance until dawn
& never worry about
her ATS Limousine
turning into
a pumpkin

ATS
has driven thousands
of Cinderellas to their
Wedding Ball and we
would like to add you
to our long list of
satisfied clients.
ATS Executive Coaches
are fully equipped with
all amenities and your
ATS Wedding Package
has some special extras.
Call today for reservations
or write to:

**ATS Limousine Service
3609-A Chain Bridge Road
Fairfax, VA 22030**

(703) 591-3366

Your Wedding Day

When you think of Luxury
and Comfort think of
Cardinal Limousine.
Luxury from our limousines,
Comfort from our prices

Cardinal Limousine

(703) 243-2578 • (703) 532-0725
Pager: (703) 597-1372

~Special~
Wedding Package
$147
Regular Package Price $168

* <u>3 Hours of Luxury Stretch Limousine Service.</u>

* <u>Choose the color of your limousine</u> *from our all new fleet.
These are top of the line luxury vehicles fully equipped
and immaculately maintained. Features include TV,
Bar, Phone, FM Cassette, and Privacy Divider.*

* <u>Complimentary Champagne.</u>

* <u>Professional uniformed chauffeur at your service.</u>

* <u>Extended service is available at a discount rate.</u>
*Package does not include 15% gratuity for driver.
Please book early to insure color and availability.*

Preferred
LIMOUSINE
703-978-1102
P.O. Box 1157, Springfield, VA 22151

REGENCY LIMOUSINE SERVICE
Whatever the affair . . . Let Regency take you there!

"Specializing in Weddings"

Luxury Limousines, Sedans and Minibuses
White Ultra Stretch Limousines Available

Models Available with Bar, TV,
Telephone, Stereo and Much More..

Anyplace • Anytime • Any Occasion

622-0200

*Champagne Wedding
Packages Available*

622-LIMO

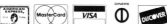

**12055 Tech Road
Silver Spring, Maryland 20904**

All Major Credit Cards Honored

*800-262-LIMO
FAX 622-0181*

1954 Steel Saloon Rolls-Royce Bentley	1941 Cadillac Grande Opera Limousine

"Joy! Those Ancient Motor Machines!"
Ye Olde Limousine Service
948-7170
Weddings, Special Occasions, Airport Transfers

_____

_____

_____

_____

_____

_____

_____

_____

_____

Don't Compromise The Most Important Day Of Your Life.

WEDDING SPECIALISTS

Act I Limousine Service
(703) 323-9509

RESERVE EARLY

BALTIMORE– WASHINGTON
Limousine Service

Luxury Limousines For All Occasions!

- White and Black Stretch Lincolns Available
- Professional and Courteous Chauffeurs
- Complimentary Champagne
- Also Available for Bachelor and Bachelorette Parties

(301) 805-5050
BOWIE, MARYLAND

Notes

_____

_____

_____

_____

_____

_____

_____

_____

_____

_____

_____

On the Day of your Dreams use...

Exclusive Limousines Service Inc.

OUR WEDDING PACKAGES INCLUDE:
First Class Lincoln Stretch Limousine
Equipped with:

AM/FM Cass. Stereo	Cellular Phones	Privacy Windows
VCR Player	Intercom Systems	Solid Divider
Color TV	Tinted Windows	Moon Roof

Also Provided Free:
Tuxedo Uniformed Chauffeur
wearing black tuxedo with tails, white shirt, red tie & cummerbund
Rolled out red carpet
Roses for the Bride & Groom
Fully Stocked Bar
gilbeys gin, smirnoff vodka, j&b scotch, bacardi rum, seagrams 7
CELEBRATION BOTTLE OF CHAMPAGNE!

SPECIAL PACKAGE DEALS
BACHELOR & BACHELORETTE PARTIES
BRIDAL SHOWERS • AIRPORT TRANSFER

(301) 856-0066
WE ACCEPT AMERICAN EXPRESS CREDIT CARDS

copyright 1993 ELS no part of this material may be reproduced without the written consent of exclusive limousine service inc.   Equipment availability subject to change

Notes

Florists

Bob's Flowers

Proudly Serving Washington Area Brides
Since 1972

© 87

the wedding & party specialists

- weddings, bar mitzvahs, banquets, luncheons - all occasions
- creative floral and/or balloon designs to suit every taste and budget
- careful attention to details
- serving the entire Metropolitan area
- FREE consultations and planning sessions (by appointment, please)

3 CONVENIENT LOCATIONS

| Leisureworld Plaza 3800 International Blvd. Silver Spring, MD 598-0900 | Congressional Plaza 1645 Rockville Pike Rockville, MD 770-1330 | Walnut Hill 16541 Frederick Road Gaithersburg, MD 869-2400 |

HERNDON FLORIST, INC.

Experienced Wedding Specialist

716 Lynn Street
Herndon, Virginia
437-4990

Mon-Fri 9-6
Sat - 9-5
Wedding Consultations
by appointment

---

*TRADITIONAL AND UNIQUE
SILK FLORAL DESIGN FOR
YOUR WEDDING DAY...
AND AFTER.*

**T
H
A
T
SPECIAL**

By appointment
(301) 977-1777

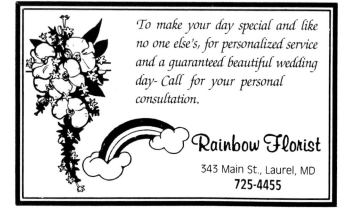

To make your day special and like no one else's, for personalized service and a guaranteed beautiful wedding day- Call for your personal consultation.

Rainbow Florist

343 Main St., Laurel, MD
725-4455

FLORAL ARRANGEMENTS

*Check with
your florist
to guarantee the
seasonal availability
of your flowers.*

floral designs

Just for You

(301) 460-6517

Silver Spring, MD

Carol Bowen & Lorraine Abrams
Please call for an appointment

Traditional and Unique

When Only The
Best Will Do!

BY APPOINTMENT
SILK FLOWER DESIGNS
301-345-6735

Touch of Silk

Specializing in Silk Flowers
Riverdale, Maryland
(301) 459-5038

Carol S. Hite   Hours by Appointment

*The most
beautiful day
in your life
deserves
The most
beautiful
flowers.*

Serving Sterling, Reston, Herndon

*Free consultation
Call for appointment*

The Flower Depot
*93 Sugarland Run Dr.
Sterling, VA 22170*

(703) 430-5807   Metro- 450-4884

FLOWER TOWNE

"An Experience In Floral Design"

Unique Floral Ideas Designed For Cherished Memories

Complete Wedding Services

Tuxedo Rental	Candelabras	Wedding Album
Invitations	Plant Rental	Engraved Announcements
Bridal Gown Preservation		Accessories

Teleflora

Indian Head Highway
301-645-6939
301-753-6222   301-743-2220

FTD

Notes

_____

_____

_____

_____

_____

_____

_____

_____

_____

_____

_____

_____

_____

_____

_____

_____

_____

Party Tents

TOPS
IN TOTAL WEDDING RENTALS...

RENTAL DEPOT

For over 15 years our Professional Reputation has been built on providing quality rental equipment to virtually hundreds of weddings and receptions.

• TENTS • TABLES and CHAIRS • DANCE FLOORS •
• BAND STANDS • CHINA and SILVER • LINEN •

Call or write for our complimentary catalog

RENTAL DEPOT®

9801 Nokesville Road ◆ *Manassas, VA 22110*
703-335-1777

Photographers

SINCE 1935...

DISTINCTIVE PHOTOGRAPHY
THAT LASTS FOREVER

Glogau

GLOGAU STUDIO

5110 Ridgefield Road at River Road, Bethesda

652-9577

OUR PRINTS ARÉ
**LIFETIME
GUARANTEED**

Finer Wedding Images

Because we Care

Boudoir Portraits • Passport Photos • Silver Images

DANIELS
PHOTOGRAPHY
INC.

Tall Oaks Shopping Center
471-7175

Reston

Our 22nd Year

VA.

"Simply Beautiful Photography"

PRESTIGE STUDIOS

585-4482 1-800-873-FOTO

91A

You made one terrific choice.
Now make another.

Henry L. Pitt Photography, Inc.

by Appointment
(703) 690-2391

Your Personal Love Story in Pictures . . .

by **Royal** COLOR PHOTO
BRIDAL PHOTOGRAPHERS

CONVENIENTLY LOCATED IN THE *Royal* FORMAL & BRIDAL STORES

Iverson Mall
423-0900

2729 University Blvd.
Wheaton, Md.
984-2344

1515 Rockville Pike
Rockville, Md.
468-5898

Columbia Mall
740-1233

Springfield Mall
922-5654

Annapolis Mall
224-2555

Main Plant ▪ 3800-34th Street ▪ Mount Rainier, Md. ▪ 927-3010

Formals!

Candids!

Special Effects!

PRICES TO FIT EVERY BUDGET
WE WELCOME TELEPHONE INQUIRIES
Call us for our SPECIALS!

The Choice of the Most Discriminating Families

© COPYRIGHT CAMELOT PHOTOGRAPHERS

(301) 340-7466

Call Max Krupka "Producer of Simcha Showcase"

Distinctive Memories

On Location and Studio Portraits

Packages to Suit Every Budget

Abstract Studios

• Photography • Video •
9723 Baltimore Blvd. College Park Md. 301-441-4600

Call for Our Brochure & Price List

95A

The beauty and excitement
of your wedding day
captured forever in
natural unposed photographs
by Roosevelt Sharpe, Jr.

Silver Spring, Maryland   *(301) 681-9217*

Carl Cox Photography

Capture those precious moments

Call for appointment to reveiw our
unique wedding albums

(301) 670-0086

Y ou see it in each other's eyes. The magic of this moment. The dreams for tomorrow. A declaration of love.
Capture the magic of your wedding with professional wedding photography.

And remember the magic.

By
Cook's Photo-Art Studio
Vienna, Va. 22180

(703) 938-5885   (703) 938-5858

Elizabethan StudioS
Fine Art Photography

860-4800

JOHN BRADY
124 MacGregor Ridge Road
Stafford, VA 2254

(703) 720-1531

Providing high quality
photography at an affordable
price for 20 years.

97A

Introducing the

of Wedding Photography

Bennett Studios lets you relive your memories of that special day in pictures. Exquisite photography that you will treasure for the rest of your life. Call today to discuss plans for your photo and video needs.

—Special combination photo and video packages—

Bennett Studios

Photography and Videotaping
245 Maple Avenue • Vienna, VA 22180

(Above Marco Polo Restaurant)

(703) 255-3500

CLASSIC ◆ PHOTOGRAPHY

Specializing in preserving your
most treasured moment

Remember Today... Tomorrow with Pictures from Classic

*ASK ABOUT OUR GUARANTEE
COMPETITVE RATES QUALITY &
SERVICE*

779-6897
**4307 JEFFERSON
SUITE 405**
HYATTSVILLE

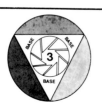

MEMBER

- Packages to suit every budget.
- Proofs included with packages.
- Great value and service at yesterday's prices.

Base 3 Photography
435-1860

Jontina

Photography

572-5129

Have Jontina Photography preserve the romance of your love by photographing those special events that make your wedding unique and memorable. No one is more qualified to capture the story of your wedding day in pictures.

Jontina is noted for its European style photography . . . a technique that is truly unique.

Call for an appointment
Serving Md. - D.C. - Va.

Petteway Photographics

Steven Petteway

Your Wedding Photography Can Be Sensational

- ⫴ *Elegant Portraits*
- ⫴ *Color Slides Included*
- ⫴ *Custom Hand Printing*
- ⫴ *Flexible Coverage*

Call (703) 690-2889

Creation Waits
Photography
For That Very Special Wedding

ALLEN THORNBURGH
703 243-0536
Residence 703 528-7984

PROPER EXPOSURES

ERIC & K.J. BRENNEMAN
PHOTOGRAPHERS

(301) 253-9249

"Memories of Distinction"
Conveniently located in Upper Montgomery County

99A

AWARD WINNING PHOTOGRAPHY
by
Daniel Whelan
681-8260
Silver Spring, Maryland

len raves studio

WEDDINGS   PORTRAITS   PORTFOLIOS

(703)659-1794
(703)631-1170

THERE ARE TIMES WHEN

ONLY **SISSON STUDIOS** WILL DO

569 - 6051

Springfield, Virginia

SIEGEL PHOTOGRAPHICS

ERWIN A. SIEGEL   (703) 960-6726

BY APPOINTMENT ONLY

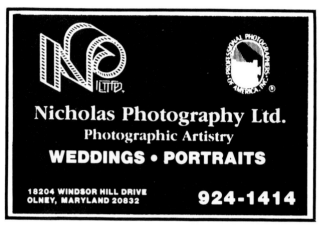

Nicholas Photography Ltd.
Photographic Artistry
WEDDINGS • PORTRAITS

18204 WINDSOR HILL DRIVE
OLNEY, MARYLAND 20832   **924-1414**

"A Soft Image of Love"

Portrait Design by Dao
(703) 680-7700

You create the moments...
We create the memories.

Weddings   Captured Moments   Portraits

"The Natural Choice"
301-870-2614

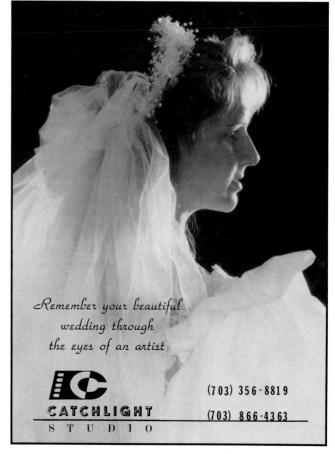

Remember your beautiful wedding through the eyes of an artist

CATCHLIGHT
S T U D I O

(703) 356-8819

(703) 866-4363

101A

Expressions Of Love On A Very Special Day

Creative Reflections (703) 435-1518

Tessmer of Fairfax Custom Photography

(703) 941-8270

Video and Photography Complete Packages

RSVP Wedding Photography & Video Quality For Less!

301-277-3166

Invitations and Wedding Supplies

Paper Images

CUSTOM INVITATIONS
WEDDING ACCESSORIES
FREE CONSULTATIONS
CALLIGRAPHY

"With personalized service, kindness and consideration, you will find our prices are competitive and our service is incomparable."

Geri Pross   340-0308

Rockville, MD

European wedding favours designed especially for you — prices for every budget!

Impress your guests with elegantly designed European style wedding favours - known as a Bomboniera!

Favour Designs For:

Bridal Showers	Weddings
Christenings	Baby Showers
Anniversaries	Birthdays

Sold separately: Tulle, Netting, Pre-Cut Circles, Flowers, Jordan Almonds, Printed Ribbons, Napkins, Rice Roses.

WRAP IT UP
240 West Broad Street
(Route 7)
Falls Church, Virginia 22046
532-3626   759-3908

When Your Dreams Come True . . . you shouldn't have to worry about everything being perfect.

Victoria's can plan the perfect wedding from start to finish

- Invitations
- Napkins
- Matches
- Favors
- Planning
- Rehersal
- Wedding
- Calligraphy
- Limousines

. . . Victoria's Will Be There
VICTORIA'S WEDDING CONSULTANTS

645-3185

Victoria Minni   Open 7 Days

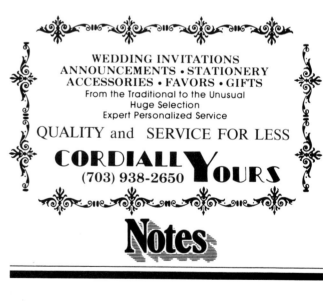

WEDDING INVITATIONS
ANNOUNCEMENTS • STATIONERY
ACCESSORIES • FAVORS • GIFTS
From the Traditional to the Unusual
Huge Selection
Expert Personalized Service

QUALITY and SERVICE FOR LESS

CORDIALLY YOURS
(703) 938-2650

Notes

_____

_____

_____

_____

_____

_____

_____

Your own Church
or chosen wedding location
on your own Wedding Stationery

"Possibly the most distinguished wedding stationery ever produced."

ST. PETER'S CHURCH, MOUNTVIEW

ALL YOU NEED IS A PHOTOGRAPH or some other picture from which artists can produce an original drawing to be printed as a delicate reproduction on your Wedding Stationery –EXCLUSIVE stationery at an ORDINARY price !

Las invitaciones tambien pueden ser in espanol.

Send or phone now to:
Illustrated Wedding Stationery
3900 Jermantown Road
Suite Number 350
Fairfax, VA 22030
Tel. (703) 934 4650

GIBBON BRIDGE COUNTRY HOUSE HOTEL

- Invitations
- Calligraphy
- Accessories
- Favors
- Balloons
- Imprinting

Rose Leaves
CUSTOM INVITATIONS

Carol Rose   (301) 493-5554
Bethesda, MD
By Appointment Only.

You are cordially invited to preview our extensive collection of Wedding Invitations and Personalized Accessories.

Select all your wedding needs from a wide range of styles and prices.

R.S.V.P.
COLOPHON PRESS
3729 University Boulevard West
Kensington, Maryland 20895
301-933-1555

Empire Printing, Inc.

COMPLETE WEDDING SERVICES

"RUSH SERVICE AVAILABLE"

- Invitations
- Announcements
- Napkins and accessories
- Thank you notes
- Wedding Programs
- Engraving
- Personalized Stationery

OPEN SATURDAY

971-3388

6118-A Franconia Road, Franconia Shopping Center
(Convenient to Springfield, Alexandria, Woodbridge)

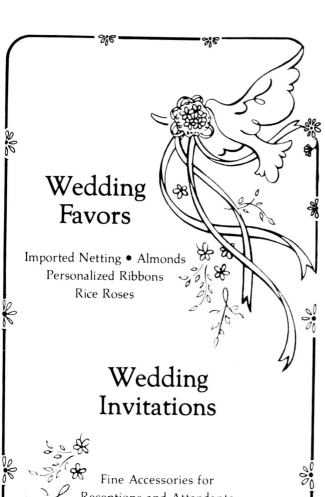

Wedding Favors

Imported Netting • Almonds
Personalized Ribbons
Rice Roses

Wedding Invitations

Fine Accessories for
Receptions and Attendants

Personalized Matches,
Napkins

TARAMINA

Casa delle Bomboniere

946-9300

In the Wheaton Triangle
2515 Enalls Avenue
Wheaton, Maryland
Across from Wheaton Plaza

Calligraphy Services

Calligraphy

CALLIGRAPHIC DESIGN

8802 GLADE HILL ROAD
FAIRFAX, VIRGINIA
2·2·0·3·1
(703) 978-7811

Add a special touch to your invitations with the beautiful style of calligraphy.

By Invitation Only

- Custom Invitations • Announcements • Accessories
- Calligraphy
- Engraved and Raised Printing • Social and Business Stationery
- Personal Touch Service

Gaithersburg, Maryland
301-963-5858

Notes

_____
_____
_____
_____
_____
_____
_____
_____
_____
_____
_____
_____

Add a special
touch to your
invitations

Together with their parents
Elizabeth Ann Martig
and
James Buchanan
share with them
...tion of love
...eenth of November
nineteen hu... ...nd eighty-seven
St. ... Luthern
510 North ... Street
Omaha, Ne...ska

with your own
beautiful style

Notes

Rental Supplies

BETTER EVENTS has everything you need to ensure perfection for all your special occasions. BETTER EVENTS is your complete source for top quality party and equipment rentals.. elegant china, silver and glassware Choose table linens with the refined grace of white and cream, or match the seasons with a spectrum of glorious colors.

Create your own special setting in one of our tents. We have the basics and all the specialty items too.

Visit our showroom! Allow yourself the luxury and the confidence of working with our highly skilled events specialist to help you create an individual look . . . one with flair and style.

Experience has taught us that understanding your needs is only the first step. Giving you the best service you've ever had is the next.

Our goal is to make all of your events. . .
BETTER EVENTS!

Better Events, Inc.

Fairfax, Virginia

703-591-0400
Open 7 Days A Week

Serving:
VA., D.C., & MD.

CANOPY RENTALS

**Everything
You Need
but the
Food and
the Guests!**

Tables • Chairs
Tents • Dance Floors
China • Chafers
Glassware • Serving Trays

**Everything you need
for a Perfect
Wedding**

WHERE **PLUS** MEANS ONE OF THE AREA'S LARGEST PARTY RENTALS

**DELIVERY AVAILABLE
PARTY CONSULTANT AVAILABLE**

SPRINGFIELD

(703) **451-6060**

LEESBURG

(703) **771-1657**

7701 FULLERTON RD.
SPRINGFIELD, VA 22153

HOURS: MON THRU SAT 7:30AM TO 6PM

237 SHENANDOAH ST.
LEESBURG, VA 22075

Take
Advantage
Of the
Experience and
Knowledge Your
Local
Professionals
Offer.

**AAA
"PARTY
RENTALS"**

Rent all your Wedding
and Reception Needs!

**WEDDING ARCHES • CANDELABRA
CHINA • GLASSWARE • CHAFERS
FOUNTAINS • TABLES • LINENS
CHAIRS • CANOPIES
QUALITY PAPER &
PLASTIC PRODUCTS**

Personalized Imprinting • Invitations

Include us in Your
Wedding Plans

6539 Annapolis Road
Landover Hills, Maryland

386-4000

111A

Wedding Rentals
Rentals and Sales

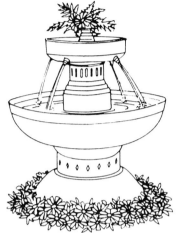

- Fountains
- China & Glassware
- Tables & Chairs
- Silver Service
- Canopies & Arches
- Linens
- Wedding Invitations & Accessories

AMEX, VISA, MC

832-1818
Delivery Available

U-RENT CO.
2204 R.I. Ave., N.E.
Washington, D.C. 20018

Here Comes The Bride...

BROOKE RENTAL center ®

We Rent The Things You Need.®

Canopies...Tents...Tables...
Chairs...China...Glasses...
Linens...Silver...and more.

243-2122 | 938-4807
Arlington | Vienna

Notes

_____
_____
_____
_____
_____
_____
_____
_____
_____
_____
_____
_____
_____

Entertainment

Bristol Sounds

Since 1976

DISC JOCKEYS...When Quality Counts

For over 14 years, Bristol Sounds Disc Jockeys has made Special Moments unforgettable with Special Music.

Call us for a free Information Package or set up an appointment to visit us at our Customer Reception Center where you can view videotapes of our Wedding Professionals, see and hear a Bristol Sounds Music System and talk to us about the Special Music for your Special Day.

Call The DEEJAY HOTLINE™
(301)474-3000
NORTHERN VIRGINIA (703) 734-0777
BALTIMORE (301) 750-2424

 MasterCard

Bob Tennyson Orchestras

Ceremony Soloists and Ensembles
Strolling Musicians
Cocktail Combos
Bands . . . 4 to 16 piece groups

Featuring Quality Music for 3 Generations

585-8317
Silver Spring

Soundman™ disc Jockeys

Let us help make your wedding reception everything you dreamed it would be. "Romantic, Exciting, Special."

This is your big day—so don't settle for anything less! Choose the finest in DJ entertainment—Soundman Disc Jockeys.

Maryland
(301) 345-5496
Virginia
(703) 691-0044

114A

When you want it to be perfect...

... call the wedding specialists

BLACK TIE D.J.'S

FEATURING ...

- **EXPERIENCED DISC JOCKEYS** who will make your wedding reception a perfect success. Your disc jockey will announce and coordinate all of the traditional events and see to it that everything runs smoothly.

- **ALL TYPES OF MUSIC** with thousands of songs to choose from. We customize the music especially for your reception and can please all ages and music tastes. Your special requests are welcome.

- **CONTINUOUS MUSIC** for the entire length of your reception. We have music for dancing as well as the perfect background music. The volume is always kept at a comfortable level.

- **PROFESSIONAL QUALITY SOUND SYSTEMS** which have been attractively designed to complement the elegance of your reception. With several sizes of systems available we can accommodate any size reception.

- **PERSONALIZED SERVICE** to assure that everything will be done exactly as you desire. We assist you in planning all of the details in advance so that your reception will be worry-free.

Call for our free brochure

(703) 425-4677

VISA

Ask about special savings on all popular lines of wedding stationery

The Lace Music

Music for All Occasions

Solo Strings
to
Complete Bands
from
Black Tie to Casual

Anthony W. Aversano
(703) 830-1060

Let Our Music
Give You
Beautiful Memories

Inter-Media, Inc. can make your dream Wedding, Bar Mitzvah, or Holiday Party a reality. Our entertainment services make it easy for you to plan the music for a perfect event.

We have all styles of music- Classical, Ethnic, Big Band, Jazz, Top 40/ Variety, Country- and all sizes of bands from 3 to 17 pieces. We also offer professional DJ Services. Our band leaders and DJs are experienced MCs who make sure that everything is just the way you want it.

We have video tapes, audio tapes and song lists that you can view in a relaxed setting. Please give us a call now and begin planning to make your dreams come true.

INTER MEDIA
Music & Entertainment Services

(703)534-5705

FLUTE & GUITAR

"The Elegant Touch"

Weddings   Parties
Receptions   Recitals

Baroque, Classical and Contemporary Chamber Music

FLUTAR PRODUCTIONS

(301) 927-1661

Spotlight Productions

Complete Live Musical Program
for Ceremony and Reception

(703) 266-3844

PM SOUNDS
D.J. ENTERTAINMENT

THE PROMISE OF MUSICAL MEMORIES WITH PM SOUNDS
FEATURING THOUSANDS OF TITLES ON COMPACT DISCS
PROFESSIONAL AND PERSONAL SERVICE

STEVEN MORGAN

(301) 384-4550

More Brides Choose...

SOUND
GRAPHICS
DJ'S

SINCE 1977

FOR WEDDING RECEPTION
ENTERTAINMENT

323-0523
SERVING VA, MD, DC
1-800-736-1606

"THE #1 CHOICE FOR WEDDING ENTERTAINMENT"

A wide variety
of musical entertainment
is available to enhance
your wedding &
reception.

WHY WOULD YOU LEAVE THE ENTERTAINMENT AT YOUR RECEPTION TO JUST ANYONE?

America's Premier DJ's Inc.

- Personalized Service—**YOU** Meet **your** DJ
- Extensive Song List—**YOU** Select **your** Music
- Professional, Experienced DJ's—**YOU** choose the personality and volume.

**CALL TODAY FOR YOUR FREE
ENTERTAINMENT PACKAGE.
MENTION THIS AD & SAVE $20.**

(703) 978-7341

Serving the Entire Metro Area

Don't know which D.J. to choose?

"RELAX"

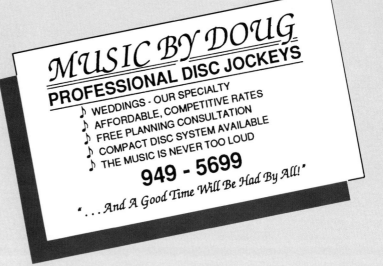

MUSIC BY DOUG
PROFESSIONAL DISC JOCKEYS
♪ WEDDINGS - OUR SPECIALTY
♪ AFFORDABLE, COMPETITIVE RATES
♪ FREE PLANNING CONSULTATION
♪ COMPACT DISC SYSTEM AVAILABLE
♪ THE MUSIC IS NEVER TOO LOUD
949 - 5699
"...And A Good Time Will Be Had By All!"

We've been doing weddings forever!

Diamond ALLEY
Music For All Occasions

Entertainment.
The most important part of a successful reception.
Don't settle for second best.

Box 246, Brookeville, MD 20833   301-854-5022

DISC JOCKEY ENTERTAINMENT

CUSTOMIZED

Your choices of music, format, attire, and details.

PERSONALIZED

*Meet your Disc Jockey **before** signing a contract.*

PROFESSIONAL

Many years experience and hundreds of references.

View our Demonstration Video with no obligation and receive a **free** in person consultation and planning guide for your reception.

dB Sound Systems
inc.

"We're More Than Just Music"

(703) 790-9144

Virginia • Maryland • District of Columbia

♪ Ceremony music also available

119A

"THE D.J. CONNECTION"

(301) 952-2002
PORTA PARTY DISC JOCKEY'S

JIM

CHRIS

The DJ Company you deal with is the key to a successful Wedding Reception and:

JOHN

We provide anything and everything any
Disk Jockey Company offers,
equal to or better. And we
"Garr on teee" what we promise you!

JIM

Features and Benefits of "The D.J. Connection"

Experience: Company owned by the GRAND POO BA of DJ's. 21 years of DJ entertaining and public speaking.

Owner of company answers phone: You deal with me personally. I have DJ'd & MC'd over 1000 Wedding Receptions.

Professional Quality DJ's & MC's: Experienced and trained. All have insight to entertain and *Play 52 Week's Yearly!*

We specialize to your needs and desires: We work with you to make *our* affair together, better. Communication assured.

Personal Concern: We try to take a personal interest in you and your affair. *"We Care"* and want your party to be a success.

Confidence: Scheduled properly to enable your DJ to be on time and not rush. Assigned Back Up DJ for your special Occasion.

Never a No Show: We have never had a DJ not show up. Depth in experienced DJ's to assure you of confidence. *And Never Late.*

We dress according to your affair: From special dress to Black Tie. Your perogative. You say how you want your DJ to dress.

Any reason, you name it!!!
Affordable, Portable, Party Disc Jockeys

Anniversary-Birthday-Banquet-Christmas-New Year-Reunion-Mitz Va-Graduation-Picnic-School-Office-Co Promo-Pool-Educational

Any music: Whatever kind of music you and your guests want know how to present it in a proficient manner.

Any time-any place: Indoors, Outdoors, 24 hours a day - seven a week. *Anywhere U.S.A.*

Written guarantee: We guarantee what you and I agree on and we promise you. Assuring you of a success with our DJ's.

See, Hear, Communicate: With your *assigned DJ.* W appropriate, after all, do you want strangers at your party?

Performing Weekly: Fairlanes Bowling Centers, Foreign Embas Club's, Business and Private Affairs in *MD, DC, VA & FLA.*

Computer controlled: All aspects of booking and busi controlled on computers to discuss and alter your needs quickly.

Wedding Reception Guidelines: Prepared and designed with of experience and thousands of parties. *Mailed upon request.*

Special Forms: We have a unique 2 page *"Music Planner"* and 2 *"Wedding Reception Planner"* to help us plan your party.

Specializing in Wedding Receptions

The DJ you select will be the entertainment at the most memorable and prestigious event of your life. Be sure of your entertainm
You are responsible for providing entertainment that you can be proud of. This event is the first day of the rest of your life and sho
not be unremembered because of an unskilled DJ.

Put your trust in a seasoned, weekly performing Disc Jockey. I can confidently say you are reading about the *BEST!* and if you want y
party to be a *SUCCESS,* there is no need to call the *REST!* **Current roster of over 40 Disc Jockey's!**

Call now! I won't call you (I hate telephone soliciting), You must call me, **Jim.** Please call to discuss your personal needs.
Book early: You must book early to reserve skilled DJ's. *Talk to me,* I will tell you what I have available.

Mention you saw our ad in "THE WEDDING PAGES", I will mail you our "WEDDING RECEPTION GUIDELINES" and "MUSIC
PLANNER." Any information you give us will be used in strict confidence in our office only and not be given out to others.

Smile its a beautiful day !!!!

952-2002   Need help with planning ?   Pick up the phone, Give **Jim** a call   Lets celebrate!   **952-200**

Purveying Prerecorded music from *1968*

Notes

To find
out why
year after
year more
couples
choose
DAVIS
DEEJAYS
for
entertainment
than any
other area
company,
call

Davis Deejays

(301) 261-2829

*as advertised
on television
and radio*

*Experienced,
not expensive* ™

call for our free brochure

A true story.

Once upon a time, in a far away place called Silver Spring, Maryland, some musicians got together and decided to form a new band....one that would be different from all the other bands, one that would be *better* than all the other bands.

But how could a band be different and better?

The musicians decided that, to be better, their band would play not just one style of music, but *all* styles of popular music from the 1940s until the present. And they would play each style of music authentically, just the way each was originally performed.

Other musicians said not to bother with that.... no one else does.

The musicians didn't listen. They decided to use more instruments and more players for better versatility in reproducing songs in their original style, so they became an eight-piece band, not the typical five pieces.

Other musicians said not to bother with that.... no one else does.

It was decided that two of the eight band members, one male and one female, should be specialists in the art of singing. Vocalists. The best vocalists. Not instrumentalists who also happen to sing.

Other musicians said not to bother with that.... no one else does.

Then the new band insisted that their music should be quieter than other bands, so that people of *all* ages would be able to enjoy the music.

Other musicians said not to bother with that.... no one else does.

It was then decided that the new band would like most of all to play music at wedding receptions, where people would really appreciate their ability to play many different styles of music authentically, and not too loudly.

Other musicians laughed. You'll never get to play any good music at wedding receptions, they said.

Not only will we play good music at wedding receptions, said the new band, we'll also learn to make every wedding reception run smoothly, and make every reception fun. And

they did. Then they said, each and every wedding must always be the most important performance we've ever done. And each was. And each still is.

Other musicians laughed. Weddings are yucky, they said.

Then, to be *really* different, the new band decided to never book themselves through talent agents. Never ever. They knew that if they could show their new ideas directly to potential clients, they would find more than enough demand for a new and better band, without the inconvenience of a middleman.

Wow! Other musicians *really* laughed at this idea. Nobody but nobody can get work without an agent, they said.

But the musicians didn't listen, and went ahead with their plans anyway. What would they call their new band? The band was called RETROSPECT, to reflect the nature of the music....all styles back through time. The name RETROSPECT became a Registered Trademark.

And soon the band became one of the Washington area's most popular and successful bands. By playing all styles of music. Authentically. By using more instruments, better musicians, better singers. By not playing too loudly. By *specializing* in wedding receptions since the beginning. By making each wedding the most important, the most fun, with the best music.

Other musicians were astonished. They couldn't understand how RETROSPECT could be so popular. What did RETROSPECT do that they didn't do?

And talent agents were astonished. They couldn't understand either, how RETROSPECT could be so successful. What did RETROSPECT do to get work?

And even to this day, they just don't understand. They probably never will. And RETROSPECT lived happily ever after.

Retrospect ® has been performing in the Washington area since 1978. Free info is available– call them at (301) 831-5700 or 649-3336. Early bookings are advised.

© 1990 Larry Elliott

122A

Disc Jockey Services

Variety Of Music

*All styles of music * Music for audiences of all ages * Continuous music
* Music styles for listening & dancing * Song requests are welcome

Expert Services

* Seasoned DJs * Serving the Washington area since 1975
* Reception announcing * Reception planning assistance

Quality Music Systems

* Professional sound reinforcement systems * Realistic sound quality
* Full, rich, & clean sound reproduction * Systems for any sized facility

CAPITAL ENTERTAINMENT
(703) 836-9390

Dance Bands
Musicians
Orchestras

*"Outstanding Musical Entertainment
For Any Gathering"*

For a wedding celebration that is special, let us provide you with the finest music presented by one of our many performers. We have groups of various sizes, music styles and fee requirements.

CAPITAL ENTERTAINMENT   (703) 836-9390

123A

Notes

Musical Entertainment
for a
Memorable Wedding Reception

EXPERIENCE . . .

Nard's is the most experienced DJ service available. Founded in the D.C. Area in 1972
and growing rapidly ever since, Nard's is a nationwide organization playing music
and entertaining from Boston to L.A. We have numerous permanent
installations in the area and welcome people to stop in and talk
to our DJs about upcoming events. Our continuing business
of supplying music and personnel to bars and nightclubs
keeps our DJs current with the latest music and
trends, as well as keeping their skills sharp
in relating varieties of music to your
special situation.

Nard's

PROFESSIONAL DJ SERVICE

821-8629   1-800-537-NARD

Notes

Video Memories

CUSTOM PRODUCTIONS.

CUSTOM PACKAGES.

MAZZEO CUSTOM VIDEO.

Bring the joy of that special day to video
with the finest in videotaping services!
Many options are available to suit your tastes—the
choice is yours!   CALL for FREE consultation

MAZZEO CUSTOM VIDEO

A videotaping and editing service serving
VA—MD—DC

(301) 890-4845
(301) 743-3022

ON BUDGET • ON TIME

WE GUARANTEE:

- Professionalism with affordable prices!

- All packages complete within 14 days!

- Some completed the same day!

If you book Mazzeo Custom Video
3 months in advance, you are
guaranteed two VHS copies FREE.

Call now before your wedding date
is booked.

TaKE ONE VIDEO

"WHEN IT COUNTS"

301 858-5100

WEDDING VIDEOS

Videography Is Our Only Business
WEDDINGS Are Our Specialty

ACE VIDEO SERVICES
(301) 990-9119

SERVING THE WASHINGTON METROPOLITAN AREA

Notes

128A

Imagine Your Wedding Is A Work Of Art

We Produce Superb Videos With Unsurpassed Picture Quality

1-800-955-6969
(301) 544-6969

P.O. Box 1521
Annapolis, MD 21404

ANNAPOLIS VIDEO PRODUCTIONS INC.

"WE FOCUS ON EXCELLENCE"

CALL FOR BROCHURE AND PRICE LIST   SERVING THE WASHINGTON, BALTIMORE, AND ANNAPOLIS AREA

ALLIED VIDEO MEDIA

Video Taping For All Social or Business Occasions

DISTINCTIVE VIDEOTAPING OF
WEDDINGS & SPECIAL EVENTS

Established 1983
Courteous & Dependable Service
100's of References & Sample Tapes

**SERVING THE
WASHINGTON METRO
AREA**

Call Kit: (301)469-8130

*Keepsake
Video
Productions*

KVP VIDEO

WEDDINGS AND PARTIES
VIDEO FOR HOME AND INDUSTRY
SUPER VHS & 3/4 FORMAT AND
STILL PHOTOGRAPHY AVAILABLE

L.H. LINDBERG

24 HR. ANS. SERVICE
703-978-1948

A+ VIDEO services

301-567-9622

FOR PERSONAL SERVICE:
★ CREATIVE & ROMANTIC VIDEOS
★ UNOBTRUSIVE
★ WEDDING SPECIALISTS
★ GREATER WASHINGTON AREA
★ EXPERIENCE SINCE 1979

FOR HIGHEST QUALITY:
★ SUPER VHS EQUIPMENT
★ DIGITAL SPECIAL EFFECTS
★ EDITING
★ FLASHBACKS
★ HIGHLIGHT & GUEST TAPES

Notes

Honeymoon
and Travel

While planning
the most important
day of your lives,
don't forget
the most important week:
YOUR HONEYMOON

At Travel World, we understand that you want your honeymoon to be just as perfect as your wedding.

We are the Washington, DC area's best source for honeymoon travel. Call us for:

- **Europe** • **Hawaii** • **Bermuda** • **Canada**
- **Australia** • **Caribbean**

- also -

- **Cruises** • **Land Packages** • **Safaris**

PERSONAL SERVICE FOR THE DISCRIMINATING COUPLE
Call Katherine for a personal consultation

TRAVEL WORLD

1500 Wilson Boulevard • Arlington, Virginia 22209

703 / 525-3605

132A

FOR THE PERFECT HONEYMOON
Call us . . .

*Don't trust the most important trip of your life
to just anyone.
Call our honeymoon specialist,
Betty Liston
at
(703) 920-2510*

Travel Horizons

1600-G Crystal Square Arcade
Arlington, Virginia 22202

Your Travel Agency Should Be
UNIGLOBE®
Herndon Sterling Travel

*"For the personal attention to
your Honeymoon needs that a small,
experienced agency can offer"*

Specializing in:
Honeymoons to Bermuda, Bahamas, Caribbean, California, Canada, Florida, Hawaii, Mexico, and Cruises.

Your Honeymoon is important – Call the Experts

437-1001

1056 Elden Street, Herndon, Virginia 22070
Convenient Evening and Saturday Hours

---

world connections travel
WCT

Honeymoon
Prices
Got
You
Down?

We're not just another Travel Agency

Give us one
hour of your time
and you will receive
complimentary accomodations
at one of these exciting destinations

Barbados • Acapulco • Majorca

Call our Honeymoon Specialist for
your no obligation consultation
Chris Nelson

(703) 237-6034   Tysons Corner, VA

Windjammer

Sail with us to sparkling emerald isles on a sea of turquoise blue. Measure time in sunrises and sunsets as you live an adventure under white sails. Race the wind and romance the sea. Travel back in time and cruise the Caribbean in a tradition long forgotten.

6 and 13 Day Cruises. Fares from $675.

Use the coupon below to request your free Great Adventures Brochure. Or call us: **1-800-432-3364** (in Florida) or **1-800-327-2601** (outside Florida) or see your 'barefoot' travel agent.

 **Windjammer** --------------
Barefoot Cruises LTD.

P.O. Box 120, Dept. 4799, Miami Beach, FL 33119-0120

Name: _____

Address: _____

City, State, Zip: _____

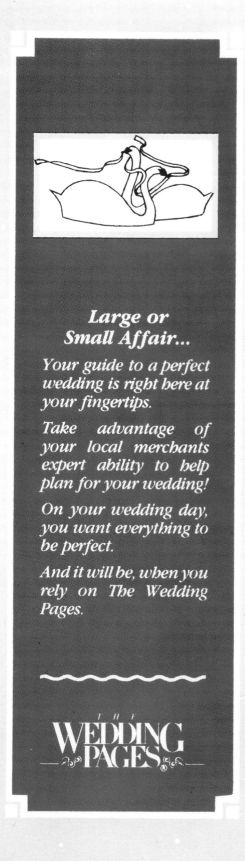

Large or Small Affair...

Your guide to a perfect wedding is right here at your fingertips.

Take advantage of your local merchants expert ability to help plan for your wedding!

On your wedding day, you want everything to be perfect.

And it will be, when you rely on The Wedding Pages.

THE WEDDING PAGES®

134A

YOU PLAN THE WEDDING WE'LL PLAN THE HONEYMOON

PERFECT HONEYMOONS LTD.

Register your honeymoon cruise with PERFECT HONEYMOON LTD. and allow your friends to contribute to your most precious gift--your Honeymoon!

The experts in honeymoons to Hawaii, Bermuda, Florida, Mexico, California, Tahiti and all Carribbean Islands.

Special Cruise packages available for the Bride and Groom-- call now for more information.

CALL OUR HONEYMOON SPECIALIST BETH MILLER AUGERINOS, CTC

703-709-0125

EVENING AND SATURDAY APPOINTMENTS • CENTRALLY LOCATED IN FAIRFAX COUNTY
FREE CONSULTATION • 20 YEARS EXPERIENCE PLANNING HONEYMOONS • FREE BROCHURE

Notes

_____

_____

_____

_____

_____

_____

_____

_____

_____

_____

_____

Relax. . . and enjoy this special time together!

Notes

Jewelers

Beautiful Beginnings...

Diamond Solitaires and Diamond Bridal
Sets priced from $299.00

Prices from $135 to $400.

His and Hers
ANNIVERSARY RINGS

★ Charge Accounts   ★ 83 Years of   ★ Lifetime
Available   Experience   Diamond Warranty

Gordon's
JEWELERS
Since 1905

Visit stores listed below or shop Gordon's Coast to Coast

Springfield Mall	Landover Mall	Prince George's Plaza	Laurel Centre	Forest Village Park Mall
Springfield, VA	Landover, MD	Hyattsville, MD	Laurel, MD	Forestville, MD
703-971-6225	301-773-4454	301-559-0333	301-953-2330	301-568-0300

KAY JEWELERS AND BEAUTIFUL DIAMONDS ...

Just Naturally Go Together

© 1987 Kay Jewelers, Inc.

We've been called The Diamond People for years. Why? Because Kay Jewelers and diamonds just naturally go together.

No other jeweler will guarantee the mounting for life, and replace it free. And guarantee the trade-in value of your diamond to increase at least fifty percent in ten years. And, take back any diamond you buy up to three months after purchase.

Not only do we offer you beautiful diamonds at beautiful prices, we offer extra assurances to help you make this important purchase with peace of mind.

Being a diamond merchant is serious business, and we've taken it seriously for over 70 years. This dedication to quality service has earned us a reputation as "The Diamond People" that we, and our customers, prize.

Manassas Mall
Manassas, VA 703-361-8239

Fair Oaks Mall
Fairfax, VA 703-591-4340

Springfield Mall
Springfield, VA 703-971-1110

Landmark Shopping Ctr.
Alexander. VA 703-354-3078

Wheaton Plaza
Wheaton, MD 301-933-6771

Montgomery Mall
Bethesda, MD 301-469-6524

Laurel Centre
Laurel, MD 301-776-9096

Prince George's Plaza
Hyattsville, MD 301-559-8700

Forest Village Park Mall
Forestville, MD 301-420-6164

Tyson's Corner
Mclean, VA 703-893-3015

Ballston Common
Arlington, VA 703-527-2024

Fashion Center
Arlington, VA 703-418-6758

Iverson Mall
Hillcrest Heights, MD 301-423-8255

Lakeforest Mall
Gaithersburg, MD 301-840-5755

White Flint Mall
Rockville, MD 301-770-5177

Beltway Plaza
Greenbelt, MD 301-474-3939

Landover Mall
Landover, MD 301-322-7722

KAY®
J E W E L E R S

The diamond people®

Four ways to buy: Cash, Charge, Bankcard, Interest Free Layaway

Plan On Saving By Shopping At Best.

Planning a wedding is exciting, yet it demands a great deal of your time and money. By shopping at Best before your wedding, you'll save time because you'll find all your needs in one place. Examine our magnificent array of sparkling diamond engagement rings and wedding bands. Choose from a delightful selection of gifts for your wedding party. Set up your new home with brand name housewares, kitchen appliances and home furnishings.

Plus, you'll save money at Best because our everyday low prices and sale prices let you get the best value for your money. And saving money is the best way to plan for the future. So visit Best today for your wedding needs, and plan on saving.

Our Quality Assurance Policy covers all our fine jewelry.

· Guarantee and Limited Warranties · 90-Day Return Policy · Free Inspection and Cleaning of Exquisite® Fine Jewelry · Free written Appraisal of Value on Exquisite® Fine Jewelry · Full Trade-in Allowance on Exquisite® Fine Jewelry · Manufacturers' Warranties on Watches · U.S. Government Standards of Purity · **Jewelry Layaway Available**

BEST ®

Best Products Co., Inc.

Best Showrooms: Bethesda, MD, 301/469-6630; **Fairfax, VA,** 703/385-2929; **Falls Church, VA,** 703/573-7150; **New Carrollton, MD,** 301/459-7400; **Rockville, MD,** 301/881-8422; **Shirlington, VA,** 703/578-4600; **Springfield, VA,** 703/644-2400; **Greenbelt, MD,** 301/474-5500;
Best Jewelry Stores: Lake Forest Mall, Gaithersburg, 301/921-0204; **Laurel Centre Mall,** 301/725-1540; **The Mall in Columbia,** 301/964-4427; **Old Town,** Alexandria, 703/836-6997; **Connecticut Ave., N.W.,** 202/293-6976.

"Unique"

The purchase of a diamond requires the guidance of an expert. When you purchase a diamond from any member of the Barlow & Eaton Family of Fine Jewelers, you can be confident that our diamond specialists will help you select the most beautiful and precious diamond in your price range. We'll show you the different kinds of cuts available (round, oval, pear, marquise, emerald). . .we'll explain the importance of color, clarity and carat weight. And every purchase comes with our unconditional 100 Day Money Back Guarantee. So you can't possibly make a mistake when you buy your jewelry from Barlow & Eaton Fine Jewelers. . . .

"A Unique Experience in Jewelry"

Barlow & Eaton

F·I·N·E J·E·W·E·L·E·R·S

BEACON MALL	SEVEN CORNERS SHOPPING CTR	LANDOVER MALL
ALEXANDRIA, VA	FALLS CHURCH, VA	LANDOVER, MD
703-765-6333	703-538-2366	301-322-4111

Partners for Life

You're committed
to each other.

We're committed
to you.

You trust each other.

You can trust us, too.

SHAW'S
Jewelers
The Perfect Diamond Store...and more.

Fine Jewelry is so easy to buy with our
handy Credit plans. We guarantee you'll
be completely satisfied with each and
every jewelry purchase. We'll even give
you 6 months to make sure.

Ballston Common Arlington, VA 703-524-0333 • Fair Oaks Mall Fairfax, VA 703-273-6300
Galleria at Tysons II McLean, VA 703-556-0371 • Springfield Mall Springfield, VA 703-971-0414
Fashion Center Arlington, VA 703-415-2350 • Mall At Manassas Manassas, VA 703-335-5117
Lakeforest Mall Gaithersburg, MD 301-258-9070

142A

Engaging Solitaires

If you're considering engagement, consider J.B. Robinson Jewelers. You'll find a beautiful selection of diamonds in a variety of sizes and shapes. Our knowledgeable salespeople can tell you about the 4C's: cut, color, clarity, and carat weight. They're the characteristics that determine the quality and rare beauty of each J.B. Robinson diamond.

You'll feel secure choosing J.B. Robinson Jewelers for your diamond purchase. We back all our diamonds with our 10 Assurances, including a lifetime warranty and three-month refund guarantee.

J.B. Robinson Jewelers - beautiful diamonds to last a lifetime.

© 1987 J.B. Robinson Jewelers, Incorporated

Ballston Common
Arlington, VA • 703-841-0770

Lakeforest Mall
Gaithersburg, MD • 301-948-4520

Springfield Mall
Springfield, VA • 703-971-3710

Wheaton Plaza
Wheaton, MD • 301-949-1776

JB • ROBINSON JEWELERS

Fair Oaks Mall
Fairfax, VA • 703-385-2650

Landover Mall
Landover, MD • 301-772-0001

Tysons Corner Center
McLean, VA • 703-356-5154

A M E R I C A ' S L E A D I N G J E W E L E R℠

Presents...

diamond bridal sets

We Offer...
- **Free Lifetime Warranty Against Diamond Loss**
- **Satisfaction Guaranteed On All Diamond Purchases**
- **Lifetime Trade-Up Policy On Diamonds And Gemstones**
- **Full Service Jeweler**
- **Interest-Free Jewelry Layaway**
- **Up To $1,500 Instant Credit**
- **Free Jewelry Inspection And Cleaning**

A Diamond Is Forever

AMERICA'S LEADING JEWELER℠

Service®
MERCHANDISE

For the Store Nearest You, Call Toll-Free Nationwide 1·800·251·1212

 4C Your guide to diamond value.

CUT. A master cutter cuts each diamond to precise angles, allowing the maximum amount of light reflection. The five most common shapes are Round, Oval, Pear, Marquise and Emerald.

COLOR. The best color is no color. Light passes effortlessly through a colorless diamond, producing rainbows of color.

CLARITY. A diamond of the highest quality is virtually free of interior and exterior flaws. Clarity is determined by expert examination of the stone under 10-power magnification.

CARAT. Diamond size is measured in carats. One carat equals 100 points; thus, a diamond of 75 points weighs .75 carats.

©Service Merchandise Company, Inc., 1989 NM189

144A

Notes

the winning team
...Bonded and you.

Prices Starting As Low As:
1/2-Carat.....from $690 * 3/4-Carat.....from $1350
2/3-Carat.....from $990 * 1-Carat.....from $1990

IF YOU'RE NOT WEARING IT-SELL IT OR TRADE IT.
Serving and Saving The Public Since 1920

1501 REISTERSTOWN ROAD
IN PIKESVILLE, MARYLAND 21208

Baltimore Beltway (695) to
Exit 20, go south Reisterstown
Road-approx. 1/4-mile

Visit our other store
at Crocker Center in
Boca Raton, Florida.

BONDED
JEWELRY CENTER

1-800-638-2083
1-800-492-1063 From Md.
653-9000 Local

Voted #1
By Balto. Mag. as
the best place to
buy diamonds.

Open Mon.-Fri. 9:15 to 6 p.m.   Thurs. 9:15 to 8 p.m., Sat. 9:15 to 6 p.m.

146A

Notes

THIS COULD BE THE START OF SOMETHING BEAUTIFUL.

Weisfield's has an outstanding selection of engagement and wedding sets. All in the latest styles, many designed just for us. We offer top quality and value, too. Plus a Diamond Bond that gives you a diamond replacement warranty that secures your investment for the future. Now, what could be more beautiful than that.

weisfield
JEWELERS THE LOOK

Lakeforest Mall Gaithersburg, MD
301-948-2845
Galleria at Tysons II McLean, VA
703-893-9337
Manassas Mall Manassas, VA
703-369-3711

147A

DO YOU HAVE A JEWELRY PROBLEM?

It doesn't fit; You aren't satisfied with it anymore; You can't seem to complement your engagement ring.

Go straight to Everhart Jewelers. They delight in helping people with special problems. Mention the *Wedding Pages* and you will receive a free gift.

 MEMBER AMERICAN GEM SOCIETY

Everhart Jewelers

9858 Main Street	6649 Old Dominion Drive
Fairfax Square	McLean Square
Fairfax, Virginia	McLean, Virginia
703 273-2550	703 821-3344

When shopping for a diamond, inquire about the purity, weight and guarantee!

Notes

_____

_____

_____

_____

_____

_____

_____

_____

_____

Lingerie

YOU'VE ONLY JUST BEGUN

Whether it be for that special
night of your life or for every
night of your married life visit

Charmeuse & Lace Corset Embellished
with pearls and musical garter which
plays "Here Comes The Bride"

NIGHT DREAMS
BOUTIQUE

8381 Leesburg Pike, Tysons, VA 22182
703-556-8839

Featuring

♥ *Honeymoon Attire*
♥ *Boudoir Playthings*
♥ *Bachelor/Bachelorett Gag Gifts*
♥ *Edible Love Potions*

LINGERIE & TOY CATALOGUE
SEND $10
NIGHT DREAMS For Adults
8381 Leesburg Pike, Tysons, VA 22182

Dance
Instruction

Special Wedding Party Dance Lessons and Program

The Bride and Groom, your family and close friends can arrange special group and private lessons for your wedding party at the studio. Learn today's popular dance steps and ballroom moves that you can use "Now and Forever."

Alexandria
751-4336

Bethesda
657-2700

Falls Church
237-8848

Gaithersburg
590-0387

Silver Spring
681-4466

Arthur Murray
Franchised Dance Studios

Credit Cards Welcome

Notes

Your New Home

Let Me Turn Your Dream of Home Ownership into a Reality . . .

Ask for:

Janelle Curths, GRI

Realtor®, Notary
Multi-Million Dollar Producer

- Pre-Purchase Consultation
- Free Market Analysis
- Professional Personal Service
- Commitment to Excellence

 **Mount Vernon** REALTY INC.

7202 Arlington Boulevard
Falls Church, Virginia 22042

(703) 698-1200

REALTOR

 EQUAL HOUSING OPPORTUNITY

Simcha
Showcase 90

"THE MOST EXCITING AND BEST"
WEDDING
and
PARTY PLANNING SHOWS OF THE YEAR

SIMCHA SHOWCASE '90
PARTY PLANNER EXTRAVAGANZAS

- DANCE   to the sounds of live bands
- TASTE   culinary delights of the areas "BEST" caterers and bakers.
- MEET   the areas premier WEDDING and party planners
- ENJOY   one of the finest Bridal and Formal wear fashion shows
- VIEW   exquisite Photography and Videography
- BE   entertained all day
- EVERYTHING   for your WEDDING under one roof at a time

March 4, 1990
THE McLEAN HILTON
11:30 A.M. - 6:00 P.M.

March 25, 1990
HYATT REGENCY ⊞ BETHESDA
11:30 A.M. - 6:00 P.M.

Camelot™
Productions

Admission at door $5.50

Advance ticket purchase available at savings.

(301) 340-7466

Bridal Shows

The Eighth Annual Washington Wedding Show

The area's oldest bridal show is still the best!

Saturday, January 20th
and
Sunday, January 21st
1990

Howard Johnson Plaza Hotel, New Carrollton, Md. (Beltway Exit 20B)
For Ticket Information call

(301) 899-4983

Notes

Exquisite Weddings, Inc. Presents:

THE WEDDING SHOW

Wedding Fashion Show

Exhibits of Everything You'll Need to Design Your Dream Wedding

- Gowns
- Caterers
- Entertainment
- Flowers
- Photographers
- And Lots More!

WIN . . . .

- A Designer Wedding Gown
- A Spectacular Honeymoon
- A Custom Wedding Cake

Come to The First Major Wedding Event of 1991

Saturday and Sunday January 5 & 6 1991

We're the Largest Show in the Area of Local Vendors

Call Now & Register: **(703) 922-1961**

Businesses: For Exhibit Information Call: (703) 922-1961

Send me _____ tickets to The Wedding Show on January _____ 1991. Enclose $5.00 per ticket. Invite your groom, families and attendents. Checks or Money Orders should be made out to:

Exquisite Weddings, Inc.
P.O. Box 8654
Alexandria, VA 22306

Name _____
Address _____
City_____State_____Zip_____
Telephone (__)____Wedding Date____

Notes

Dance Instruction

Weddings often include dancing as part of the reception festivities. Don't let your or your spouse's inability to dance keep you from enjoying this special time. Learn to dance.

Dancing is an excellent form of relaxation and recreation. Whether it's a nice slow dance with someone you love, or one of today's popular rock and roll styles, you will look and feel much more confident if you learn the proper steps.

> **"Dancing is an excellent form of relaxation and recreation."**

A series of dance lessons during your engagement is a great opportunity for both of you to be together and forget about the pressures of wedding planning. The lessons can be purchased from a dance studio or professional instructor. They can often be tailored to the level of proficiency you wish to obtain and at a time most convenient for you.

Your honeymoon will also be greatly enhanced if you have the ability to dance to any type of music.

Dancing is something you can enjoy together for the rest of your lives.

Formal Wear

The Groom and His Attendants

The groom, his groomsmen, ushers and the fathers may or may not dress identically. Their attire however, should complement your dress and follow the formality of the wedding.

The style and color of tuxedo the groom selects will depend on several variables — his coloring and build, the bride's and bridesmaids' dress color and style, the season, and the tastes of the bridal couple.

Select a style that flatters the groom's build. If he is not very tall, a tux with tails may make him appear shorter. A lot of ruffles on a thin high-necked shirt can make a husky man appear larger. Darker colors have a slimming effect. Bring it all together by having the groom and his attendants wear ties and cummerbunds or suspenders that are the same color as the bridesmaids' dresses. The formal wear professional can work with you to select the perfect tuxedo.

If all the men in the wedding are dressing identically, you may wish to distinguish between the groom and the rest of the party. This can be done by having him wear a slightly different boutonniere or neckwear or a tuxedo with tails.

To get an idea of what is available and appropriate, consult a men's formal wear professional. They can provide you with brochures reflecting different styles.

Make arrangements for the party to have measurements taken. If a member lives out-of-town, have him get his measurements taken there and give the rental specialist the necessary information. The tuxedos should be reserved two to three months prior to the wedding.

A rental tuxedo usually includes a jacket, vest or cummerbund, pants, suspenders, shirt, cufflinks, studs and a tie. Shoes are usually rented from the formal wear store in order to maintain consistency.

Be sure to find out when the attire can be picked up and when it must be returned. Have the groom and ushers try their tuxedos on a few days before the ceremony in case there are any last minute adjustments.

Purchasing a Tuxedo

Just as the bride has a gown that she can treasure forever, a groom may want to purchase his formal wear or have a tuxedo that is tailor-made. There are many professionals in your area with a wide range of fashions, colors and fabrics to choose from. Purchasing a tux allows the groom a suit of clothes permanently altered to fit him. Should another formal occasion arise, he will already have his own great-looking apparel.

Formal Wear Questions

When selecting your formal wear, ask these questions:

1) What formal wear styles best suit the style and time of day of my wedding?
2) Are shoes, studs, cummerbund and cufflinks included?
3) When should the tuxedos and accessories be reserved?
4) Are alterations included?
5) When should the appointments for fittings be made?
6) When should the formal wear be picked up?
7) When must it be returned?
8) When the groomsmen pick up the tuxedos, can they try them on?
9) Do you have the stock on hand?

Formal Wear Checklist

Formal Wear Shop: _____

Address: _____

Phone Number: _____

Formal Wear Specialist: _____

GROOM

Tuxedo — Style: _____

                            Color: _____ Size: _____

Package Includes: _____

_____

Fitting Date: _____ Time: _____

Pick-up Date: _____ Return Date: _____

GROOMSMAN: _____ Phone No: _____

Tuxedo — Style: _____

                            Color: _____ Size: _____

Fitting Date: _____ Time: _____

Pick-up Date: _____ Return Date: _____

GROOMSMAN: _____ Phone No: _____

Tuxedo — Style: _____

                            Color: _____ Size: _____

Fitting Date: _____ Time: _____

Pick-up Date: _____ Return Date: _____

Formal Wear Checklist

GROOMSMAN: _____ Phone No: _____

Tuxedo — Style:_____

              Color: _____ Size:_____

Fitting Date: _____ Time:_____

Pick-up Date: _____ Return Date: _____

GROOMSMAN: _____ Phone No: _____

Tuxedo — Style:_____

              Color: _____ Size:_____

Fitting Date: _____ Time:_____

Pick-up Date: _____ Return Date: _____

GROOMSMAN: _____ Phone No: _____

Tuxedo — Style:_____

              Color: _____ Size:_____

Fitting Date: _____ Time:_____

Pick-up Date: _____ Return Date: _____

GROOMSMAN: _____ Phone No: _____

Tuxedo — Style:_____

              Color: _____ Size:_____

Fitting Date: _____ Time:_____

Pick-up Date: _____ Return Date: _____

Formal Wear Checklist

USHER: _____ Phone No: _____

Tuxedo — Style:_____

             Color: _____ Size:_____

Fitting Date: _____ Time:_____

Pick-up Date: _____ Return Date: _____

USHER: _____ Phone No: _____

Tuxedo — Style:_____

             Color: _____ Size:_____

Fitting Date: _____ Time:_____

Pick-up Date: _____ Return Date: _____

USHER: _____ Phone No: _____

Tuxedo — Style:_____

             Color: _____ Size:_____

Fitting Date: _____ Time:_____

Pick-up Date: _____ Return Date: _____

USHER: _____ Phone No: _____

Tuxedo — Style:_____

             Color: _____ Size:_____

Fitting Date: _____ Time:_____

Pick-up Date: _____ Return Date: _____

Formal Wear Checklist

FATHER OF THE BRIDE:

Tuxedo — Style:_____

               Color: _____ Size:_____

Fitting Date: _____ Time:_____

Pick-up Date: _____ Return Date: _____

FATHER OF THE GROOM:

Tuxedo — Style:_____

               Color: _____ Size:_____

Fitting Date: _____ Time:_____

Pick-up Date: _____ Return Date: _____

Photographer

Selecting Your Photographer

For months you have been planning this day . . . a day that will be over in a matter of hours. There will be only one chance to capture the excitement and memories in print. This chance should not be left to an amateur photographer. A professional photographer who specializes in weddings will not get caught up in the festivities of the day. Using his creativity, he will be able to provide proper lighting in a variety of settings to capture all those special moments of your wedding day.

In selecting your photographer, look at his portfolio pictures of past weddings. Make sure he has not just made a picture, but that he has captured the emotion and excitement of the moment and the subjects.

Another important factor in your selection should be the photographer's personality. He should be sensitive to your needs. Also, make sure he will be prompt, discreet and dressed properly.

Once you find the photographer you would like, there are several points you will need to clarify with him. First, make sure he is available on the date and at the times needed. Second, get the delivery dates of the proofs and prints. Third, talk about the types of pictures you want, both candid and posed. Fourth, compile a list of not-to-be-missed pictures for your photographer. Finally, if you are also hiring a video crew, tell your photographer so he can plan ahead and coordinate the work.

Formal Portraits

Formal portraits are made weeks in advance either at the bridal salon or at the photographer's studio. Be sure you have all of your jewelry and accessories. The photographer will also need a description of your bouquet in order to provide a similar dummy.

You will, of course, want to have pictures made with your groom, your parents and the wedding party. If you are not bothered by superstition, they can be taken before the ceremony. Otherwise, you will want to set aside time before or during the reception.

You will also want candid shots taken during the ceremony and reception. If you have requested certain photos including relatives or friends, it may be a good idea to have your host or hostess assist the photographer in finding the right people and answer any of his questions.

It is always nice for your guests if you display an enlarged print of your formal portrait at the reception.

Oil Portraits. A beautiful way to enhance your formal portrait is with oils. An oil portrait highlights so much of your natural beauty.

The procedure for such a portrait begins with several poses taken in black and white with flat lighting. An artist then uses either a light oil or brush oil to fill in the details.

The light oil involves putting the paint on with cotton and then smoothing it with dacron. Brush oil is applied with paint brushes. The brush oil has a longer drying time. You should be sure of the artist's timetable if you wish to display the portrait on your wedding day.

Reflections

Many brides and grooms are adding a new dimension to their wedding ceremony or reception with a multi-media slide show. Sometimes called Reflections, the slide presentation reflects the lives of the bride and groom through pictures.

A photographer or photo finishing center uses original photographs, negatives or slides and develops a presentation. Often, there will be two screens, side by side, or across the ceremony area. This show will visually tell the story of the bride and groom. A selection of your favorite music can be a wonderful addition to the program.

The presentation can be appropriate during the wedding ceremony or reception depending on your personal tastes.

Boudoir Photograph

Do you want something special for your groom that shows your sensual side? The boudoir photograph is taken by a boudoir photographer with you wearing soft, luxurious lingerie in a bedroom setting.

The photographer can provide the setting or you may feel more comfortable in a more familiar setting of your choosing. The result can become a romantic treasure for your groom.

Obviously, this type of photograph is not for everyone. If you do have the inclination, there are professionals available.

Restrictions

Be sure to ask your clergymember if there are any restrictions on picture taking. Some forbid the use of a flash and some forbid picture taking altogether. If there are any restrictions, discuss them with your photographer ahead of time.

Cost

Although you may be cost conscious when shopping for a photographer, beware of hard-to-believe deals. They usually are. Package deals should be carefully examined to compare true costs. Most photographers require a deposit when booking. The balance is usually due upon receipt of your prints.

When storing your wedding pictures, be sure to keep them in an album away from direct sunlight.

Photographer Questions

When selecting your photographer, ask these questions:

1) Do you have a portfolio I can look at?
2) Do you have skill in diffused lighting, soft focus, split framing, and multiple exposures?
3) Is your equipment capable of shooting in any light available?
4) Do you do portraits?
5) Are oil portraits available?
6) What other photo services are available?
7) What package plans are available?
8) Do you do negative retouching?
9) How much are reprints?
10) What are the delivery dates for prints?
11) What is the cost?
12) Is a desposit required? How much is it? When must it be paid? When is the balance due?
13) When should I book my photographer?

Know what you're paying for by asking the following questions:

1) How many photographs will be taken in all?
2) What sizes of prints are offered?
3) What is the cost breakdown per print?
4) Are special mountings used an additional expense?
5) How many photographs am I obliged to purchase? Is there a minimum order requirement?
6) What album styles are available and what is the cost of each? (Albums are usually tailor-made to hold the exact number of prints selected.)
7) How long will you stay at the ceremony and the reception?
8) Is a travel cost included?
9) What extra services are available? Do you have photo invitations and thank you notes? Do you make special mini gift albums for relatives?

Special Shots and Guests
Not To Be Missed by Photographer

CEREMONY

_____

_____

_____

_____

_____

_____

_____

_____

_____

RECEPTION

_____

_____

_____

_____

_____

_____

_____

_____

_____

_____

Videographer

Selecting a Videographer

Capture all the magic moments of your wedding on video. A professional videographer can create a documentary of your special day by capturing all the sights and sounds.

A videographer should be selected at least nine to twelve months before the wedding. Use a professional! A home movie is not the way to capture all of the moments of the day. Meet with the videographer and review some of his prior work to make sure it meets your standards. It is important to feel comfortable with the person who will actually be doing the shooting. Request a meeting with that person if you are not dealing with him when you contract for the work.

Special Effects Terminology

To liven up the videotape, many people add special effects. The professional videographer can often provide these options for you:

Multiple Screens—Placing up to five images on the screen at once.

Split Screens—Placing two different full-action images on the screen at one time.

Dissolving—The current image dissolves into the next image.

Freeze-Frame—Making a video frame appear like a still photograph.

Digital Slides—One image slides off one side of the screen and another frame slides on from the opposite side.

Skip-Frame—This allows a series of frames to skip at regular intervals and give a sort of strobe effect.

Audio Dubbing and Mixing—This al-lows you to replace the taped audio sound with something different. For instance, you may want a musical soundtrack during a scene.

Titling—If the videographer has a title generator, titles and subtitles can be included during or after the actual filming.

The use of panning, zooming and close-ups will spice up your video. Some videographers also have multiple camera capabilities which help ensure the best shots possible. Precision editing systems take you from scene to scene smoothly without jumps, static or snow and allow you to incorporate favorite wedding photographs.

Ask plenty of questions and make sure you provide the videographer with a listing of those special people and moments you want to capture during the wedding and reception.

Be sure the contract you sign clearly states all of the terms and conditions of the shoot, the dates and times you have reserved, the price, what should appear in the video and the approximate delivery date.

The officiant should be informed that you are planning to have a videographer. There are some locations that restrict the use of lights or limit the filming locations. You should also make arrangements for the videographer to visit the site. This will allow him to plan his shooting positions. If the videographer is familiar with the location, there may be no need for the visit.

Copies of the tape should be made professionally. The quality is much better than anything that can be produced at home.

Videographer Questions

When selecting your videographer, ask these questions:

1) Can I see samples of your past work?

2) What types of videos do you offer?

3) Will you use panning, zooming, and close-ups to enhance my video?

4) What packages are offered?

5) How much are they?

6) Are duplicate tapes available?

7) How soon should I reserve the date?

Special Shots and Guests
Not To Be Missed by Videographer

CEREMONY

_____

_____

_____

_____

_____

_____

_____

_____

_____

_____

RECEPTION

_____

_____

_____

_____

_____

_____

_____

_____

_____

_____

_____

Florist

Flowers will play an important role in enhancing your wedding style, bringing beauty and elegance to the ceremony as well as the reception. Since not all florists specialize in weddings, you must choose your florist carefully.

You should visit several florists and look at photographs of their past work. This will give you a taste of their abilities to create the look you want. Describe the style of your gown, your attendants' dresses and the wedding. You might also want to bring fabric swatches to build a flower scheme around.

> ## "Make sure your flowers suit your style."

Traditionally, the bride's bouquet is made of white flowers such as stephanotis, orchids, roses, lilies of the valley, gardenias, carnations, or sweet peas. Included in the bouquet are fillers like baby's breath and ferns or ivy for greenery. Make sure your flowers not only suit your style, but also yourself. If you're small, a large bouquet will look too overwhelming. You might also want to wear some soft delicate flowers in your hair.

The bouquets your attendants carry should be identical. To set your maid of honor apart, you might want to vary the style or color slightly. Instead of bouquets, you could have them carry long-stemmed roses in their arms. Use baby's breath and greenery for fillers and hold it together with ribbons matching their dresses. A wreath of flowers in the hair could add just the right touch.

The men in the wedding party should wear boutonnieres. These may be white roses, carnations or maybe even a colorful flower. They should be worn on the left lapel. The groom's boutonniere should differ from the groomsmens', possibly a carnation with a rose embedded in its center.

When ordering your flowers, don't forget corsages for the mothers and grandmothers. They need not be identical, but should be coordinated with the color of their dresses.

Flowers for the Site

Before deciding on the flower arrangements for the wedding site, consult the clergymember or officiant to see if altar arrangements are allowed. Because they will bring attention to the front, they should be tastefully done. Consider using smaller arrangements of flowers as pew markers. If your florist is not familiar with the site, suggest a visit to get an idea of what is needed.

These same altar arrangements may be used to decorate the reception hall. In addition, flowers in vases make beautiful table decorations. Plants and greenery can also provide an added touch. Be sure to ask your florist for suggestions.

Silk Flowers

A popular alternative to fresh flowers is silk flowers. Elegant replicas, they have several advantages. They do not turn brown and there is no preserving cost in making them a permanent keepsake. Your florist can do beautiful silk arrangements if you request them.

Selecting Your Florist

Whatever you select, final arrangements should be made at least three to six months ahead of time. Ordering ahead will insure the availability of the flowers you want, especially during holiday seasons when they are in great demand.

Be sure to have their delivery time before the arrival of the photographer. Also, check with the florist early on the day of your wedding to make sure there will be no surprises.

Preserving Fresh Flowers

Because you will want to preserve your bouquet, arrangements should be made for this. You should make arrangements to have a toss-away bouquet made to substitute in the bouquet tossing ritual. The florist must have the wedding bouquet within a day or two of the wedding. If the florist will not collect your bouquet at the end of the day, have someone drop it off.

First, the moisture is removed to preserve the shape and color. A protective solution is then sprayed on the flowers. It is then displayed in a glass case or mounted on a satin pillow. The process takes about three weeks.

Floral Questions

When selecting your florist, ask these questions:

1) Do you have pictures or samples of your work?

2) Will you build a flower scheme around fabric swatches?

3) Is a deposit required to reserve your services? How much is the deposit? When is it due? When is the balance due?

4) Are you familiar with the advantages and disadvantages of our wedding and reception sites?

5) Can you coordinate the flowers for the wedding party, mothers and special guests?

6) Will you deliver or must the flowers be picked up? Additional charge for delivery?

7) What do your services include?

8) What other kinds of decorating can you provide?

9) Can you provide rental services?

10) Can you preserve my bouquet? For how much? If not, is there someone you can recommend?

11) Will you perform set-up at the ceremony and reception locations? Additional charge for set-up?

Floral Checklist

Florist:_____ Phone No: _____

Address:_____

Floral Specialist: _____

WEDDING PARTY

Bride's bouquet style: _____

Bouquet color:_____ Ribbon color:_____

Kinds of flowers used: _____

_____ Cost: _____

Maid of Honor's bouquet style:_____

Bouquet color:_____ Ribbon color:_____

Kinds of flowers used: _____

_____ Cost: _____

Bridesmaid's bouquet style: _____

Bouquet color:_____ Ribbon color:_____

Kinds of flowers used: _____

_____ Quantity:_____ Cost: _____

Mother of bride's corsage style: _____

Corsage color: _____ Ribbon color:_____

Kinds of flowers used: _____

_____ Cost: _____

Floral Checklist

Mother of groom's corsage style: _____

Corsage color: _____ Ribbon color: _____

Kinds of flowers used: _____

_____ Cost: _____

Grandmother's corsage style: _____

Corsage color: _____ Ribbon color: _____

Kinds of flowers used: _____

_____ Cost: _____

Groom's boutonniere style: _____ Color: _____

Kind of flowers used:_____ Cost: _____

Men's boutonniere style:_____ Color: _____

Kind of flowers used:_____ Quantity:_____ Cost: _____

Hostess' corsage:_____ Cost: _____

Host's boutonniere: _____ Cost: _____

Cake cutter's corsage: _____ Cost: _____

Wedding book attendant's corsage: _____ Cost: _____

DELIVERY

Which flowers: _____

Date:_____ Time: _____ Address: _____

Which flowers: _____

Date:_____ Time: _____ Address: _____

Floral Checklist

CEREMONY

Altar arrangements: _____ Color: _____

Kind of flowers used: _____

Number of arrangements: _____ Cost: _____

Pew marker arrangements: _____ Color: _____

Kind of flowers used: _____

Number of arrangements: _____ Cost: _____

OTHER

Aisle runner: _____ Knee cushion: _____

DELIVERY

Which flowers: _____

Date: _____ Time: _____ Address: _____

RECEPTION

Head table arrangements: _____ Color: _____

Kind of flowers used: _____

Number of arrangements: _____ Cost: _____

Guest table arrangements: _____ Color: _____

Kind of flowers used: _____

Number of arrangements: _____ Cost: _____

Floral Checklist

Buffet table arrangements: _____ _____ Color: _____

Kind of flowers used: _____

Number of arrangements: _____ Cost: _____

Receiving line arrangements: _____ _____ Color: _____

Kind of flowers used: _____

Number of arrangements: _____ Cost: _____

Wedding cake table arrangements: _____ Color: _____

Kind of flowers used: _____

Number of arrangements: _____ Cost: _____

Other table arrangements:_____ Color: _____

Kind of flowers used: _____

Number of arrangements: _____ Cost: _____

Other table arrangements:_____ Color: _____

Kind of flowers used: _____

Number of arrangements: _____ Cost: _____

DELIVERY

Which flowers: _____

Date:_____ Time: _____ Address: _____

Total Cost of flowers and floral arrangements:_____

Balloonist

Selecting Your Balloonist

Balloons can add a festive atmosphere to your special occasion. Balloon professionals have numerous decorating ideas and designs available. They can decorate the entire hall, create a balloon arch backdrop for the wedding cake ceremony or design floral and balloon centerpieces for the reception tables. A balloon release at the church or reception site can add a dramatic touch.

Because balloons are available in so many colors, the supplier may be able to use your wedding color schemes throughout decorating.

You do not need to limit your use of balloon decorations to the wedding and reception. Balloons liven up showers, rehearsal dinners and your bachelor and bachelorette parties.

Whatever you select, final arrangements should be made three to six months ahead of time. Be sure to have their delivery before the arrival of the photographer. Also check with the balloonist the day before your wedding to make sure there will be no surprises.

Balloonist Questions

When selecting your balloonist, ask these questions:

1) Do you have a working portfolio?

2) What professional training have you received?

3) Can you include symbolism in the decorations?

4) Can you incorporate balloons with flowers?

5) What designs or styles of centerpieces can you create?

6) What types of sculptures can you make?

7) How are your prices structured and what are your terms?

Balloonist Checklist

Balloonist: _____ Phone No: _____

Address: _____

Balloon Specialist: _____

CEREMONY

Altar arrangements: _____ Color: _____

Kind of balloons used: _____

Number of arrangements: _____ Cost: _____

Pew marker arrangements: _____ Color: _____

Kind of balloons used: _____

Number of arrangements: _____ Cost: _____

RECEPTION

Head table arrangements: _____ Color: _____

Kind of balloons used: _____

Number of arrangements: _____ Cost: _____

Guest table arrangements: _____ Color: _____

Kind of balloons used: _____

Number of arrangements: _____ Cost: _____

Buffet table arrangements: _____ Color: _____

Kind of balloons used: _____

Number of arrangements: _____ Cost: _____

Balloonist Checklist

Other table arrangements:_____ Color: _____

Kind of balloons used: _____

Number of arrangements: _____ Cost: _____

Other decorations: _____

Color: _____

Cost: _____

DELIVERY

Date:_____ Time: _____ Address: _____

Total Cost of balloons and balloon arrangements:_____

Invitations and Stationery

Once you have determined the number of guests you plan to invite to your wedding, you should start thinking about the invitations. Here too, you will have many options to choose from. Meeting with a reputable printer or stationer who specializes in wedding stationery will help you in many ways.

Types of Invitations

There are several types of invitations to consider — wedding, reception, wedding/reception, and announcements. The wedding invitation requests the presence of a person to the ceremony. Traditionally, it is a double sheet of white or ivory card stock. If you wish to have the message on the inside, the front may be plain or designed.

Wedding invitations may be printed or engraved. Engraving gives the invitation a distinct quality and richness. Thermography gives the same quality at a lower price. A variety of type styles are available. You may select the style you prefer.

The invitations should be mailed four weeks before the ceremony. Informal wedding invitations should be mailed at least 10 days before.

If you wish to invite the person only to your reception, a reception invitation is used. It should match the wedding invitation in color type and stock, but is only a single sheet of paper.

Enclosure Cards

The reception invitation may be the same size as the wedding invitation or it may be an enclosure card. In the lower left corner should be printed the R.S.V.P.

The standard form may be used, but phrases such as "Kindly send response to (your parents' address)" or "The favor of a reply is requested" are also acceptable. Giving an address to reply to isn't essential, as it's usually engraved or embossed on an already stamped envelope.

When the guests are invited to both the wedding ceremony and reception, a wedding/reception invitation is used. The information on the invitation includes the location and time of the ceremony and reception.

The request for a response is in the lower left hand corner. A response card and matching stamped, addressed envelope should be enclosed.

Announcements

There may be some people who are unable to attend or whom you are unable to invite. Announcements inform them of your wedding plans.

The paper, lettering, addressing and size are the same as the invitations. They are addressed and prepared for mailing before your wedding day. They are mailed on your wedding day.

Wording

Formal invitations and announcements use traditional phrasing and styles. Names should always be written out. In most places, it is acceptable to omit the middle name or to use only an initial. Abbreviations are used only for the following titles: Dr., Mr., Mrs., Ms., Jr., and Lt. if combined with Colonel.

The date is also written out. The year does not have to be included, but if you do, it is written out. The time is spelled out, for example "two o'clock." If it is on the half hour, the words "half past" or "half after" are used. To distinguish between a.m. and p.m., use phrases such as "in the afternoon" or "in the evening."

All numbers in the addresses are spelled out unless the street number is very long. In this case, it is acceptable to use numerals. If the street name is a number, it should always be written out. If the city is not easily recognized, both the city and state should be included.

The traditional wording on the wedding and reception invitations usually reads "request the honor of your presence." If it's just a reception invitation, the words "request the pleasure of your company" are used. The word "to" joins the bride and groom on the wedding invitation. "And" joins them on the reception invitation.

Paper

Traditionally, the paper is white or ivory. It is priced according to quality and weight. Contemporary invitations come in many colors, and colored inks are also used.

Size

Invitations are folded and are available in two sizes. The 5 by 7½ inches size is folded a second time before inserting into the envelope. It is for the very formal wedding. The smaller size, 4½ by 5½ inches, is more popular. It fits exactly into the envelope. Both come with a tissue to prevent smudging of the engraving. It should be left in place.

Envelopes

Formal invitations come with two envelopes. The outer one is gummed and carries the full name and address of the guest with no abbreviations. A return address may be printed, embossed, or written on the back flap or in the upper left hand corner. Pre-printed, gummed labels should not be used.

The inner envelope is slightly smaller and is not gummed. It carries the guest's name and contains the invitation and any enclosures or reply cards.

Insertion of Invitations

The fold of the invitation should be placed at the bottom of the inner envelope with the lettering facing the flap. The enclosures should be inside the fold of the invitation. The inner envelope with the invitation should then be inserted into the outer one so that the name is upright and faces the flap of the outer envelope.

Addressing Invitations

To get a headstart on addressing, ask the stationer to send the envelopes to you early. They should be handwritten in black or blue ink. If you are having several people help you address them, make sure both envelopes are addressed in the same handwriting. An added professional touch may be achieved by engaging a calligrapher to do this.

Guidelines

1. Both envelopes should be done in the same handwriting.
2. Use "Ms." only when you know how this particular person feels about it.
3. Titles such as Reverend or Colonel should be written out. Titles such as Dr., Mr., Mrs., Ms., and Lt. if combined with Colonel may be abbreviated.
4. Write out "and" in between titles. "Mr. and Mrs."
5. Write out names in full if possible. An initial is acceptable for the middle name if you do not know the person's middle name or are unsure of its spelling.
6. Do not use "and family." The childrens' names appear on the inner envelope on a second line. If their names do not appear, they are not invited.
7. Persons over the age of sixteen are entitled to a separate invitation.
8. All parts of the address should be written out completely, except house numbers.
9. Use zip codes!
10. Address stickers or labels should never be used.
11. R.S.V.P. cards should be stamped with postage.
12. If you prefer, it has become acceptable practice to word the inner envelope of a single guest's invitation: Miss Brown and Guest.
13. Order additional envelopes to allow for errors.

Keepsakes

Your guests will often want to preserve more than just the memories of your special day. Printed ceremony programs or personalized napkins and matchbooks make perfect keepsakes. Your stationer can provide you with samples and ideas.

Thank You Notes

Receiving wedding gifts is an exciting part of getting married. It is important that they are acknowledged promptly. The wedding gift list is incorporated with the wedding guest list in order to prevent duplication of information. This will help you maintain accurate records of the giver's name, address, gift description, date received, and date the acknowledgement was sent.

When writing thank you notes, you should mention the gift by name and include comments beyond the gift itself. You might also include a comment about the wedding, an invitation for dinner or any other personal touch. If you're not sure what the gift is, you may simply refer to it as "the lovely engraved silver or crystal piece." You may have received cash or a check. In this case, let the giver know how you will use it.

To get your groom involved in the wedding responsibilities, you might want to put him in charge of the thank you notes or share the responsibility.

Ceremony Program

It has become increasingly popular to provide the wedding guests with a ceremony program. This program includes details about the ceremony such as titles of songs, names of the participants and sometimes a wedding message from the bride and groom.

An example of a ceremony program is included on the following pages.

Stationery Questions

When selecting your stationer, ask these questions:

1) Do you have samples I can look at?

2) Will you set time aside to help me with my decision? Are appointments available?

3) Can you supply thank you notes, napkins, matchbooks, scrolls, and ceremony programs?

4) When must they be ordered?

5) When will they be ready?

6) May I receive my envelopes early for addressing?

7) Is a deposit required? How much is it? When is it due? When is the remainder due?

8) Do you have gift ideas for my attendants?

9) Do you have any suggestions that might be helpful to me?

Stationery Checklist

Stationer's Name: _____ Phone No: _____

Address: _____

Stationer Representative: _____

COST

Guaranteed Rate? _____ Deposit?_____ Amount:_____

Deposit Due?_____ Balance Due?_____

Cancellation terms:_____

QUANTITIES

Ceremony: _____ Reception: _____ R.S.V.P. _____ Tissues: _____

Thank You Notes: _____ Ceremony Programs: _____ Napkins: _____

Matches: _____ Outer Envelopes: _____ Inner Envelopes: _____

Reception Favors: _____ Accessories: _____

IMPORTANT INFORMATION

Paper Stock: _____ Paper Color: _____

Style of Lettering:_____ Ink Color:_____

When will I be able to pick up my order? _____

Can I pick up my envelopes early for addressing? _____

What kind of a selection of wedding favors do they have? _____

_____

Invitation Wording Worksheet

Ceremony Program Worksheet

_____
_____
_____
_____
_____
_____
_____
_____
_____
_____
_____
_____
_____
_____
_____
_____
_____
_____
_____
_____
_____
_____
_____
_____
_____
_____
_____
_____
_____

R.S.V.P Worksheet

_____

_____

_____

_____

_____

Reception Card Worksheet

_____

_____

_____

_____

_____

Matches Worksheet

_____

_____

_____

_____

_____

Napkin Worksheet

_____

_____

_____

_____

_____

Guide to Addressing Invitations

GUESTS	INNER ENVELOPE	OUTER ENVELOPE
Husband and wife	Mr. and Mrs. Jones	Mr. and Mrs. David Jones
Husband, wife & children under 16	Mr. and Mrs. Jones John, Sue and James (in order of age)	Mr. and Mrs. David Jones
Married, but wife has kept maiden name	Ms. Johnson Mr. Jones	Ms. Mary Johnson Mr. David Jones
Single woman	Miss Jones	Miss Mary Jones
Single woman and guest	Miss Jones and Guest	Miss Mary Jones
Single man	Mr. Smith (Master if young boy)	Mr. James Smith
Single man and guest	Mr. Smith and Guest	Mr. James Smith
Engaged Couple	Mr. Green and Miss White	Mr. Robert Green
Widow	Mrs. Brown	Mrs. Robert Brown
Divorcee	Mrs. Brown (if retaining former husband's name)	Mrs. Smith Brown (maiden name and former husband's surname)
Two sisters over 16, but still at home	The Misses Jones	The Misses Sue and Mary Jones
Two brothers over 16, but still at home	The Messrs. Brown	The Messrs. James and Michael Brown
Unmarried couple living together	Miss White Mr. Green	Miss Teresa White Mr. Robert Green

On the following pages are some examples of formal invitations, showing both traditional and contemporary wordings.

Traditional Wording of Invitations

By Mother and Father

> Mr. and Mrs. James Brown
> request the honour of your presence
> at the marriage of their daughter
> Marian Elise
> to
> Alan Robert Jones
> Saturday, the twenty-fourth of June
> nineteen hundred and eighty-eight
> at five o'clock
> Saint Thomas Church
> Sunnyvale, California

One Parent Deceased: Father Issuing Invitation

> Mr. James Brown
> requests the honour of your presence
> at the marriage of his daughter
> Marian Elise
> to
> Alan Robert Jones
> Saturday, the twenty-fourth of June
> nineteen hundred and eighty-eight
> at five o'clock
> Saint Thomas Church
> Sunnyvale, California

One Parent Deceased: Mother Issuing Invitation

> Mrs. James Brown
> requests the honour of your presence
> at the marriage of her daughter
> Marian Elise
> to
> Alan Robert Jones
> Saturday, the twenty-fourth of June
> nineteen hundred and eighty-eight
> at five o'clock
> Saint Thomas Church
> Sunnyvale, California

One Parent Deceased (living parent remarried)
Mother remarried

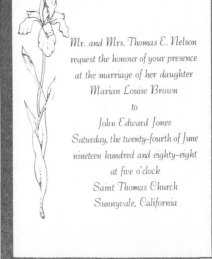

> Mr. and Mrs. Thomas E. Nelson
> request the honour of your presence
> at the marriage of her daughter
> Marian Louise Brown
> to
> John Edward Jones
> Saturday, the twenty-fourth of June
> nineteen hundred and eighty-eight
> at five o'clock
> Saint Thomas Church
> Sunnyvale, California

By Groom's Family

Mr. and Mrs. Kenneth E. Johnson
request the honour of your presence
at the marriage of
Miss Marian Elise Brown
to their son
Mr. Richard Edmund Johnson
Saturday, the fourth of June
nineteen hundred and eighty-eight
at five o'clock
Saint Thomas Church
Sunnyvale, California

One Parent Deceased (living parent remarried)
Father remarried

Mr. and Mrs. David Brown
request the honour of your presence
at the marriage of his daughter
Marian Louise Brown
to
John Edward Jones
Saturday, the twenty-fourth of June
nineteen hundred and eighty-eight
at five o'clock
Saint Thomas Church
Sunnyvale, California

Divorced Parents
Divorced Father issuing invitation

Mr. William Jefferson
requests the honour of your presence
at the marriage of his daughter
Elizabeth Anne
to
Alan Robert Jones
Saturday, the twenty-fourth of June
nineteen hundred and eighty-eight
at five o'clock
Saint Thomas Church
Sunnyvale, California

Divorced Parents
Divorced Mother issuing invitation

Mrs. Bernice Jefferson
requests the honour of your presence
at the marriage of her daughter
Elizabeth Anne
to
Alan Robert Jones
Saturday, the twenty-fourth of June
nineteen hundred and eighty-eight
at five o'clock
Saint Thomas Church
Sunnyvale, California

Both Parents Deceased
Married brother or married sister
issuing invitation

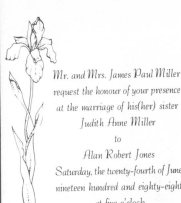

Mr. and Mrs. James Paul Miller
request the honour of your presence
at the marriage of his(her) sister
Judith Anne Miller
to
Alan Robert Jones
Saturday, the twenty-fourth of June
nineteen hundred and eighty-eight
at five o'clock
Saint Thomas Church
Sunnyvale, California

Both Parents Deceased
Older brother issuing invitation

Mr. William E. Peters
requests the honour of your presence
at the marriage of his sister
Marian Elise
to
Alan Robert Jones
Saturday, the twenty-fourth of June
nineteen hundred and eighty-eight
at five o'clock
Saint Thomas Church
Sunnyvale, California

Second Marriages

Invitations are worded the same,
except that the bride's married
name is used.

By Bride and Groom

Miss Susan Leigh Bradigan
and
Mr. Anthony David Jones
request the honour of your presence
at their marriage
Saturday, the twenty-fourth of June
nineteen hundred and eighty-eight
at five o'clock
Saint Thomas Church
Sunnyvale, California

Invitations

Traditional Wording of Invitations

Double wedding
When brides are not sisters

Mr. and Mrs. Vincent Randall
and
Mr. and Mrs. Mark L. Matthews
request the honour of your presence
at the marriage of their daughters
Judith Ann Randall
to
Mr. Joseph Samuel Ashman
and Marian Elise Matthews
to
Mr. John Edward Spencer
Saturday, the twenty-fourth of June
nineteen hundred and eighty-eight
at five o'clock
Saint Thomas Church
Sunnyvale, California

Double Wedding
When brides are sisters

Mr. and Mrs. Mark L. Matthews
request the honour of your presence
at the marriage of their daughters
Jennifer Lynn
to
Mr. Gregory Alan Forbes
and
Suzanne Kaye
to
Mr. Jeremy Edmund Jefferson
Saturday, the twenty-fourth of June
nineteen hundred and eighty-eight
at five o'clock
Saint Thomas Church
Sunnyvale, California

Contemporary Wording of Invitations

Dr. and Mrs. David Bradley
and
Mr. and Mrs. Keith Whitney
invite you to witness as their children
Marie and Bruce
share the Sacrament of Matrimony
A wedding mass will celebrate
this union
Saturday, the tenth of June
nineteen hundred and eighty-nine
at ten o'clock in the morning
Queen of the Holy Rosary Church
Lincoln, Nebraska

Contemporary Wording of Invitations

Our daughter, Susan
will be married to
Bryan Andrew Brady
on Saturday, the eleventh of June
nineteen hundred and ninety
at three o'clock in the afternoon at
Gorham United Methodist Church
Arlington, Texas
We invite you to worship with us,
witness their vows, and be our guest
at the reception and buffet to follow.
If you are unable to attend we ask
your presence in thought and prayer.

Mr. and Mrs. Roger Peterson

Invitations

Beautiful is the miracle of love
they will give to each other.
The holy ceremony uniting our
daughter Teresa Maria
and William Lee Keats
will take place Saturday,
June sixteenth
nineteen hundred and ninety
at four o'clock
Queen of Angels Church
2330 West Sunnyside
Sacramento, California
We joyfully ask you to witness
this celebration of life.

Mr. and Mrs. Anthony Evans

Our love is the flower that blossoms,
Our joy...its lasting perfume
We invite you to be with us
as we begin our new life together
on Saturday, April first
nineteen hundred and eighty-nine
. at six o'clock
First Congregational
Church of Vernon
695 Hartford Road
Philadelphia, Pennsylvania

Catherine Ann Armstrong
and
William Edward Ashley

The sun, the stars, the sky, the earth
and all of God's creatures
join in His divine plan of the universe
Come celebrate with us one
special part
the marriage of our daughter
Carol Ann
to
Stephen Louis Conrad
Saturday, July fourteenth
nineteen hundred and ninety
at one o'clock
Saint Luke Lutheran Church
340 Wilshire Boulevard
Omaha, Nebraska

Richard and Elaine Armstrong

The most joyous of occasions
is the union of man and woman
in celebration of life...
Mr. and Mrs. Jonathan Winfield
invite you to share in the ceremony
uniting their daughter
Nancy Elaine
and
Mr. David Alan Nelson
on Saturday, December fifteenth
nineteen hundred and ninety
at two o'clock
First Church of God
San Clements, Parkway
Denver, Colorado

Mr. and Mrs. George Whitman

Invitations

Our joy will be more complete
if you can share in the ceremony
uniting our daughter
Susan Marie
and
Mr. Christopher Andrew Barrows
Saturday, the ninth of July
nineteen hundred and eighty-eight
at two o'clock
Saint Margaret Church
552 Crescent Boulevard
Falls Church, Virginia

Mr. and Mrs. Vincent A. Edwards

A fresh new day...and it is ours
a day of happy beginnings
when we, Susan Marie Edwards
and Christopher Andrew Barrows
pledge our love as one
on Saturday, October eighth
nineteen hundred and eighty-eight
at seven o'clock p.m.
Church of Christ
11512 South Normandy
Minneapolis, Minnesota

Our joy will be more complete if you
can share in this celebration of life

Carol Ann Stillman
and
Robert Alan Remington
invite you to share the joy of the
beginning of their new life together
when on Saturday, July first
nineteen hundred and eighty-nine
at one o'clock
they exchange marriage vows
Saint Paul University Chapel
723 State Street
Dallas, Texas

The more love is shared,
the more quickly it grows
Tracy L. Weber
and
Daniel J. Bristol
invite you to join them in celebrating
the beginning
of a new life together
on Saturday, the fifth of August
nineteen hundred and eighty-nine
at two o'clock in the afternoon
Saint Edwards Catholic Church
3826 Eleventh Street
Seattle, Washington

Sample Ceremony Program

THE MARRIAGE SERVICE OF
SUSAN LEE BROWN
AND
ALAN ROBERT JONES
SATURDAY, MARCH 21, 1990
ST. JOHN'S CHURCH
MINNEAPOLIS, MINNESOTA
PASTOR JAMES F. WALLACE
OFFICIATING

PRELUDE OF ORGAN MUSIC
SEATING OF PARENTS
LIGHTING OF CANDLES
VOCAL SOLO .... SUNRISE SUNSET
PROCESSIONAL
"Jesu Joy of Man's Desiring" .... J. S. Bach
"Trumpet Tune" .... Purcell
THE CALL TO CELEBRATION
THE CHARGE TO THE COUPLE
THE DECLARATION OF INTENT
THE VOWS
THE EXCHANGING OF THE RINGS
THE SERMON
VOCAL SOLO .... LORD'S PRAYER
LIGHTING OF THE CANDLE
VOCAL SOLO .... LOVE ONE ANOTHER
RECESSIONAL
"Trumpet Voluntary" .... Purcell
POSTLUDE

PARENTS

Mr. and Mrs. James Brown

GRANDPARENTS

Mr. and Mrs. Robert Brown

Mrs. Alan Jones

Mrs. Michael Smith

ORGANIST

Anthony Grasso

SOLOIST

Suzanne Mitchell

ATTENDANTS

Maid of Honor . . . . Carol Chandler
Friend of Bride

Bridesmaids . . . . Nancy Doyle
Friend of Bride

Jeri Brown
Cousin of Bride

Pamela Jones
Sister of Groom

Best Man . . . . David Jones
Brother of Groom

Groomsmen . . . . Robert Jones
Cousin of Groom

Lawrence Brown
Brother of Bride

Randy Johnson
Friend of Groom

Host and Hostess . . . . Mr. and Mrs. John Smith
Uncle and Aunt of Bride

Mr. and Mrs. Randolph Johnson
Friends of Couple

Guest Book . . . . Dawn Johnson
Friend of Couple

Bridal Gift Registry

To insure you will receive exactly what you want and to avoid duplicating gifts, register your choices and preferences in the bridal registry at your favorite department, china, jewelry or gift store.

The bridal registry lists all the gifts you would like to receive. The store will show it to anyone who asks to see it. As the items are bought, they are crossed off the list and the gift is sent to you. Most major department stores maintain registries, circulating your selections to all their branches, and updating as needed, making it more convenient for gift givers.

Many registries today are computerized, which makes the updating of your selections much more reliable and keeps the number of duplicate gifts to a minimum.

When making your list, there are several things to keep in mind. First, shop with your groom so that you can make choices together. Second, list all the patterns, quantities, designs, colors, shapes and sizes that you have chosen from appliances to linens. Finally, make sure your selections cover a wide price range in order to accommodate all your guests.

"Many registries are computerized."

Part of the reason for the registry is to help those sharing in your special day to know what gifts you most desire. Once your registry or registries have been selected, make sure you inform your family and friends where you are registered so they can tell other guests.

The hostesses of your showers may want to let everyone know where you are registered on the shower invitations. Re-member to call or stop in to update this list after showers, holidays and the wedding itself. Gift lists for your showers are provided.

Even with the registry, you may still receive duplicate gifts. These can be returned or exchanged. There is no need to notify the giver. Send a thank you note for the gift received.

Should you receive a damaged gift directly from the store, return it immediately with its original packing material. Reputable stores replace them with no hassle.

Gifts should be acknowledged within one month through a thank you note.

Use the bridal registry checklist provided as a worksheet to reflect items you already have and those you need. Most bridal registries will provide you with their checklist. Take "The Wedding Pages" checklist with you to the bridal registry to assure your list is accurate and complete.

Bridal Gift Registry Questions

When selecting your gift registry, ask these questions:

1) Do you circulate my choices to all branches of your store?

2) Do you update my selections as items are purchased?

3) What is your policy regarding returns?

4) Do you wrap and deliver the gifts?

5) Is there an additional charge for this?

Gift Registry Worksheet

Formal Dinnerware

Store:

Brand:

Pattern:

Have	Need	Description
		Dinner plate
		Salad plate
		Bread & butter plate
		Soup bowl
		Cereal bowl
		Fruit bowl
		Cup & saucer
		Small platter
		Medium platter
		Large platter
		Oval vegetable
		Round vegetable
		Gravy boat
		Sugar & creamer
		Butter dish
		Salt & pepper
		Tea pot
		Coffee pot

Formal Flatware

Store:

Brand:

Pattern:

Have	Need	Description
		Dinner knife
		Steak knife
		Butter knife
		Dinner fork
		Salad fork
		Cocktail fork
		Tea spoon
		Soup spoon
		Table spoon
		Iced tea spoon
		Pierced tablespoon
		Gravy ladle
		Carving set
		Sugar spoon
		Casserole spoon
		Dessert server
		Salad set

Formal Stemware

Store:

Brand:

Pattern:

Have	Need	Description
		Goblet
		Wine
		Champagne
		Sherbet
		Cordial
		Cocktail
		Brandy

Formal Accessories

Store:

Brand:

Pattern:

Have	Need	Description
		Candlesticks
		Vase
		Decanter
		Paperweights
		Objects of art
		Pitcher
		Bar sets
		Candles
		TV trays
		Candelabra
		Salad bowl
		Decorative plates
		Ice bucket
		Bon Bon dish
		Relish serving tray
		Roll tray

Informal Dinnerware

Store:

Brand:

Pattern:

Have	Need	Description
		Dinner plate
		Salad plate
		Bread & butter plate
		Soup bowl
		Cereal bowl
		Fruit bowl
		Cup & saucer
		Small platter
		Medium platter
		Large platter
		Oval vegetable
		Round vegetable
		Gravy boat
		Sugar & creamer
		Butter dish
		Salt & pepper
		Tea pot
		Coffee pot
		Mugs

Informal Flatware

Store:

Brand:

Pattern:

Have	Need	Description
		Dinner knife
		Steak knife
		Butter knife
		Dinner fork
		Salad fork
		Cocktail fork
		Tea spoon
		Soup spoon
		Table spoon
		Iced tea spoon
		Pierced tablespoon
		Gravy ladle
		Carving set
		Sugar spoon
		Casserole spoon
		Dessert server
		Salad set

Informal Glassware

Store:

Brand:

Pattern:

Have	Need	Description
		Goblet
		Wine
		Low tumbler
		High tumbler
		Juice
		Iced tea
		Champagne

Gift Registry Worksheet

Cookware

Have	Need	Description
		Covered casserole
		Fry Pan - small
		large
		Double boiler
		Microwave ware
		Omelette pan
		Roaster
		Sauce pan - 1 qt. 2 qt. 3 qt. 5 qt.
		Bakeware
		Pans
		Bread
		Cake
		Cupcake
		Lasagne
		Loaf
		Pizza
		Popover
		Souffle'
		Spring form
		Quiche
		Cookie sheets
		Casseroles 1 qt. 2 qt. 3 qt. 5 qt.
		Stock pot 4 qt. 6 qt. 8 qt. 12 qt.
		Pasta machine

Bath Linens & Accessories

Have	Need	Description	Color
		Bath towel	
		Hand towel	
		Fingertip towel	
		Washcloth	
		Body sheet	
		Contour rug	
		Bath rug	
		Tank set	
		Lid cover	
		Fingertip holder	
		Hamper	
		Mirror	
		Scale	
		Shower curtain	
		Soap dish	
		Tissue cover	
		Toothbrush holder	
		Towel stand	
		Wall shelf	
		Wastebasket	

Fine Accessories

Have	Need	Description
		Chafing dish
		Cheese boards
		Chip 'n dip
		Coasters
		Copper items
		Cutting boards
		Decorative glasses
		Decorative plates
		Fondue pot
		Ice buckets
		Punch bowl sets
		Serving bowl
		Trivet
		Trays
		Wicker items
		Wine cooler
		Unique collectibles

Bed Linens

Have	Need	Description	Size
		Sheets	
		Fitted	
		Flat	
		Flannel	
		Waterbed	
		Pillowcases	
		Blankets	
		Thermal	
		Conventional	
		Electric	
		Comforter	
		Mattress pad	
		Pillows	
		Synthetic	
		Down	
		Bedspread	

Gift Registry Worksheet

Kitchen Accessories

Have	Need	Description
		Mug
		Coasters
		Cutting boards
		Ice bucket
		Apron
		Canister set
		Charcoal grill
		Cookie jar
		Copper molds
		Cutlery
		Knife set
		Ironing board
		Kitchen gadgets
		Mitts
		Mixing bowls
		Picnic basket
		Spice rack
		Tea kettle
		Wok
		Gourmet items
		Dinnerware sets
		Glassware sets
		Flatware sets

Small Electrics

Have	Need	Description	Have	Need	Description
		Blender			Ice cream freezer
		Can opener			Iron
		Coffee maker			Regular
		Crock pot			Steam
		Deep fat fryer			Mixer
		Electric fry pan			Smoke detector
		Electric knife			Toaster
		Food processor			Toaster oven
		Hot food server			Waffle baker
					Electric fan
					Corn popper

Luggage

Have	Need	Description			Color
		Pullman			
		24″ 26″ 29″			
		Companion 24″			
		3 suiter			
		Garment bag M/F			
		Travel kit M/F			
		Carry on			
		Overnight			

Table Linens

Have	Need	Description	Size
		Tablecloth	
		Formal	
		Casual	
		Lace	
		Placemats	
		Fabric	
		Straw	
		Woven	
		Vinyl	
		Napkins	
		Napkin rings	
		Kitchen ensembles	

Special Gifts

Have	Need	Description	Color
		Camera	
		Microwave oven	
		Microwave or TV cart	
		Telephones	
		Wall hangings	
		Lamps	
		Vacuum	
		Radio alarm clock	
		Fireplace accessories	
		Card table & chairs	
		Sofa pillows	
		Objects of art	
		Television	
		Stereo	
		Gas grill	

Pre-Wedding Celebrations

Although planning a wedding can get hectic, one of the things no one seems to tire of is all the parties that precede it. The engagement party, bridal showers and the bachelor and bachelorette parties are usually built around a theme. Celebrate as many as you have the time and energy for.

Engagement Party

The engagement party can be as casual or formal as you like. It can be held whenever and wherever you and your guests feel most comfortable: indoors or outdoors, at a restaurant or club, or catered to a private home. Have a dinner party, barbecue or brunch.

Anyone may host the engagement party including your parents, a close friend or relative, or even you and your groom. Get creative with the decorations. Balloons, a decorated cake and party favors are just a few suggestions. The theme of the party you choose will provide more ideas.

Traditionally, it is the bride's father who announces the engagement with a toast to the couple. The groom then stands to make a short speech of thanks.

Those who attend the engagement party are not expected to bring gifts. They should also be invited to the wedding.

Bridal Showers

As a rule, anyone may host a bridal shower. It is likely that there will be more than one shower in your honor. These too may be held anywhere at any time and on any day of the week.

Invitations may be handwritten, commercial fill-in or they may be handled by telephone.

Guests should be notified several weeks in advance.

Themes are usually built around the types of gifts to be given such as lingerie, kitchen, bathroom, bedroom, sport and recreation, plant, or beauty and health. If the gifts are clothing related, you will want the host to put your size and color preferences on the invitations. For household and other gifts, the host should note the store that has your bridal registry.

Many of the guests will be invited to more than one shower. This can get quite expensive. You might want to let them know that you would like them to attend all of them, but that only one gift is necessary.

Attendants' Parties

The Bride's

A week or so before the wedding, the bride should host a party as a thank you to her attendants. There is no rule on the type of party it can be. Many choose to have a lunch, dinner or cocktails, however, some choose to treat it like the last night out as a single woman. It's up to you.

This is a good time for you to give your attendants their gifts and discuss any last-minute details.

The attendants' gifts can be any one of a variety of items such as engraved items reflecting the wedding day, porcelain or ceramic gifts or even a pen and pencil set. A practical gift would be the jewelry you want the attendants to wear during the wedding ceremony. This allows you to select the proper jewelry to set off the bridesmaids' gowns.

You may wish to have the party with the groom and his attendants so everyone has a chance to get to know each other before the wedding day.

The Groom's

Everyone has heard exaggerated stories about the adventures of the groom and his attendants at his bachelor party. Although many of these stories are not to be believed, the result of having it the night before the ceremony is a bleary-eyed groom. To avoid this, the best man, his attendants or the groom should host the celebration a few nights before the wedding day.

At the end of the party, the groom toasts his bride with champagne. This is a good time for him to distribute his gifts to his attendants.

The groom's gifts to his attendants will depend on the attendants and their backgrounds. Gifts could include engraved knives reflecting the wedding date, pen and pencil sets, a bottle of liquor, wine or champagne, or even a gym bag.

As an added touch and to insure safety, a limousine service can be used to transport celebrants.

Transportation

Limousine Service

Scheduling and planning the transportation for you and your wedding party and out-of-town guests is crucial in making your wedding day run smoothly.

Private or rented vehicles might serve for the wedding party and guests, but you, the bride, should ride in style. What better way than in a chauffeur-driven limousine? Choose between the standard service with stereo and a glass divider separating the driver and passengers or a "stretch" or Rolls Royce with the works: stereo, bar and television.

When ordering yours, ask about the price, the minimum rental time, how they deal with overtime, and cancellation policies. Reserve the limousine as soon as possible in order to assure that you can get the limousine of your choice. Many firms require a deposit with the balance paid at pick-up time.

The procession to the church begins with your mother, your maid of honor, and perhaps an attendant or two. The second car should include the rest of the attendants. You and your father should follow in the third car.

> ## "Reserve the limousine as soon as possible."

The groom and his best man should make their own arrangements, arriving at the ceremony site at least 30 minutes before it is scheduled to begin. If pictures are to be taken before the ceremony, the groom, his groomsmen, and ushers should arrive approximately two hours before the ceremony.

Friends and relatives should make themselves available for the transportation of out-of-town guests. The details should be written out and given to all the drivers. They must know where they are to be, whom they are to transport and when they must be at each location. Maps and directions to the church and reception site may either be mailed with the invitations or distributed at the ceremony.

When leaving the church, you and your new husband will ride in the same car that brought you and your father to the church. Your parents will travel in the same car. The rest of the wedding party will go in the remaining cars.

During the reception, your friends will very likely give your car the traditional decorating. Whatever is used should be easily washable and not harm the car's finish. Better yet, use balloons or already made up signs and streamers. The decorating should not obstruct the driver's view.

You can also arrange to have the limousine service pick you up after the reception and take you to your hotel in style. Be sure to tip the driver.

Horse-Drawn Carriages

As an added personal touch, you may wish to use a horse-drawn carriage on your wedding day. Carriages are a welcome and exciting subject for both photographers and videographers. The variety of carriages often allows this service to be available year-round. You may wish to use an open carriage for weddings during the summer months or a closed carriage during winter months. Service may vary from a simple horse and carriage to an elaborate coach.

When making arrangements, you should ask about carriage styles, prices, minimum rental time and overtime charges. You should provide information regarding the number of people traveling in the coach and any special requirements you might wish to make.

A carriage ride might also be a welcome treat for some of your special guests.

Often, carriages are used in connection with limousine or vintage car services. Don't hesitate to ask for recommendations. Wedding suppliers will guide you to respectable companies which can provide the desired service.

Vintage Car Rental

Picture yourself riding to your wedding or reception in a 1953 Corvette or a 1954 Ford Thunderbird. Maybe a 1963 Cadillac better suits your style. Whatever your taste, there are car rental companies that offer vintage car rentals as an exciting way for the couple and wedding party to get around on the wedding day.

As with other wedding plans, check with the rental company on the availability of the cars you are interested in and make your reservations well in advance.

Sports and Luxury Car Rentals

There are also rental companies that now offer sport and luxury cars. Mercedes Benz, Porsche, Ferrari and even Lamborghini in some cases, are available on a rental basis. If you like sport or luxury cars, this may be one way to enjoy them.

Availability should be checked as soon as you select the type of vehicle. Reservations should be made as far in advance as possible.

Transportation Questions

When selecting your transportation, ask these questions:

1) What types of limousine or horse-drawn carriage services can you offer?
2) How do you base your charges? Time? Distance?
3) Is there a minimum rental time?
4) After the minimum, how do you base your charges?
5) When must reservations be made?
6) Is a deposit required? How much is it? When must it be paid? When is the balance due?
7) What is your cancellation policy?
8) What are the policies on decorating the vehicles or carriages?
9) Can I use the same vehicle to pick up several people?
10) Are the vehicles available to see prior to the wedding?

Driver's Checklist

Name of driver: _____ Vehicle: _____

Address:_____ Phone No: _____

PASSENGERS

1. Name:_____ Pickup time: _____

   Pickup location: _____

2. Name:_____ Pickup time: _____

   Pickup location: _____

3. Name:_____ Pickup time: _____

   Pickup location: _____

4. Name:_____ Pickup time: _____

   Pickup location: _____

5. Name:_____ Pickup time: _____

   Pickup location: _____

6. Name:_____ Pickup time: _____

   Pickup location: _____

Ceremony address:_____ Arrival time: _____

Directions:_____

_____

Reception address:_____ Arrival time: _____

Directions:_____

_____

Out-Of-Town Guests

Most weddings include participants, family members, and guests from out-of-town. It is usually an inconvenience for the direct wedding party and their families to be running to and from the airport and making accommodation and transportation arrangements for all of them.

Accommodations

In order to simplify this procedure, make arrangements with a local hotel or motel to take care of accommodations for all of your out-of-town guests. Oftentimes, they will be willing to give them a special rate. This will also allow several of them to travel to the ceremony together or make it more convenient to pick them up before the ceremony.

Some hotels and motels will provide a special service. They will accommodate your guests and use their limousine service as a means of getting them to the ceremony.

Transportation

Another way to help your out-of-town guests is to set up a rental car for them. Rental car companies often have special weekend rates and will be glad to accommodate the entire out-of-town wedding party. Find out which guests need cars and then make the reservations at one time. Your guests will appreciate this gesture.

Travel Agency

Many travel agencies will work out both accommodation and transportation details for your out-of-town guests. This can save them time. It is especially helpful for your out-of-town attendants.

Anything you can do to help those who travel to share in your special day will be appreciated by them and make the day even more special.

Your Honeymoon

Your married life together begins with your honeymoon. This is not only a time to relax after all the pre-wedding and wedding pressures, but also a time to enjoy each other's company and dream about the rest of your lives together.

Because this is a time of sharing, you will want to plan your honeymoon together. Decide how each of you would like to spend this time. If you have different ideas, compromise. There are so many places to go and things to do that this should not be difficult.

Get caught up in the excitement of an exotic island. Sail through Caribbean waters or spend a romantic week at a resort close to home. Rent a cabin overlooking a lake. Ski down hills layered in snow. Whatever you plan to do, stick to your budget.

Arrangements

Start by seeing a travel agency. They can give you ideas about how to spend your time at no charge. Not only will you hear what is available, but by looking through the brochures provided, you can find the perfect setting for your romantic interlude.

Planning with an agency helps you save money. They can give you information on many kinds of vacation packages, reduced airline fares and resort specials. Many vacation areas have off-season rates that they can help you take advantage of.

As with other wedding professionals you will rely on, a travel agent should be selected carefully. You may want to talk with friends and relatives for their suggestions. The agent should be willing to work with your ideas and within your budget. Good travel agents will also make suggestions and offer useful tips on clothing requirements, currency exchange, inoculations, passports, etc.

Because you will have so much on your mind while planning your wedding, a travel agency helps ease some of the burden. They will make your reservations and arrange your transportation. Most important, they will attend to all the details.

During your trip, do not be bashful about telling the hotel management that you are newlyweds. Many hotels will extend extra courtesies to you. Begin making arrangements at least six months ahead of time. This will give you less to worry about as your wedding day gets closer. Leave a copy of your itinerary and phone numbers with parents or friends, and arrange for someone to check your home while you are gone. If you are driving your own car on your honeymoon, it should be in top condition. Have it thoroughly checked before your trip. Also, have your route all planned out ahead of time.

Your honeymoon begins the night of your wedding and usually includes at least one night's stay in a local hotel. Many hotels offer "Wedding Night Packages." A complimentary bridal suite may be included in a reception package.

Because some hotels end room service at 10 p.m. and you may not have had a chance to eat, ask if there is special consideration given for the wedding night or if the hotel provides gift baskets.

Traveling Abroad

Requirements for traveling abroad differ from country to country. While the details may differ, the general categories are similar.

A passport proving your citizenship is a necessity in nearly all foreign countries. There may also be additional identification required. Passports are issued by the U.S. Government. If children will be a part of your trip abroad, you will want to find out the types of identification that are required for them.

A variety of inoculations may also be needed. The number and types required will depend on your shot record and the country you are visiting.

Most foreign countries have their own currency system. The rates of exchange (how much U.S. currency is needed to purchase foreign currency) can differ from day to day. Talk to your travel agent for banks and other locations that exchange currency. Also, have them provide a list of locations that exchange currency near your accommodations overseas.

Chances are there will be many differences between the U.S. and foreign countries. Check with your travel agent about foreign customs. Remember, you are a visitor in their country and you will want to ensure your stay is pleasant.

If you or your groom use any electrical devices such as a blow dryer, curlers or electric shaver, make sure you have an electrical adapter that can convert electrical current to the same one these devices were designed for.

The Bride's Trousseau

In days past, when marriages were arranged by the families, the bride entered the commitment with a dowry, or trousseau. This acted as compensation for the groom's responsibility of providing a good home for his wife and their children.

Today, much has changed. A trousseau may still include a hope chest with family heirlooms or other housewarming items. It is more likely that the term will apply to the clothing and accessories you will need for your honeymoon and the early stages of your life together. This is the beginning of a new stage in your life. New clothes will make you feel more special about your recent union.

The items you choose should not be purchased during a haphazard shopping spree. Rather, select carefully. Professionals in many stores or boutiques can help you select items that fit with your particular style and coloring. Give them the details of your honeymoon plans. They will be able to provide ideas for a wardrobe that will be appropriate for the climate and season of your destination.

While traveling, you will want to pack a minimum of items, but still allow yourself a variety of choices. The store attendant should be able to coordinate a selection that you can mix and match for the look you want.

Accessories go a long way when your wardrobe is limited. Just the right scarf, belt, jewelry or other accessory can be all that is needed to change the outfit. The clothing professional can also help you to accentuate flattering features or hide other features.

Lingerie is a big part of the honeymoon attire. Be sure to get undergarments that can be worn under clothing in addition to negligees, nighties and teddies that will be worn alone. New lingerie can make you feel good about you, not to mention its affect on your groom.

Clothing and Accessories for the Groom

The bride is not the only one who will need new clothes. This is a new and exciting time for the groom, too. He should have the same special treatment.

Your groom may already have a favorite place to shop. If not, look around for stores that have the styles he is interested in and feels comfortable wearing.

He, too, should coordinate his new purchases for greater variety. Depending on your honeymoon itinerary, he may need to get both casual and dress clothes. Neckties, jewelry, belts and hats can work wonders for his wardrobe.

Enticing undergarments are not just for the bride. Many stores carry a wide array of unmentionables for men that will spice up the honeymoon. You may want to surprise him with articles that will flatter him and appeal to you.

The number of items each of you will need depends on where you are going and the length of time you will be away. The following chart can act as a checklist and help you figure out how much you will need.

Packing Checklist

CLOTHING		TOILETRIES		EQUIPMENT	
Underwear		Toothbrush/Paste		Camera/Film	
Socks/Nylons		Lotion/Moisturizer		Games/Books	
T-Shirts		Brush/Comb		Address Book	
Pajamas/Bathrobes		Contact Lens/Glasses		Journal/Diary	
Lingerie		Make-up Purse		Tickets/Itinerary	
Bathing Suit/Trunks		Hair Clips/Pins		Passport/Credit Card	
Shorts		Razor/Aftershave		Suitcases	
Comfortable Pants		Perfume/Cologne		Traveler's Checks	
Dress Clothing		Suntan Lotion		Cash	
Evening Purse		Tampons/Pads		Swim Gear	
Sweater/Sweatshirts		Birth Control		Ski Gear	
Jacket/Coat and Tie		Soap		Hiking Gear	
Dress Shoes		Nail Polish/Remover		Tennis Gear	
Tennis Shoes		Nail File			
Sandals		Cotton Balls/Q-Tips			
Jewelry		Nail Clipper			
Jogging Suits		Hair Rollers			
Hats/Visors		Hair Spray			
Sunglasses		Curling Iron/Dryer			
		Towels			
		Shampoo/Rinse			
		Mouthwash			
		Aspirin			
		First Aid Kit (Travel)			
		Dental Floss			

Packing

Chances are, you will be tempted to take as much clothing as you can fit in your bags. This is a temptation you will want to avoid. Remember, it will be you that has to carry the heavy baggage. While there are some situations you will need to anticipate, it can be done without trying to fit your entire wardrobe into a few pieces of luggage.

Luggage/Suitcases

The type of luggage you choose will depend on the type of trip you have planned and your own personal preferences. A luggage sales representative can offer advice on what is best for you.

Some people prefer a hard-bodied pullman style. The divider in the middle allows it to act as two cases in one. Put shoes, lingerie, sportswear or separates in one side; and suits and dresses in the other. You may also want to put your clothing in one section and your spouse's clothing in the other.

Softsided cases are also popular. They are flexible and the side and edge pockets allow you to cushion the belongings inside.

Many larger pieces of luggage come with wheels and handles or straps. These features will make carrying your bags easier.

In addition to a large case, you will also want a smaller carry-on piece. Look for a case that is small and lightweight, but still holds all the items you cannot do without temporarily.

Luggage is available in a variety of brands, colors, styles and materials. The professional sales representative can provide information about quality, durability and cost. Do not be fooled by fancy styles or colors. They may not last. Also, do not compromise quality for cost. A good set of luggage can last a lifetime.

What to Bring

To allow yourself a variety of clothing combinations and yet still pack light, organize your travel wardrobe around a single color. This will allow you to mix and match clothes. It will also make it easier for you to eliminate clothes that are not compatible with your color. The individual items should be basic styles so that they can be dressed up or down simply by adding accessories. For example, a simple black skirt can be worn with comfortable walking shoes and a blouse during the day. At night, add black hose, heels, jewelry or other accessories.

Do not worry about running out of fresh clothing. Skirts, blouses and undergarments can often be washed in your hotel room sink. Hotel laundries and self-service laundromats are usually available also.

Be prepared for any weather changes by dressing in layers — a T-shirt, shirt, sweater, jacket, etc. You can then stay warm or take off layers of clothing in response to temperature changes.

For dressier occasions, your groom should bring a jacket or blazer, a tie and dress shoes. The bride can bring a nice dress that does not take up much room in the case or a dressy blouse that can be worn with a basic skirt and dressed up with accessories. Even your dress clothes should be compatible with the color you have selected for your travel wardrobe.

And, of course, comfortable shoes are a must for any trip.

> ## "Be prepared for weather changes."

Carry-on luggage should not be stuffed with all the items that would not fit in your other bags. Instead, it should contain those things that you need to keep with you while traveling. It can include: eyeglasses, prescription medications, passports, tickets and other travel documents, an easy-to-read book or magazine, crossword puzzles or a deck of cards, a pen or pencil and paper, tissues or moistened towelettes for freshening up, skin moisturizer, aspirin, candies or gum, one dollar bills for tips or in-flight purchases.

If you will be traveling for a long period of time before reaching your destination, you and your groom will each want to bring a small grooming kit. It will not only help you to look your best, but it will also help you feel fresh. The bride's kit should include small supplies of beauty care items, a comb or brush, and a toothbrush and toothpaste. For the groom, bring a light razor and shaving cream, a toothbrush and toothpaste, and a comb or brush. When you feel fresh while traveling, you feel less tired.

How to Pack

The fold and cushion method of packing will allow you to get everything into your bag with as few wrinkles as possible. Put cosmetics and heavy items such as electric rollers on the bottom of your case. Stuff sides and corners with socks, underclothing, shoes, accessories and purses. Instead of rolling belts, place them along the inside edge of your bag. Lingerie, stockings, swimwear and scarves should be folded and rolled to take up less space.

Items that wrinkle easily — suits, shirts, jackets, blouses and pants — should be placed on top. Pack these with as few folds as possible. And layer sheets of white tissue paper within the folds to reduce wrinkles. Make sure the contents are firm and full to keep them from shifting while en route. Unpack your clothes as soon as you reach your destination.

Despite your preparation, you may still experience some wrinkles. You can steam the wrinkles out by filling a bathtub with hot water and hanging the garment overnight in the bathroom with the door closed. There are also many types of travel irons that need little space in your luggage.

Gearing Up for the Honeymoon Mentally and Physically

You and your new husband will want to enjoy every moment of your honeymoon instead of wasting time recovering from your journey there. You will be more relaxed and comfortable if you take time to prepare and plan before you leave.

First of all, plan your trip well in advance and begin gathering your supplies at this time also. Any last minute rushing around can cause stress.

A few days before the honeymoon, slow down. Try to go to bed a little earlier or get up later. Eat lighter foods such as poultry, fish and greens. Indulge in a little exercise and most important, relax.

While traveling, drink a lot of water to offset the effects of dehydration or "jet lag." Excessive intake of coffee, tea, cola or alcohol upset the body's processes.

Freshening up periodically with a splash of water on the face or some light grooming can always make you feel better.

Once there, try to adapt to your new time zone. You may want to nap for a couple of hours, take a short walk and then eat a light supper before retiring early. When you awake, you should be ready to enjoy the new day with your new husband.

Borrowing Money — It's OK

A honeymoon is a special time set aside for the newly married couple to begin a lifetime of happiness together. You will want it to be a time the two of you will never forget.

Because many couples are just starting out and because other wedding expenses are great, there is not always enough extra money available for the honeymoon you envisioned for yourselves. Just remember, it's all right to borrow the money to finance your trip.

Depending on your credit history, many banks, savings and loans, credit unions or other financial institutions can make the funds available to you. This also allows you to pay for your honeymoon in installments instead of in a lump sum. Credit cards are also a ready source of cash.

Bring . . .

Money . . . use traveler's checks or credit cards instead of large sums of cash. Keep a list of your traveler's checks and credit card numbers in case they are lost or stolen.

Proof of age . . . your driver's license and a copy of your birth certificate.

Proof of marriage . . . a copy of your marriage license.

Proof of citizenship if necessary . . . a passport, visa or birth certificate.

Health insurance card . . . bring your physician's telephone number.

In case of emergency . . . carry a list of phone numbers of family members that should be notified in an emergency.

Don't forget your tickets!

Travel Agent Questions

When selecting your travel agent, ask the following questions:

1) What ideas can you offer for our honeymoon?
2) Can you work within our budget?
3) Will all the arrangements be taken care of for us?
4) If not, what do we have to do?
5) When should the arrangements be made?
6) If we are leaving the country, what will we need?

Honeymoon Checklist

WEDDING NIGHT ACCOMMODATIONS

Hotel Name: _____ Phone No: _____

Address: _____

_____

Estimated Time of Arrival: _____

Confirmation No: _____

Departure Date: _____ Departure Time: _____

TRAVEL AGENCY

Company: _____

Address: _____

_____

Representative: _____ Phone No: _____

TRANSPORTATION

Mode of Transportation: _____ Pick up tickets: _____

Departure Date & Time: _____

Arrival Date & Time: _____

Car Rental Agency: _____ Phone No: _____

Address: _____

_____

Confirmation No: _____

HONEYMOON LOCATION

Name of Resort: _____ Phone No: _____

Address: _____

_____

Arrival Date & Time: _____

Confirmation No: _____

Departure Date & Time: _____

CHAPTER

V

Legalities

Legalities

Prenuptial Agreement

In the past, prenuptial agreements were used to allow assets given to the couple to become the property of the family again in the event of a divorce. Today, the importance of these agreements has grown with the number of people getting married later in life and coming into the marriage with a career and assets. They are an effective way to encourage communication so that both parties know what the other's expectations are.

Prenuptial agreements today define items such as dividing property in the event of a divorce, the type of life-style the couple wishes to work towards, when children will be conceived and even where the couple has decided to live.

Legally speaking, the prenuptial agreement can supersede state property distribution laws in the event of divorce. There is never a guarantee that the agreement will be enforced. To give you the most concise and legally binding agreement, go to an attorney with experience in this area in the state in which you will be residing.

Marriage License Requirements

By law, all states require a marriage license. Both of you may apply together or separately (check on state regulations) at the license bureau in the location of your wedding.

You will need to provide proof of age. This can be done with your birth certificate, immigration record, adoption record or passport. Only certified photocopies are accepted.

If you are under the age of consent (it varies from state to state), you will need parental consent. Find out what type of proof is necessary.

If you were not born in the United States, you will need proof of citizenship. Bring a copy of your divorce papers if applicable.

In most states, blood tests are required. Be sure to find out how long the results are valid and bring the results of the test with you when applying for your license.

There is a waiting period before the license is valid. Be sure you keep the time limit in mind when applying.

Finally, there is a fee, although the amount varies. It's a good idea to call or write your local government official's office to get detailed information.

Choosing Your Name

Traditionally, brides have taken the husband's family name upon marriage. Today, however, you have a few options. Some women prefer to keep their names, having built a professional reputation before marriage. If so, you need not change any of your records, credit card accounts, etc.

You may also wish to hyphenate your name. In this case, your surname comes first followed by your husband's. However, you may have it the other way around. Be sure to talk about your choices with your husband, making sure it is what you both want and that you are comfortable with it.

If you choose to take your husband's surname, be sure to change your name on all these important documents:

- Driver's license.
- Car registration and title.
- Social security card.
- Insurance . . . health, life, car, and homeowners.
- Voter's registration.
- Bank accounts . . . checking, savings, etc.
- Credit cards.
- Passports or visas.
- Personal records . . . school and office.
- Business cards, memos and letterheads.
- Post office . . . don't forget that change of address card.
- Your last will and testament.

Wills

Your marriage is the beginning of a lifetime together. The last thing you want to think about is the death of your spouse. Yet, a majority of Americans die without wills, creating many difficulties for the loved ones they leave behind.

Without a will, the state of residence can use its rules and regulations to dictate the division of your property. It is doubtful your spouse will receive all your assets. In most cases, the distribution is not handled in a swift or cost effective manner.

It is not difficult to protect yourself from this situation. Preparation of a will is simple and inexpensive when you compare the benefits if death does occur.

The will is an important planning item for you and your spouse. It should be dealt with as soon as possible after the wedding. A qualified attorney with experience in writing wills can assist you in every step of developing a will. Using an expert will also ensure your will is in compliance with the local laws and is a legally binding document.

Prepaid Legal

Many Americans are not able to afford an attorney when they need one or do not know how to use one. This results in huge losses for some people. Newlyweds, as a rule, are not in tune with their legal needs. As we mentioned earlier, few have wills, which are an absolute necessity. One way to have legal services any time is to enter into a prepaid legal contract which will provide you with an attorney. It is similar to purchasing an insurance policy.

Different companies vary in their coverage, but the majority include phone consultations with an attorney, phone calls by an attorney on your behalf, review of contracts and documents, wills and legal expenses for trial defense or IRS audits.

These services could prove to be invaluable to you and your spouse from the time you sign your first lease, buy your first home or set up your first will, to the time you retire.

Notes

CHAPTER

VI

Premarital Counseling

Premarital Counseling

Planning a wedding is no small task. You and your future spouse may begin to feel great stress. The natural attitude may be, "everything will be fine after the wedding." But you may be surprised.

Wedding planning may be the first real test of your ability to work with and cope with your spouse. If problems and disagreements arise during your engagement, you may want to look into premarital counseling.

A premarital counselor can help you isolate the problems and then teach you techniques to overcome them. You will also learn more about each other's personality and the kind of support each of you need.

You may be worried about seeing a counselor. What if you find a major problem? Does that mean the wedding must be called off? This is very unlikely. However, if a problem is serious enough to end the engagement, it is better to find out now rather than after you are married.

Many religions provide premarital counseling through the church or through organized groups. Some even require counseling before the ceremony can be performed. This is often a sound idea. If counseling is not available, a reference for outside professionals will be provided.

Remember, the more a couple knows about each other, the stronger their marriage will be.

CHAPTER

VII

Your New Home

Your New Home

Finding Your New Home

Your new home is a reflection of your taste and style. But what is best for the two of you? Should you rent an apartment, buy a house, a condominium, a cooperative or rent a house? Your decision will depend on your income and desires. The first step is to make some important general decisions about where you would like to live and begin saving right after your engagement.

Location. What are your priorities? Do you want to be close to work, relatives or maybe recreational activities?

Cost. First, determine your gross monthly income. As a general rule, you should not look at spending more than 35 percent of your combined gross monthly income for mortgage payments, rent, homeowner's insurance, real estate taxes and any existing debt, including car or school loans and credit cards.

Needs Versus Wants. Decide what is most important to you. If you entertain a lot, make sure you have plenty of room. If you are a gourmet cook, make sure the kitchen fulfills your needs. If recreational activities are important, make sure the apartment or condominium complex has such facilities or make sure the sports or fitness clubs are close by. Do not let yourself be forced into a situation that does not satisfy your needs.

Size and Layout. If you already have furniture, make sure the size and layout of your home can accommodate it. What is the situation for electrical outlets, cable television, and other conveniences?

Once these initial questions have been answered, it will be possible for you to begin the decision process. Amazing as it seems, it may be possible for you to buy your own home. The average combined income of newlyweds today is high enough to allow the purchase of a home right after or even before the wedding.

To see if you are qualified to purchase a home, talk to a real estate broker. They can look at your current financial situation and judge what kind of house payment you could comfortably afford to make. Then they will show you what is available in the way of homes, condominiums or cooperatives in the areas you are interested. This service costs you nothing. You may be surprised at what you can afford.

Another option for new homes is to go directly to a developer. A developer can often offer incentives to make either a house, condominium or cooperative a reality. Instead of 10-20 percent down, a developer will sometimes offer 5 percent down. You can also negotiate partial payments of points by the developer. Sometimes they will offer incentives such as a washer and dryer, carpeting upgrades or increased light fixture allowances.

> *"You may be surprised at what you can afford."*

Apartments are often the most affordable option for the new couple. There are many ways to look for an apartment. One of the quickest ways is to use an apartment finder service. They specialize in locating apartments for people and are familiar with what is available in your city. You can also use printed apartment directories which are usually free and can be found in grocery stores, newsstands, shopping malls, etc. The newspaper is also a source for apartments and breaks the listings down by area or location.

When looking for an apartment, you should review the lease carefully before signing. Look into the following areas:

Maintenance. Are on-site personnel available? If not, how is maintenance handled? Are emergency services provided?

Talk to Residents. If possible, talk with a few residents to see if they are content with the situation.

Talk to the Manager. Ask the manager questions that are important to you. What are the neighbors like? What is the average age of the residents? Can guests use the sports facilities? How far away is the church, grocery store, shopping mall? What is the parking situation? Can we have two cars? Are the spots assigned? What incentives are offered if any? Are a washer and dryer provided or is there a laundromat close at hand?

The Lease. Make sure you review a blank copy of the lease and that you understand it. Remember, this is a binding legal document.

Restrictions. Because many apartment complexes do not allow children or pets, it is a good idea to know this up front. Some complexes also restrict the use of waterbeds, motorcycles, campers or pick-up trucks.

This advice should help you to find that perfect place to start your married life. Be sure to think through all the possibilities before making a long-term commitment.

Moving

After selecting your home, the next step is to move. Most people do not enjoy moving. If you are one of these people, a professional mover might be the answer.

Movers can move you across the country or across the street. Many specialize in one area of moving, such as apartment movers. They can even perform all of the packing functions for you.

Truck rental is another possibility if you are interested in performing your own move. Trucks of all different sizes are available.

Furnishing Your New Home

The furniture in your new home should express your combined tastes. Furniture selection can be a real challenge, but professionals are available to assist you.

A full-service furniture store will have representatives available for decorating advice. They can help you select the styles and colors that give your home the look you want. Stereos, televisions, VCRs and major appliances are also offered. They may carry a full line of carpeting and other floor coverings that can be just what is needed in your new home.

Most stores offer finance options that allow you to make payments over a period of time. This allows you to get the quality and style you want now, instead of working your way up to what you want.

Rent-to-own centers are another way to furnish your home. They offer furniture, stereos, televisions, VCRs, microwaves, major appliances and other types of furnishings you will need. These centers set up monthly or weekly payments. You

pay these for a fixed period of time and at the end, you own the items. Renting-to-own is an ideal option if you do not have a strong credit history.

Stereo and television centers can provide you with an entertainment center that can become the centerpiece of your new family room. Their representatives are specialists in sight and sound. They can give you advice on quality equipment that meets your expectations.

New floor and wall covering can tie your style together. Floor covering centers specialize in carpeting and other floor coverings. They provide assistance in selecting colors and have installation services available. This type of store gives you the opportunity to look over several manufacturers' products so that you can make the right choice.

> *"Your new home should express your combined tastes."*

Wall covering stores help you determine the wall coverings that should grace your home. Sometimes, a change in wall coverings can change the whole feel of a room. These stores often offer interior decorating services and installation.

It is unlikely that your new home will have a color scheme that is exactly what you want. Painting is an economical way to change the look of your new home. A paint store can give guidance on matching colors and selecting combinations that work well with your furnishings. The representatives may also have ideas on ways to liven up a room with paint combinations or with a border.

Draperies are an item that few have experience in choosing. A drapery specialist will make your selection easier. They have styles on display or catalogues featuring different styles. Custom-made draperies are available in any material you select. Draperies are not an extravagance. They have a long life and can really enhance the atmosphere of your home.

Interior Decorators

You may be unsure about your ability to match colors and styles to furnish your new home. An interior decorator's abilities may be just what you need. Their knowledge in design and interpreting your tastes will enable them to find the coverings and furnishings for the look you want.

Using an interior decorator can save you an enormous amount of time. You will also have the satisfaction of having the job done right the first time.

Long Distance Services

Today there are many alternatives for long distance services. When you move into your new home, you will want to review the possibilities. You will have the choice of national or local long distance companies.

Many will offer special services. If you use long distance often, it will pay to find the plan that best reflects your needs.

You can find out about the choices available by researching the options in your area.

Cable Television Services

Many couples enjoy having cable television in their homes. Find out if your home is wired for cable and if service is available in your area.

Some cable companies require you to use their tuner boxes. See how yours operates. If you are able to use a cable-ready television, you will not need to have the box sitting out.

Premium channels are also available for movies and specials. Your cable company can tell you about all of the services it offers. They offer a variety of alternatives to network programming such as sports, weather and news 24 hours a day.

Newspapers and Magazines

It is important to keep up with current events. One of the best methods is subscribing to your local newspapers. Not only do they offer up-to-date news, they also provide information on sales at local area retail establishments, coupons for various stores and information about the local community.

Magazines can also be useful for current news and topics that are of interest to you and your spouse. There are magazines that give you tips on decorating and cooking, tell you about sports, and provide information on almost any subject you can imagine.

CHAPTER

VIII

Financial Planning

Financial Planning

Although this is just the beginning of a happy life together, it is never too early to begin thinking of your future financial security. In the past, most couples put their money in a savings account earning nominal interest, if they saved at all. Today, the key is to begin an overall financial plan that will help you realize your future goals as a couple and, if you choose, as a family.

Banking

An important step for all newlyweds is to set up checking accounts. You should discuss whether you will use a joint checking account, separate accounts or a combination of both. You should also set up the guidelines for who is responsible for bill paying, etc. You can establish your account at a bank, a savings bank, savings and loan, credit union, mutual fund money market or other institution that offers checking services. You should be sure you understand the charges for the services and their limitations (for example, the number of checks you may write monthly). Automatic Teller Machines (ATM) are becoming more important and popular all the time. If you feel you need this service, be sure it is offered as a part of the institution's checking program.

Credit Cards

Credit cards should also be obtained as soon as possible. It is often advisable to obtain cards before your wedding. This will allow you to have extra funds available should they be needed for the wedding or the honeymoon. Remember, this is a once-in-a-lifetime affair and you do not want to shortchange yourselves. After the wedding, you can add the name of your spouse on your card and he can add yours on his or you may wish to maintain your own accounts. The cards can be obtained through various financial institutions.

Loans

It is very common for you and your groom to be paying for a part or even all of your wedding. Sometimes you will need assistance in paying for the type of wedding and reception you want or to make the honeymoon everything you dreamed.

A loan for your wedding and/or honeymoon is not wrong when you consider the importance of the wedding day and the special time you will share during your honeymoon.

Loans can be obtained through banks, savings banks, savings and loans and other financial institutions that specialize in consumer loans. Many of these institutions are willing to provide you with the funds you need for the wedding, the honeymoon and getting established in your first home.

Sometimes couples will own at least one house between them. If this is the case, the financial institution can provide you with a home equity loan. This loan allows you to borrow against the equity you have in your house. It is an excellent way to get credit if needed.

Financial Planners

What are your financial goals? Have you ever really considered where you want to be in one year, five years, ten years? In the past, financial planning was not common among newlyweds, but today it is different. In order to have a family, own a home, have all of the creature comforts, and a comfortable retirement, financial planning must begin as early as possible in your life as a couple.

> ## "What are your financial goals?"

Today's brokerage firms specialize in financial planning and have programs available for any economic class and any financial situation. Some offer check writing services, mutual funds, certificates of deposit and a number of other investment opportunities. The individual brokers go through extensive training to provide counseling services to you.

Financial planning consultants, once geared toward the affluent, are now offering their services to those with less money to invest and to those just beginning to invest for the future. These planners are normally independents offering a number of investment products from several different companies. This allows them to tailor investments to your particular needs and tolerance for risk.

Insurance companies are also becoming heavily involved in this area. They offer customized life insurance policies with various investment possibilities and many offer mutual funds. Their agents are trained in financial consulting and can be helpful in finding the right investments for you.

Brokerage firms, financial planning consultants and insurance companies may provide profile surveys which analyze your situation and help you to better understand your goals financially.

Another source of financial planning is a tax adviser. Certified Public Accountants are becoming more and more involved in financial planning because they are so involved with their clients' tax planning finances.

Insurance

Financial planning includes many things such as prenuptial agreements, wills and the areas already touched on in this section on financial planning. But it also includes insurance.

When you are in love and thinking about your wedding and honeymoon, it is hard to think about such mundane subjects, but insurance is a necessary part of any household.

Life. The death of your spouse is probably the last thing on your mind, but marriage brings new responsibilities for both of you. You should think about your spouse's situation if a death does occur. This is especially important if you unexpectedly discover that your family is going to grow. Additionally, your youth will allow the coverage you need now. Many people are declined or have to pay higher premiums because of health problems, high risk or hazardous sports and hobbies. Any current policies you have should be changed to name you or your spouse as the beneficiary.

Automobile. Now that you are married, your rates may be lower, especially if you are a two or more car family. Check with an agent to consolidate your policies.

Home. It is important to protect your assets. Home insurance can consist of structural insurance if you own a house or just the contents, and liability insurance if you rent.

Health. Health problems can be a drain on any family. If neither of you is covered by a group health program at your place of employment or if the coverage is only available to one of you, you should look into health insurance immediately. Dental insurance is also becoming popular and is available. More information on health insurance is provided in the Health and Beauty Section.

Disability Income. This insurance provides you with income if you become disabled and cannot work. Many people are not aware of the importance of this type of insurance. If you are relying on a single income or need both of your incomes to make ends meet, you should look into this coverage.

The types of insurance listed above are made available through insurance agents. They can help you design the proper insurance program to suit your particular needs.

Tax Services

As a couple, there will be changes in your financial situation. You and your spouse may purchase a home together or you may now have two incomes instead of one. What was once a simple tax return may now need the expertise of a professional tax preparer.

Certified Public Accountants (CPA), tax preparation services, and some bookkeeping services can provide tax preparation, tax planning and even financial services. Not only can they save you time, but they can get you all the deductions to which you are entitled.

Employment Agencies

If one, or both, of you is moving to a new city, an employment agency can be helpful in finding a position with a local company.

Entering a job market you are not familiar with can be difficult. Professionals at an employment agency can advise you on interviewing techniques, help you prepare a resume and arrange interviews with employers interested in someone with your qualifications.

In fact, many employers go directly to an agency instead of advertising in a newspaper. This way, they do not have to take the time to screen a great number of applicants.

An employment agency may be a viable alternative for you.

Notes

CHAPTER

IX

Bridal Shower Guest/Gift Lists

1st Shower Guest/Gift List

Given by: _____ Location: _____

Date: _____ Time: _____ Theme: _____

1. Name: _____

    Address: _____

    Description: _____ DATE: (_____) (_____)
    RECEIVED   ACKNOWLEDGED

2. Name: _____

    Address: _____

    Description: _____ DATE: (_____) (_____)
    RECEIVED   ACKNOWLEDGED

3. Name: _____

    Address: _____

    Description: _____ DATE: (_____) (_____)
    RECEIVED   ACKNOWLEDGED

4. Name: _____

    Address: _____

    Description: _____ DATE: (_____) (_____)
    RECEIVED   ACKNOWLEDGED

5. Name: _____

    Address: _____

    Description: _____ DATE: (_____) (_____)
    RECEIVED   ACKNOWLEDGED

6. Name: _____

    Address: _____

    Description: _____ DATE: (_____) (_____)
    RECEIVED   ACKNOWLEDGED

7. Name: _____

    Address: _____

    Description: _____ DATE: (_____) (_____)
    RECEIVED   ACKNOWLEDGED

8. Name: _____

    Address: _____

    Description: _____ DATE: (_____) (_____)
    RECEIVED   ACKNOWLEDGED

9. Name: _____

    Address: _____

    Description: _____ DATE: (_____) (_____)
    RECEIVED   ACKNOWLEDGED

10. Name: _____

    Address: _____

    Description: _____ DATE: (_____) (_____)
    RECEIVED   ACKNOWLEDGED

11. Name: _____
    Address: _____
    Description:_____ (_____) (_____)
    DATE: RECEIVED   ACKNOWLEDGED

12. Name: _____
    Address: _____
    Description:_____ (_____) (_____)
    DATE: RECEIVED   ACKNOWLEDGED

13. Name: _____
    Address: _____
    Description:_____ (_____) (_____)
    DATE: RECEIVED   ACKNOWLEDGED

14. Name: _____
    Address: _____
    Description:_____ (_____) (_____)
    DATE: RECEIVED   ACKNOWLEDGED

15. Name: _____
    Address: _____
    Description:_____ (_____) (_____)
    DATE: RECEIVED   ACKNOWLEDGED

16. Name: _____
    Address: _____
    Description:_____ (_____) (_____)
    DATE: RECEIVED   ACKNOWLEDGED

17. Name: _____
    Address: _____
    Description:_____ (_____) (_____)
    DATE: RECEIVED   ACKNOWLEDGED

18. Name: _____
    Address: _____
    Description:_____ (_____) (_____)
    DATE: RECEIVED   ACKNOWLEDGED

19. Name: _____
    Address: _____
    Description:_____ (_____) (_____)
    DATE: RECEIVED   ACKNOWLEDGED

20. Name: _____
    Address: _____
    Description:_____ (_____) (_____)
    DATE: RECEIVED   ACKNOWLEDGED

2nd Shower Guest/Gift List

Given by: _____ Location: _____

Date: _____ Time: _____ Theme: _____

1. Name: _____

    Address: _____

    Description: _____ DATE: (_____) (_____)
    RECEIVED   ACKNOWLEDGED

2. Name: _____

    Address: _____

    Description: _____ DATE: (_____) (_____)
    RECEIVED   ACKNOWLEDGED

3. Name: _____

    Address: _____

    Description: _____ DATE: (_____) (_____)
    RECEIVED   ACKNOWLEDGED

4. Name: _____

    Address: _____

    Description: _____ DATE: (_____) (_____)
    RECEIVED   ACKNOWLEDGED

5. Name: _____

    Address: _____

    Description: _____ DATE: (_____) (_____)
    RECEIVED   ACKNOWLEDGED

6. Name: _____

    Address: _____

    Description: _____ DATE: (_____) (_____)
    RECEIVED   ACKNOWLEDGED

7. Name: _____

    Address: _____

    Description: _____ DATE: (_____) (_____)
    RECEIVED   ACKNOWLEDGED

8. Name: _____

    Address: _____

    Description: _____ DATE: (_____) (_____)
    RECEIVED   ACKNOWLEDGED

9. Name: _____

    Address: _____

    Description: _____ DATE: (_____) (_____)
    RECEIVED   ACKNOWLEDGED

10. Name: _____

    Address: _____

    Description: _____ DATE: (_____) (_____)
    RECEIVED   ACKNOWLEDGED

2nd Shower Guest/Gift List

11. Name: _____

 Address: _____

 Description: _____ DATE: (_____) (_____)
 RECEIVED   ACKNOWLEDGED

12. Name: _____

 Address: _____

 Description: _____ DATE: (_____) (_____)
 RECEIVED   ACKNOWLEDGED

13. Name: _____

 Address: _____

 Description: _____ DATE: (_____) (_____)
 RECEIVED   ACKNOWLEDGED

14. Name: _____

 Address: _____

 Description: _____ DATE: (_____) (_____)
 RECEIVED   ACKNOWLEDGED

15. Name: _____

 Address: _____

 Description: _____ DATE: (_____) (_____)
 RECEIVED   ACKNOWLEDGED

16. Name: _____

 Address: _____

 Description: _____ DATE: (_____) (_____)
 RECEIVED   ACKNOWLEDGED

17. Name: _____

 Address: _____

 Description: _____ DATE: (_____) (_____)
 RECEIVED   ACKNOWLEDGED

18. Name: _____

 Address: _____

 Description: _____ DATE: (_____) (_____)
 RECEIVED   ACKNOWLEDGED

19. Name: _____

 Address: _____

 Description: _____ DATE: (_____) (_____)
 RECEIVED   ACKNOWLEDGED

20. Name: _____

 Address: _____

 Description: _____ DATE: (_____) (_____)
 RECEIVED   ACKNOWLEDGED

3rd Shower Guest/Gift List

Given by: _____ Location: _____

Date: _____ Time: _____ Theme: _____

1. Name: _____

   Address: _____

   Description: _____ DATE: ____ (____ RECEIVED) (____ ACKNOWLEDGED)

2. Name: _____

   Address: _____

   Description: _____ DATE: ____ (____ RECEIVED) (____ ACKNOWLEDGED)

3. Name: _____

   Address: _____

   Description: _____ DATE: ____ (____ RECEIVED) (____ ACKNOWLEDGED)

4. Name: _____

   Address: _____

   Description: _____ DATE: ____ (____ RECEIVED) (____ ACKNOWLEDGED)

5. Name: _____

   Address: _____

   Description: _____ DATE: ____ (____ RECEIVED) (____ ACKNOWLEDGED)

6. Name: _____

   Address: _____

   Description: _____ DATE: ____ (____ RECEIVED) (____ ACKNOWLEDGED)

7. Name: _____

   Address: _____

   Description: _____ DATE: ____ (____ RECEIVED) (____ ACKNOWLEDGED)

8. Name: _____

   Address: _____

   Description: _____ DATE: ____ (____ RECEIVED) (____ ACKNOWLEDGED)

9. Name: _____

   Address: _____

   Description: _____ DATE: ____ (____ RECEIVED) (____ ACKNOWLEDGED)

10. Name: _____

    Address: _____

    Description: _____ DATE: ____ (____ RECEIVED) (____ ACKNOWLEDGED)

3rd Shower Guest/Gift List

11. Name: _____

    Address: _____

    Description: _____ DATE: (_____) (_____)
                                          RECEIVED   ACKNOWLEDGED

12. Name: _____

    Address: _____

    Description: _____ DATE: (_____) (_____)
                                          RECEIVED   ACKNOWLEDGED

13. Name: _____

    Address: _____

    Description: _____ DATE: (_____) (_____)
                                          RECEIVED   ACKNOWLEDGED

14. Name: _____

    Address: _____

    Description: _____ DATE: (_____) (_____)
                                          RECEIVED   ACKNOWLEDGED

15. Name: _____

    Address: _____

    Description: _____ DATE: (_____) (_____)
                                          RECEIVED   ACKNOWLEDGED

16. Name: _____

    Address: _____

    Description: _____ DATE: (_____) (_____)
                                          RECEIVED   ACKNOWLEDGED

17. Name: _____

    Address: _____

    Description: _____ DATE: (_____) (_____)
                                          RECEIVED   ACKNOWLEDGED

18. Name: _____

    Address: _____

    Description: _____ DATE: (_____) (_____)
                                          RECEIVED   ACKNOWLEDGED

19. Name: _____

    Address: _____

    Description: _____ DATE: (_____) (_____)
                                          RECEIVED   ACKNOWLEDGED

20. Name: _____

    Address: _____

    Description: _____ DATE: (_____) (_____)
                                          RECEIVED   ACKNOWLEDGED

Notes

CHAPTER X

Wedding Guest/Gift List

Wedding Guest/Gift List

1. Name:_____ (_____) (_____) (_____)
   CEREMONY   RECEPTION   R.S.V.P.
   Address:_____
   Gift: _____ (_____) (_____)
   DATE: RECEIVED   ACKNOWLEDGED

2. Name:_____ (_____) (_____) (_____)
   CEREMONY   RECEPTION   R.S.V.P.
   Address:_____
   Gift: _____ (_____) (_____)
   DATE: RECEIVED   ACKNOWLEDGED

3. Name:_____ (_____) (_____) (_____)
   CEREMONY   RECEPTION   R.S.V.P.
   Address:_____
   Gift: _____ (_____) (_____)
   DATE: RECEIVED   ACKNOWLEDGED

4. Name:_____ (_____) (_____) (_____)
   CEREMONY   RECEPTION   R.S.V.P.
   Address:_____
   Gift: _____ (_____) (_____)
   DATE: RECEIVED   ACKNOWLEDGED

5. Name:_____ (_____) (_____) (_____)
   CEREMONY   RECEPTION   R.S.V.P.
   Address:_____
   Gift: _____ (_____) (_____)
   DATE: RECEIVED   ACKNOWLEDGED

6. Name:_____ (_____) (_____) (_____)
   CEREMONY   RECEPTION   R.S.V.P.
   Address:_____
   Gift: _____ (_____) (_____)
   DATE: RECEIVED   ACKNOWLEDGED

7. Name:_____ (_____) (_____) (_____)
   CEREMONY   RECEPTION   R.S.V.P.
   Address:_____
   Gift: _____ (_____) (_____)
   DATE: RECEIVED   ACKNOWLEDGED

8. Name:_____ (_____) (_____) (_____)
   CEREMONY   RECEPTION   R.S.V.P.
   Address:_____
   Gift: _____ (_____) (_____)
   DATE: RECEIVED   ACKNOWLEDGED

9. Name:_____ (_____) (_____) (_____)
   CEREMONY   RECEPTION   R.S.V.P.
   Address:_____
   Gift: _____ (_____) (_____)
   DATE: RECEIVED   ACKNOWLEDGED

10. Name:_____ (_____) (_____) (_____)
    CEREMONY   RECEPTION   R.S.V.P.
    Address:_____
    Gift: _____ (_____) (_____)
    DATE: RECEIVED   ACKNOWLEDGED

Wedding Guest/Gift List

11. Name:_____ (_____) (_____) (_____)
                                                    CEREMONY   RECEPTION   R.S.V.P.

     Address:_____

     Gift: _____ _____ (_____)   (_____)
                                              DATE: RECEIVED   ACKNOWLEDGED

12. Name:_____ (_____) (_____) (_____)
                                                    CEREMONY   RECEPTION   R.S.V.P.

     Address:_____

     Gift: _____ _____ (_____)   (_____)
                                              DATE: RECEIVED   ACKNOWLEDGED

13. Name:_____ (_____) (_____) (_____)
                                                    CEREMONY   RECEPTION   R.S.V.P.

     Address:_____

     Gift: _____ _____ (_____)   (_____)
                                              DATE: RECEIVED   ACKNOWLEDGED

14. Name:_____ (_____) (_____) (_____)
                                                    CEREMONY   RECEPTION   R.S.V.P.

     Address:_____

     Gift: _____ _____ (_____)   (_____)
                                              DATE: RECEIVED   ACKNOWLEDGED

15. Name:_____ (_____) (_____) (_____)
                                                    CEREMONY   RECEPTION   R.S.V.P.

     Address:_____

     Gift: _____ _____ (_____)   (_____)
                                              DATE: RECEIVED   ACKNOWLEDGED

16. Name:_____ (_____) (_____) (_____)
                                                    CEREMONY   RECEPTION   R.S.V.P.

     Address:_____

     Gift: _____ _____ (_____)   (_____)
                                              DATE: RECEIVED   ACKNOWLEDGED

17. Name:_____ (_____) (_____) (_____)
                                                    CEREMONY   RECEPTION   R.S.V.P.

     Address:_____

     Gift: _____ _____ (_____)   (_____)
                                              DATE: RECEIVED   ACKNOWLEDGED

18. Name:_____ (_____) (_____) (_____)
                                                    CEREMONY   RECEPTION   R.S.V.P.

     Address:_____

     Gift: _____ _____ (_____)   (_____)
                                              DATE: RECEIVED   ACKNOWLEDGED

19. Name:_____ (_____) (_____) (_____)
                                                    CEREMONY   RECEPTION   R.S.V.P.

     Address:_____

     Gift: _____ _____ (_____)   (_____)
                                              DATE: RECEIVED   ACKNOWLEDGED

20. Name:_____ (_____) (_____) (_____)
                                                    CEREMONY   RECEPTION   R.S.V.P.

     Address:_____

     Gift: _____ _____ (_____)   (_____)
                                              DATE: RECEIVED   ACKNOWLEDGED

Wedding Guest/Gift List

21. Name:_____ (_____) (_____) (_____)
    CEREMONY   RECEPTION   R.S.V.P.
    Address:_____
    Gift: _____ (_____) (_____)
    DATE: RECEIVED   ACKNOWLEDGED

22. Name:_____ (_____) (_____) (_____)
    CEREMONY   RECEPTION   R.S.V.P.
    Address:_____
    Gift: _____ (_____) (_____)
    DATE: RECEIVED   ACKNOWLEDGED

23. Name:_____ (_____) (_____) (_____)
    CEREMONY   RECEPTION   R.S.V.P.
    Address:_____
    Gift: _____ (_____) (_____)
    DATE: RECEIVED   ACKNOWLEDGED

24. Name:_____ (_____) (_____) (_____)
    CEREMONY   RECEPTION   R.S.V.P.
    Address:_____
    Gift: _____ (_____) (_____)
    DATE: RECEIVED   ACKNOWLEDGED

25. Name:_____ (_____) (_____) (_____)
    CEREMONY   RECEPTION   R.S.V.P.
    Address:_____
    Gift: _____ (_____) (_____)
    DATE: RECEIVED   ACKNOWLEDGED

26. Name:_____ (_____) (_____) (_____)
    CEREMONY   RECEPTION   R.S.V.P.
    Address:_____
    Gift: _____ (_____) (_____)
    DATE: RECEIVED   ACKNOWLEDGED

27. Name:_____ (_____) (_____) (_____)
    CEREMONY   RECEPTION   R.S.V.P.
    Address:_____
    Gift: _____ (_____) (_____)
    DATE: RECEIVED   ACKNOWLEDGED

28. Name:_____ (_____) (_____) (_____)
    CEREMONY   RECEPTION   R.S.V.P.
    Address:_____
    Gift: _____ (_____) (_____)
    DATE: RECEIVED   ACKNOWLEDGED

29. Name:_____ (_____) (_____) (_____)
    CEREMONY   RECEPTION   R.S.V.P.
    Address:_____
    Gift: _____ (_____) (_____)
    DATE: RECEIVED   ACKNOWLEDGED

30. Name:_____ (_____) (_____) (_____)
    CEREMONY   RECEPTION   R.S.V.P.
    Address:_____
    Gift: _____ (_____) (_____)
    DATE: RECEIVED   ACKNOWLEDGED

Wedding Guest/Gift List

31. Name:_____ (_____) (_____) (_____)
    CEREMONY   RECEPTION   R.S.V.P.
    Address:_____
    Gift: _____
    DATE: (_____)   (_____)
    RECEIVED   ACKNOWLEDGED

32. Name:_____ (_____) (_____) (_____)
    CEREMONY   RECEPTION   R.S.V.P.
    Address:_____
    Gift: _____
    DATE: (_____)   (_____)
    RECEIVED   ACKNOWLEDGED

33. Name:_____ (_____) (_____) (_____)
    CEREMONY   RECEPTION   R.S.V.P.
    Address:_____
    Gift: _____
    DATE: (_____)   (_____)
    RECEIVED   ACKNOWLEDGED

34. Name:_____ (_____) (_____) (_____)
    CEREMONY   RECEPTION   R.S.V.P.
    Address:_____
    Gift: _____
    DATE: (_____)   (_____)
    RECEIVED   ACKNOWLEDGED

35. Name:_____ (_____) (_____) (_____)
    CEREMONY   RECEPTION   R.S.V.P.
    Address:_____
    Gift: _____
    DATE: (_____)   (_____)
    RECEIVED   ACKNOWLEDGED

36. Name:_____ (_____) (_____) (_____)
    CEREMONY   RECEPTION   R.S.V.P.
    Address:_____
    Gift: _____
    DATE: (_____)   (_____)
    RECEIVED   ACKNOWLEDGED

37. Name:_____ (_____) (_____) (_____)
    CEREMONY   RECEPTION   R.S.V.P.
    Address:_____
    Gift: _____
    DATE: (_____)   (_____)
    RECEIVED   ACKNOWLEDGED

38. Name:_____ (_____) (_____) (_____)
    CEREMONY   RECEPTION   R.S.V.P.
    Address:_____
    Gift: _____
    DATE: (_____)   (_____)
    RECEIVED   ACKNOWLEDGED

39. Name:_____ (_____) (_____) (_____)
    CEREMONY   RECEPTION   R.S.V.P.
    Address:_____
    Gift: _____
    DATE: (_____)   (_____)
    RECEIVED   ACKNOWLEDGED

40. Name:_____ (_____) (_____) (_____)
    CEREMONY   RECEPTION   R.S.V.P.
    Address:_____
    Gift: _____
    DATE: (_____)   (_____)
    RECEIVED   ACKNOWLEDGED

Wedding Guest/Gift List

41. Name:_____ (_____) (_____) (_____)
    CEREMONY   RECEPTION   R.S.V.P.
    Address:_____
    Gift: _____ (_____) (_____)
    DATE: RECEIVED   ACKNOWLEDGED

42. Name:_____ (_____) (_____) (_____)
    CEREMONY   RECEPTION   R.S.V.P.
    Address:_____
    Gift: _____ (_____) (_____)
    DATE: RECEIVED   ACKNOWLEDGED

43. Name:_____ (_____) (_____) (_____)
    CEREMONY   RECEPTION   R.S.V.P.
    Address:_____
    Gift: _____ (_____) (_____)
    DATE: RECEIVED   ACKNOWLEDGED

44. Name:_____ (_____) (_____) (_____)
    CEREMONY   RECEPTION   R.S.V.P.
    Address:_____
    Gift: _____ (_____) (_____)
    DATE: RECEIVED   ACKNOWLEDGED

45. Name:_____ (_____) (_____) (_____)
    CEREMONY   RECEPTION   R.S.V.P.
    Address:_____
    Gift: _____ (_____) (_____)
    DATE: RECEIVED   ACKNOWLEDGED

46. Name:_____ (_____) (_____) (_____)
    CEREMONY   RECEPTION   R.S.V.P.
    Address:_____
    Gift: _____ (_____) (_____)
    DATE: RECEIVED   ACKNOWLEDGED

47. Name:_____ (_____) (_____) (_____)
    CEREMONY   RECEPTION   R.S.V.P.
    Address:_____
    Gift: _____ (_____) (_____)
    DATE: RECEIVED   ACKNOWLEDGED

48. Name:_____ (_____) (_____) (_____)
    CEREMONY   RECEPTION   R.S.V.P.
    Address:_____
    Gift: _____ (_____) (_____)
    DATE: RECEIVED   ACKNOWLEDGED

49. Name:_____ (_____) (_____) (_____)
    CEREMONY   RECEPTION   R.S.V.P.
    Address:_____
    Gift: _____ (_____) (_____)
    DATE: RECEIVED   ACKNOWLEDGED

50. Name:_____ (_____) (_____) (_____)
    CEREMONY   RECEPTION   R.S.V.P.
    Address:_____
    Gift: _____ (_____) (_____)
    DATE: RECEIVED   ACKNOWLEDGED

Wedding Guest/Gift List

51. Name:_____ (_____) (_____) (_____)
    CEREMONY   RECEPTION   R.S.V.P.
    Address:_____
    Gift: _____ (_____)   (_____)
    DATE: RECEIVED   ACKNOWLEDGED

52. Name:_____ (_____) (_____) (_____)
    CEREMONY   RECEPTION   R.S.V.P.
    Address:_____
    Gift: _____ (_____)   (_____)
    DATE: RECEIVED   ACKNOWLEDGED

53. Name:_____ (_____) (_____) (_____)
    CEREMONY   RECEPTION   R.S.V.P.
    Address:_____
    Gift: _____ (_____)   (_____)
    DATE: RECEIVED   ACKNOWLEDGED

54. Name:_____ (_____) (_____) (_____)
    CEREMONY   RECEPTION   R.S.V.P.
    Address:_____
    Gift: _____ (_____)   (_____)
    DATE: RECEIVED   ACKNOWLEDGED

55. Name:_____ (_____) (_____) (_____)
    CEREMONY   RECEPTION   R.S.V.P.
    Address:_____
    Gift: _____ (_____)   (_____)
    DATE: RECEIVED   ACKNOWLEDGED

56. Name:_____ (_____) (_____) (_____)
    CEREMONY   RECEPTION   R.S.V.P.
    Address:_____
    Gift: _____ (_____)   (_____)
    DATE: RECEIVED   ACKNOWLEDGED

57. Name:_____ (_____) (_____) (_____)
    CEREMONY   RECEPTION   R.S.V.P.
    Address:_____
    Gift: _____ (_____)   (_____)
    DATE: RECEIVED   ACKNOWLEDGED

58. Name:_____ (_____) (_____) (_____)
    CEREMONY   RECEPTION   R.S.V.P.
    Address:_____
    Gift: _____ (_____)   (_____)
    DATE: RECEIVED   ACKNOWLEDGED

59. Name:_____ (_____) (_____) (_____)
    CEREMONY   RECEPTION   R.S.V.P.
    Address:_____
    Gift: _____ (_____)   (_____)
    DATE: RECEIVED   ACKNOWLEDGED

60. Name:_____ (_____) (_____) (_____)
    CEREMONY   RECEPTION   R.S.V.P.
    Address:_____
    Gift: _____ (_____)   (_____)
    DATE: RECEIVED   ACKNOWLEDGED

Wedding Guest/Gift List

61. Name:_____ (_____) (_____) (_____)
    CEREMONY   RECEPTION   R.S.V.P.
    Address:_____
    Gift: _____ (_____) (_____)
    DATE: RECEIVED   ACKNOWLEDGED

62. Name:_____ (_____) (_____) (_____)
    CEREMONY   RECEPTION   R.S.V.P.
    Address:_____
    Gift: _____ (_____) (_____)
    DATE: RECEIVED   ACKNOWLEDGED

63. Name:_____ (_____) (_____) (_____)
    CEREMONY   RECEPTION   R.S.V.P.
    Address:_____
    Gift: _____ (_____) (_____)
    DATE: RECEIVED   ACKNOWLEDGED

64. Name:_____ (_____) (_____) (_____)
    CEREMONY   RECEPTION   R.S.V.P.
    Address:_____
    Gift: _____ (_____) (_____)
    DATE: RECEIVED   ACKNOWLEDGED

65. Name:_____ (_____) (_____) (_____)
    CEREMONY   RECEPTION   R.S.V.P.
    Address:_____
    Gift: _____ (_____) (_____)
    DATE: RECEIVED   ACKNOWLEDGED

66. Name:_____ (_____) (_____) (_____)
    CEREMONY   RECEPTION   R.S.V.P.
    Address:_____
    Gift: _____ (_____) (_____)
    DATE: RECEIVED   ACKNOWLEDGED

67. Name:_____ (_____) (_____) (_____)
    CEREMONY   RECEPTION   R.S.V.P.
    Address:_____
    Gift: _____ (_____) (_____)
    DATE: RECEIVED   ACKNOWLEDGED

68. Name:_____ (_____) (_____) (_____)
    CEREMONY   RECEPTION   R.S.V.P.
    Address:_____
    Gift: _____ (_____) (_____)
    DATE: RECEIVED   ACKNOWLEDGED

69. Name:_____ (_____) (_____) (_____)
    CEREMONY   RECEPTION   R.S.V.P.
    Address:_____
    Gift: _____ (_____) (_____)
    DATE: RECEIVED   ACKNOWLEDGED

70. Name:_____ (_____) (_____) (_____)
    CEREMONY   RECEPTION   R.S.V.P.
    Address:_____
    Gift: _____ (_____) (_____)
    DATE: RECEIVED   ACKNOWLEDGED

Wedding Guest/Gift List

71. Name:_____ (_____) (_____) (_____)
                                              CEREMONY   RECEPTION   R.S.V.P.
    Address:_____
    Gift: _____ (_____) (_____)
                                         DATE: RECEIVED   ACKNOWLEDGED

72. Name:_____ (_____) (_____) (_____)
                                              CEREMONY   RECEPTION   R.S.V.P.
    Address:_____
    Gift: _____ (_____) (_____)
                                         DATE: RECEIVED   ACKNOWLEDGED

73. Name:_____ (_____) (_____) (_____)
                                              CEREMONY   RECEPTION   R.S.V.P.
    Address:_____
    Gift: _____ (_____) (_____)
                                         DATE: RECEIVED   ACKNOWLEDGED

74. Name:_____ (_____) (_____) (_____)
                                              CEREMONY   RECEPTION   R.S.V.P.
    Address:_____
    Gift: _____ (_____) (_____)
                                         DATE: RECEIVED   ACKNOWLEDGED

75. Name:_____ (_____) (_____) (_____)
                                              CEREMONY   RECEPTION   R.S.V.P.
    Address:_____
    Gift: _____ (_____) (_____)
                                         DATE: RECEIVED   ACKNOWLEDGED

76. Name:_____ (_____) (_____) (_____)
                                              CEREMONY   RECEPTION   R.S.V.P.
    Address:_____
    Gift: _____ (_____) (_____)
                                         DATE: RECEIVED   ACKNOWLEDGED

77. Name:_____ (_____) (_____) (_____)
                                              CEREMONY   RECEPTION   R.S.V.P.
    Address:_____
    Gift: _____ (_____) (_____)
                                         DATE: RECEIVED   ACKNOWLEDGED

78. Name:_____ (_____) (_____) (_____)
                                              CEREMONY   RECEPTION   R.S.V.P.
    Address:_____
    Gift: _____ (_____) (_____)
                                         DATE: RECEIVED   ACKNOWLEDGED

79. Name:_____ (_____) (_____) (_____)
                                              CEREMONY   RECEPTION   R.S.V.P.
    Address:_____
    Gift: _____ (_____) (_____)
                                         DATE: RECEIVED   ACKNOWLEDGED

80. Name:_____ (_____) (_____) (_____)
                                              CEREMONY   RECEPTION   R.S.V.P.
    Address:_____
    Gift: _____ (_____) (_____)
                                         DATE: RECEIVED   ACKNOWLEDGED

Wedding Guest/Gift List

81. Name:_____ (_____) (_____) (_____)
    CEREMONY   RECEPTION   R.S.V.P.
    Address:_____
    Gift: _____ (_____)   (_____)
    DATE: RECEIVED   ACKNOWLEDGED

82. Name:_____ (_____) (_____) (_____)
    CEREMONY   RECEPTION   R.S.V.P.
    Address:_____
    Gift: _____ (_____)   (_____)
    DATE: RECEIVED   ACKNOWLEDGED

83. Name:_____ (_____) (_____) (_____)
    CEREMONY   RECEPTION   R.S.V.P.
    Address:_____
    Gift: _____ (_____)   (_____)
    DATE: RECEIVED   ACKNOWLEDGED

84. Name:_____ (_____) (_____) (_____)
    CEREMONY   RECEPTION   R.S.V.P.
    Address:_____
    Gift: _____ (_____)   (_____)
    DATE: RECEIVED   ACKNOWLEDGED

85. Name:_____ (_____) (_____) (_____)
    CEREMONY   RECEPTION   R.S.V.P.
    Address:_____
    Gift: _____ (_____)   (_____)
    DATE: RECEIVED   ACKNOWLEDGED

86. Name:_____ (_____) (_____) (_____)
    CEREMONY   RECEPTION   R.S.V.P.
    Address:_____
    Gift: _____ (_____)   (_____)
    DATE: RECEIVED   ACKNOWLEDGED

87. Name:_____ (_____) (_____) (_____)
    CEREMONY   RECEPTION   R.S.V.P.
    Address:_____
    Gift: _____ (_____)   (_____)
    DATE: RECEIVED   ACKNOWLEDGED

88. Name:_____ (_____) (_____) (_____)
    CEREMONY   RECEPTION   R.S.V.P.
    Address:_____
    Gift: _____ (_____)   (_____)
    DATE: RECEIVED   ACKNOWLEDGED

89. Name:_____ (_____) (_____) (_____)
    CEREMONY   RECEPTION   R.S.V.P.
    Address:_____
    Gift: _____ (_____)   (_____)
    DATE: RECEIVED   ACKNOWLEDGED

90. Name:_____ (_____) (_____) (_____)
    CEREMONY   RECEPTION   R.S.V.P.
    Address:_____
    Gift: _____ (_____)   (_____)
    DATE: RECEIVED   ACKNOWLEDGED

Wedding Guest/Gift List

91. Name:_____ (_____) (_____) (_____)
    CEREMONY   RECEPTION   R.S.V.P.
    Address:_____
    Gift: _____ (_____)   (_____)
    DATE: RECEIVED   ACKNOWLEDGED

92. Name:_____ (_____) (_____) (_____)
    CEREMONY   RECEPTION   R.S.V.P.
    Address:_____
    Gift: _____ (_____)   (_____)
    DATE: RECEIVED   ACKNOWLEDGED

93. Name:_____ (_____) (_____) (_____)
    CEREMONY   RECEPTION   R.S.V.P.
    Address:_____
    Gift: _____ (_____)   (_____)
    DATE: RECEIVED   ACKNOWLEDGED

94. Name:_____ (_____) (_____) (_____)
    CEREMONY   RECEPTION   R.S.V.P.
    Address:_____
    Gift: _____ (_____)   (_____)
    DATE: RECEIVED   ACKNOWLEDGED

95. Name:_____ (_____) (_____) (_____)
    CEREMONY   RECEPTION   R.S.V.P.
    Address:_____
    Gift: _____ (_____)   (_____)
    DATE: RECEIVED   ACKNOWLEDGED

96. Name:_____ (_____) (_____) (_____)
    CEREMONY   RECEPTION   R.S.V.P.
    Address:_____
    Gift: _____ (_____)   (_____)
    DATE: RECEIVED   ACKNOWLEDGED

97. Name:_____ (_____) (_____) (_____)
    CEREMONY   RECEPTION   R.S.V.P.
    Address:_____
    Gift: _____ (_____)   (_____)
    DATE: RECEIVED   ACKNOWLEDGED

98. Name:_____ (_____) (_____) (_____)
    CEREMONY   RECEPTION   R.S.V.P.
    Address:_____
    Gift: _____ (_____)   (_____)
    DATE: RECEIVED   ACKNOWLEDGED

99. Name:_____ (_____) (_____) (_____)
    CEREMONY   RECEPTION   R.S.V.P.
    Address:_____
    Gift: _____ (_____)   (_____)
    DATE: RECEIVED   ACKNOWLEDGED

100. Name:_____ (_____) (_____) (_____)
    CEREMONY   RECEPTION   R.S.V.P.
    Address:_____
    Gift: _____ (_____)   (_____)
    DATE: RECEIVED   ACKNOWLEDGED

Wedding Guest/Gift List

101. Name: _____ (_____) (_____) (_____)
     CEREMONY   RECEPTION   R.S.V.P.
     Address: _____
     Gift: _____ (_____)   (_____)
     DATE: RECEIVED   ACKNOWLEDGED

102. Name: _____ (_____) (_____) (_____)
     CEREMONY   RECEPTION   R.S.V.P.
     Address: _____
     Gift: _____ (_____)   (_____)
     DATE: RECEIVED   ACKNOWLEDGED

103. Name: _____ (_____) (_____) (_____)
     CEREMONY   RECEPTION   R.S.V.P.
     Address: _____
     Gift: _____ (_____)   (_____)
     DATE: RECEIVED   ACKNOWLEDGED

104. Name: _____ (_____) (_____) (_____)
     CEREMONY   RECEPTION   R.S.V.P.
     Address: _____
     Gift: _____ (_____)   (_____)
     DATE: RECEIVED   ACKNOWLEDGED

105. Name: _____ (_____) (_____) (_____)
     CEREMONY   RECEPTION   R.S.V.P.
     Address: _____
     Gift: _____ (_____)   (_____)
     DATE: RECEIVED   ACKNOWLEDGED

106. Name: _____ (_____) (_____) (_____)
     CEREMONY   RECEPTION   R.S.V.P.
     Address: _____
     Gift: _____ (_____)   (_____)
     DATE: RECEIVED   ACKNOWLEDGED

107. Name: _____ (_____) (_____) (_____)
     CEREMONY   RECEPTION   R.S.V.P.
     Address: _____
     Gift: _____ (_____)   (_____)
     DATE: RECEIVED   ACKNOWLEDGED

108. Name: _____ (_____) (_____) (_____)
     CEREMONY   RECEPTION   R.S.V.P.
     Address: _____
     Gift: _____ (_____)   (_____)
     DATE: RECEIVED   ACKNOWLEDGED

109. Name: _____ (_____) (_____) (_____)
     CEREMONY   RECEPTION   R.S.V.P.
     Address: _____
     Gift: _____ (_____)   (_____)
     DATE: RECEIVED   ACKNOWLEDGED

110. Name: _____ (_____) (_____) (_____)
     CEREMONY   RECEPTION   R.S.V.P.
     Address: _____
     Gift: _____ (_____)   (_____)
     DATE: RECEIVED   ACKNOWLEDGED

Wedding Guest/Gift List

111. Name:_____ (_____) (_____) (_____)
     CEREMONY   RECEPTION   R.S.V.P.
     Address:_____
     Gift: _____ (_____)   (_____)
                                      DATE: RECEIVED   ACKNOWLEDGED

112. Name:_____ (_____) (_____) (_____)
     CEREMONY   RECEPTION   R.S.V.P.
     Address:_____
     Gift: _____ (_____)   (_____)
                                      DATE: RECEIVED   ACKNOWLEDGED

113. Name:_____ (_____) (_____) (_____)
     CEREMONY   RECEPTION   R.S.V.P.
     Address:_____
     Gift: _____ (_____)   (_____)
                                      DATE: RECEIVED   ACKNOWLEDGED

114. Name:_____ (_____) (_____) (_____)
     CEREMONY   RECEPTION   R.S.V.P.
     Address:_____
     Gift: _____ (_____)   (_____)
                                      DATE: RECEIVED   ACKNOWLEDGED

115. Name:_____ (_____) (_____) (_____)
     CEREMONY   RECEPTION   R.S.V.P.
     Address:_____
     Gift: _____ (_____)   (_____)
                                      DATE: RECEIVED   ACKNOWLEDGED

116. Name:_____ (_____) (_____) (_____)
     CEREMONY   RECEPTION   R.S.V.P.
     Address:_____
     Gift: _____ (_____)   (_____)
                                      DATE: RECEIVED   ACKNOWLEDGED

117. Name:_____ (_____) (_____) (_____)
     CEREMONY   RECEPTION   R.S.V.P.
     Address:_____
     Gift: _____ (_____)   (_____)
                                      DATE: RECEIVED   ACKNOWLEDGED

118. Name:_____ (_____) (_____) (_____)
     CEREMONY   RECEPTION   R.S.V.P.
     Address:_____
     Gift: _____ (_____)   (_____)
                                      DATE: RECEIVED   ACKNOWLEDGED

119. Name:_____ (_____) (_____) (_____)
     CEREMONY   RECEPTION   R.S.V.P.
     Address:_____
     Gift: _____ (_____)   (_____)
                                      DATE: RECEIVED   ACKNOWLEDGED

120. Name:_____ (_____) (_____) (_____)
     CEREMONY   RECEPTION   R.S.V.P.
     Address:_____
     Gift: _____ (_____)   (_____)
                                      DATE: RECEIVED   ACKNOWLEDGED

Wedding Guest/Gift List

121. Name:_____ (___CEREMONY___) (___RECEPTION___) (___R.S.V.P.___)

Address:_____

Gift: _____ DATE: (___RECEIVED___) (___ACKNOWLEDGED___)

122. Name:_____ (___CEREMONY___) (___RECEPTION___) (___R.S.V.P.___)

Address:_____

Gift: _____ DATE: (___RECEIVED___) (___ACKNOWLEDGED___)

123. Name:_____ (___CEREMONY___) (___RECEPTION___) (___R.S.V.P.___)

Address:_____

Gift: _____ DATE: (___RECEIVED___) (___ACKNOWLEDGED___)

124. Name:_____ (___CEREMONY___) (___RECEPTION___) (___R.S.V.P.___)

Address:_____

Gift: _____ DATE: (___RECEIVED___) (___ACKNOWLEDGED___)

125. Name:_____ (___CEREMONY___) (___RECEPTION___) (___R.S.V.P.___)

Address:_____

Gift: _____ DATE: (___RECEIVED___) (___ACKNOWLEDGED___)

126. Name:_____ (___CEREMONY___) (___RECEPTION___) (___R.S.V.P.___)

Address:_____

Gift: _____ DATE: (___RECEIVED___) (___ACKNOWLEDGED___)

127. Name:_____ (___CEREMONY___) (___RECEPTION___) (___R.S.V.P.___)

Address:_____

Gift: _____ DATE: (___RECEIVED___) (___ACKNOWLEDGED___)

128. Name:_____ (___CEREMONY___) (___RECEPTION___) (___R.S.V.P.___)

Address:_____

Gift: _____ DATE: (___RECEIVED___) (___ACKNOWLEDGED___)

129. Name:_____ (___CEREMONY___) (___RECEPTION___) (___R.S.V.P.___)

Address:_____

Gift: _____ DATE: (___RECEIVED___) (___ACKNOWLEDGED___)

130. Name:_____ (___CEREMONY___) (___RECEPTION___) (___R.S.V.P.___)

Address:_____

Gift: _____ DATE: (___RECEIVED___) (___ACKNOWLEDGED___)

Wedding Guest/Gift List

131. Name:_____ (_____) (_____) (_____)
                                       CEREMONY   RECEPTION   R.S.V.P.
     Address:_____
     Gift: _____ (_____)   (_____)
                                 DATE: RECEIVED   ACKNOWLEDGED

132. Name:_____ (_____) (_____) (_____)
                                       CEREMONY   RECEPTION   R.S.V.P.
     Address:_____
     Gift: _____ (_____)   (_____)
                                 DATE: RECEIVED   ACKNOWLEDGED

133. Name:_____ (_____) (_____) (_____)
                                       CEREMONY   RECEPTION   R.S.V.P.
     Address:_____
     Gift: _____ (_____)   (_____)
                                 DATE: RECEIVED   ACKNOWLEDGED

134. Name:_____ (_____) (_____) (_____)
                                       CEREMONY   RECEPTION   R.S.V.P.
     Address:_____
     Gift: _____ (_____)   (_____)
                                 DATE: RECEIVED   ACKNOWLEDGED

135. Name:_____ (_____) (_____) (_____)
                                       CEREMONY   RECEPTION   R.S.V.P.
     Address:_____
     Gift: _____ (_____)   (_____)
                                 DATE: RECEIVED   ACKNOWLEDGED

136. Name:_____ (_____) (_____) (_____)
                                       CEREMONY   RECEPTION   R.S.V.P.
     Address:_____
     Gift: _____ (_____)   (_____)
                                 DATE: RECEIVED   ACKNOWLEDGED

137. Name:_____ (_____) (_____) (_____)
                                       CEREMONY   RECEPTION   R.S.V.P.
     Address:_____
     Gift: _____ (_____)   (_____)
                                 DATE: RECEIVED   ACKNOWLEDGED

138. Name:_____ (_____) (_____) (_____)
                                       CEREMONY   RECEPTION   R.S.V.P.
     Address:_____
     Gift: _____ (_____)   (_____)
                                 DATE: RECEIVED   ACKNOWLEDGED

139. Name:_____ (_____) (_____) (_____)
                                       CEREMONY   RECEPTION   R.S.V.P.
     Address:_____
     Gift: _____ (_____)   (_____)
                                 DATE: RECEIVED   ACKNOWLEDGED

140. Name:_____ (_____) (_____) (_____)
                                       CEREMONY   RECEPTION   R.S.V.P.
     Address:_____
     Gift: _____ (_____)   (_____)
                                 DATE: RECEIVED   ACKNOWLEDGED

Wedding Guest/Gift List

141. Name:_____ (_____) (_____) (_____)
     CEREMONY   RECEPTION   R.S.V.P.
     Address:_____
     Gift: _____ (_____) (_____)
     DATE: RECEIVED   ACKNOWLEDGED

142. Name:_____ (_____) (_____) (_____)
     CEREMONY   RECEPTION   R.S.V.P.
     Address:_____
     Gift: _____ (_____) (_____)
     DATE: RECEIVED   ACKNOWLEDGED

143. Name:_____ (_____) (_____) (_____)
     CEREMONY   RECEPTION   R.S.V.P.
     Address:_____
     Gift: _____ (_____) (_____)
     DATE: RECEIVED   ACKNOWLEDGED

144. Name:_____ (_____) (_____) (_____)
     CEREMONY   RECEPTION   R.S.V.P.
     Address:_____
     Gift: _____ (_____) (_____)
     DATE: RECEIVED   ACKNOWLEDGED

145. Name:_____ (_____) (_____) (_____)
     CEREMONY   RECEPTION   R.S.V.P.
     Address:_____
     Gift: _____ (_____) (_____)
     DATE: RECEIVED   ACKNOWLEDGED

146. Name:_____ (_____) (_____) (_____)
     CEREMONY   RECEPTION   R.S.V.P.
     Address:_____
     Gift: _____ (_____) (_____)
     DATE: RECEIVED   ACKNOWLEDGED

147. Name:_____ (_____) (_____) (_____)
     CEREMONY   RECEPTION   R.S.V.P.
     Address:_____
     Gift: _____ (_____) (_____)
     DATE: RECEIVED   ACKNOWLEDGED

148. Name:_____ (_____) (_____) (_____)
     CEREMONY   RECEPTION   R.S.V.P.
     Address:_____
     Gift: _____ (_____) (_____)
     DATE: RECEIVED   ACKNOWLEDGED

149. Name:_____ (_____) (_____) (_____)
     CEREMONY   RECEPTION   R.S.V.P.
     Address:_____
     Gift: _____ (_____) (_____)
     DATE: RECEIVED   ACKNOWLEDGED

150. Name:_____ (_____) (_____) (_____)
     CEREMONY   RECEPTION   R.S.V.P.
     Address:_____
     Gift: _____ (_____) (_____)
     DATE: RECEIVED   ACKNOWLEDGED

Wedding Guest/Gift List

151. Name:_____ (_____) (_____) (_____)
     CEREMONY   RECEPTION   R.S.V.P.
     Address:_____
     Gift: _____ (_____)   (_____)
     DATE: RECEIVED   ACKNOWLEDGED

152. Name:_____ (_____) (_____) (_____)
     CEREMONY   RECEPTION   R.S.V.P.
     Address:_____
     Gift: _____ (_____)   (_____)
     DATE: RECEIVED   ACKNOWLEDGED

153. Name:_____ (_____) (_____) (_____)
     CEREMONY   RECEPTION   R.S.V.P.
     Address:_____
     Gift: _____ (_____)   (_____)
     DATE: RECEIVED   ACKNOWLEDGED

154. Name:_____ (_____) (_____) (_____)
     CEREMONY   RECEPTION   R.S.V.P.
     Address:_____
     Gift: _____ (_____)   (_____)
     DATE: RECEIVED   ACKNOWLEDGED

155. Name:_____ (_____) (_____) (_____)
     CEREMONY   RECEPTION   R.S.V.P.
     Address:_____
     Gift: _____ (_____)   (_____)
     DATE: RECEIVED   ACKNOWLEDGED

156. Name:_____ (_____) (_____) (_____)
     CEREMONY   RECEPTION   R.S.V.P.
     Address:_____
     Gift: _____ (_____)   (_____)
     DATE: RECEIVED   ACKNOWLEDGED

157. Name:_____ (_____) (_____) (_____)
     CEREMONY   RECEPTION   R.S.V.P.
     Address:_____
     Gift: _____ (_____)   (_____)
     DATE: RECEIVED   ACKNOWLEDGED

158. Name:_____ (_____) (_____) (_____)
     CEREMONY   RECEPTION   R.S.V.P.
     Address:_____
     Gift: _____ (_____)   (_____)
     DATE: RECEIVED   ACKNOWLEDGED

159. Name:_____ (_____) (_____) (_____)
     CEREMONY   RECEPTION   R.S.V.P.
     Address:_____
     Gift: _____ (_____)   (_____)
     DATE: RECEIVED   ACKNOWLEDGED

160. Name:_____ (_____) (_____) (_____)
     CEREMONY   RECEPTION   R.S.V.P.
     Address:_____
     Gift: _____ (_____)   (_____)
     DATE: RECEIVED   ACKNOWLEDGED

Wedding Guest/Gift List

161. Name:_____ (___CEREMONY___) (___RECEPTION___) (___R.S.V.P.___)
Address:_____
Gift: _____ DATE: (___RECEIVED___)   (___ACKNOWLEDGED___)

162. Name:_____ (___CEREMONY___) (___RECEPTION___) (___R.S.V.P.___)
Address:_____
Gift: _____ DATE: (___RECEIVED___)   (___ACKNOWLEDGED___)

163. Name:_____ (___CEREMONY___) (___RECEPTION___) (___R.S.V.P.___)
Address:_____
Gift: _____ DATE: (___RECEIVED___)   (___ACKNOWLEDGED___)

164. Name:_____ (___CEREMONY___) (___RECEPTION___) (___R.S.V.P.___)
Address:_____
Gift: _____ DATE: (___RECEIVED___)   (___ACKNOWLEDGED___)

165. Name:_____ (___CEREMONY___) (___RECEPTION___) (___R.S.V.P.___)
Address:_____
Gift: _____ DATE: (___RECEIVED___)   (___ACKNOWLEDGED___)

166. Name:_____ (___CEREMONY___) (___RECEPTION___) (___R.S.V.P.___)
Address:_____
Gift: _____ DATE: (___RECEIVED___)   (___ACKNOWLEDGED___)

167. Name:_____ (___CEREMONY___) (___RECEPTION___) (___R.S.V.P.___)
Address:_____
Gift: _____ DATE: (___RECEIVED___)   (___ACKNOWLEDGED___)

168. Name:_____ (___CEREMONY___) (___RECEPTION___) (___R.S.V.P.___)
Address:_____
Gift: _____ DATE: (___RECEIVED___)   (___ACKNOWLEDGED___)

169. Name:_____ (___CEREMONY___) (___RECEPTION___) (___R.S.V.P.___)
Address:_____
Gift: _____ DATE: (___RECEIVED___)   (___ACKNOWLEDGED___)

170. Name:_____ (___CEREMONY___) (___RECEPTION___) (___R.S.V.P.___)
Address:_____
Gift: _____ DATE: (___RECEIVED___)   (___ACKNOWLEDGED___)

Wedding Guest/Gift List

171. Name: _____ (___CEREMONY___) (___RECEPTION___) (___R.S.V.P.___)
Address: _____
Gift: _____ DATE: (___RECEIVED___) (___ACKNOWLEDGED___)

172. Name: _____ (___CEREMONY___) (___RECEPTION___) (___R.S.V.P.___)
Address: _____
Gift: _____ DATE: (___RECEIVED___) (___ACKNOWLEDGED___)

173. Name: _____ (___CEREMONY___) (___RECEPTION___) (___R.S.V.P.___)
Address: _____
Gift: _____ DATE: (___RECEIVED___) (___ACKNOWLEDGED___)

174. Name: _____ (___CEREMONY___) (___RECEPTION___) (___R.S.V.P.___)
Address: _____
Gift: _____ DATE: (___RECEIVED___) (___ACKNOWLEDGED___)

175. Name: _____ (___CEREMONY___) (___RECEPTION___) (___R.S.V.P.___)
Address: _____
Gift: _____ DATE: (___RECEIVED___) (___ACKNOWLEDGED___)

176. Name: _____ (___CEREMONY___) (___RECEPTION___) (___R.S.V.P.___)
Address: _____
Gift: _____ DATE: (___RECEIVED___) (___ACKNOWLEDGED___)

177. Name: _____ (___CEREMONY___) (___RECEPTION___) (___R.S.V.P.___)
Address: _____
Gift: _____ DATE: (___RECEIVED___) (___ACKNOWLEDGED___)

178. Name: _____ (___CEREMONY___) (___RECEPTION___) (___R.S.V.P.___)
Address: _____
Gift: _____ DATE: (___RECEIVED___) (___ACKNOWLEDGED___)

179. Name: _____ (___CEREMONY___) (___RECEPTION___) (___R.S.V.P.___)
Address: _____
Gift: _____ DATE: (___RECEIVED___) (___ACKNOWLEDGED___)

180. Name: _____ (___CEREMONY___) (___RECEPTION___) (___R.S.V.P.___)
Address: _____
Gift: _____ DATE: (___RECEIVED___) (___ACKNOWLEDGED___)

Wedding Guest/Gift List

181. Name:_____ (_____) (_____) (_____)
     CEREMONY   RECEPTION   R.S.V.P.
     Address:_____
     Gift: _____ (_____)   (_____)
     DATE: RECEIVED   ACKNOWLEDGED

182. Name:_____ (_____) (_____) (_____)
     CEREMONY   RECEPTION   R.S.V.P.
     Address:_____
     Gift: _____ (_____)   (_____)
     DATE: RECEIVED   ACKNOWLEDGED

183. Name:_____ (_____) (_____) (_____)
     CEREMONY   RECEPTION   R.S.V.P.
     Address:_____
     Gift: _____ (_____)   (_____)
     DATE: RECEIVED   ACKNOWLEDGED

184. Name:_____ (_____) (_____) (_____)
     CEREMONY   RECEPTION   R.S.V.P.
     Address:_____
     Gift: _____ (_____)   (_____)
     DATE: RECEIVED   ACKNOWLEDGED

185. Name:_____ (_____) (_____) (_____)
     CEREMONY   RECEPTION   R.S.V.P.
     Address:_____
     Gift: _____ (_____)   (_____)
     DATE: RECEIVED   ACKNOWLEDGED

186. Name:_____ (_____) (_____) (_____)
     CEREMONY   RECEPTION   R.S.V.P.
     Address:_____
     Gift: _____ (_____)   (_____)
     DATE: RECEIVED   ACKNOWLEDGED

187. Name:_____ (_____) (_____) (_____)
     CEREMONY   RECEPTION   R.S.V.P.
     Address:_____
     Gift: _____ (_____)   (_____)
     DATE: RECEIVED   ACKNOWLEDGED

188. Name:_____ (_____) (_____) (_____)
     CEREMONY   RECEPTION   R.S.V.P.
     Address:_____
     Gift: _____ (_____)   (_____)
     DATE: RECEIVED   ACKNOWLEDGED

189. Name:_____ (_____) (_____) (_____)
     CEREMONY   RECEPTION   R.S.V.P.
     Address:_____
     Gift: _____ (_____)   (_____)
     DATE: RECEIVED   ACKNOWLEDGED

190. Name:_____ (_____) (_____) (_____)
     CEREMONY   RECEPTION   R.S.V.P.
     Address:_____
     Gift: _____ (_____)   (_____)
     DATE: RECEIVED   ACKNOWLEDGED

Wedding Guest/Gift List

191. Name:_____ (_____) (_____) (_____)
     CEREMONY   RECEPTION   R.S.V.P.
     Address:_____
     Gift: _____ (_____) (_____)
     DATE: RECEIVED   ACKNOWLEDGED

192. Name:_____ (_____) (_____) (_____)
     CEREMONY   RECEPTION   R.S.V.P.
     Address:_____
     Gift: _____ (_____) (_____)
     DATE: RECEIVED   ACKNOWLEDGED

193. Name:_____ (_____) (_____) (_____)
     CEREMONY   RECEPTION   R.S.V.P.
     Address:_____
     Gift: _____ (_____) (_____)
     DATE: RECEIVED   ACKNOWLEDGED

194. Name:_____ (_____) (_____) (_____)
     CEREMONY   RECEPTION   R.S.V.P.
     Address:_____
     Gift: _____ (_____) (_____)
     DATE: RECEIVED   ACKNOWLEDGED

195. Name:_____ (_____) (_____) (_____)
     CEREMONY   RECEPTION   R.S.V.P.
     Address:_____
     Gift: _____ (_____) (_____)
     DATE: RECEIVED   ACKNOWLEDGED

196. Name:_____ (_____) (_____) (_____)
     CEREMONY   RECEPTION   R.S.V.P.
     Address:_____
     Gift: _____ (_____) (_____)
     DATE: RECEIVED   ACKNOWLEDGED

197. Name:_____ (_____) (_____) (_____)
     CEREMONY   RECEPTION   R.S.V.P.
     Address:_____
     Gift: _____ (_____) (_____)
     DATE: RECEIVED   ACKNOWLEDGED

198. Name:_____ (_____) (_____) (_____)
     CEREMONY   RECEPTION   R.S.V.P.
     Address:_____
     Gift: _____ (_____) (_____)
     DATE: RECEIVED   ACKNOWLEDGED

199. Name:_____ (_____) (_____) (_____)
     CEREMONY   RECEPTION   R.S.V.P.
     Address:_____
     Gift: _____ (_____) (_____)
     DATE: RECEIVED   ACKNOWLEDGED

200. Name:_____ (_____) (_____) (_____)
     CEREMONY   RECEPTION   R.S.V.P.
     Address:_____
     Gift: _____ (_____) (_____)
     DATE: RECEIVED   ACKNOWLEDGED

Wedding Guest/Gift List

201. Name:_____ (_____) (_____) (_____)
       CEREMONY   RECEPTION   R.S.V.P.
    Address:_____
    Gift: _____ (_____) (_____)
           DATE: RECEIVED   ACKNOWLEDGED

202. Name:_____ (_____) (_____) (_____)
       CEREMONY   RECEPTION   R.S.V.P.
    Address:_____
    Gift: _____ (_____) (_____)
           DATE: RECEIVED   ACKNOWLEDGED

203. Name:_____ (_____) (_____) (_____)
       CEREMONY   RECEPTION   R.S.V.P.
    Address:_____
    Gift: _____ (_____) (_____)
           DATE: RECEIVED   ACKNOWLEDGED

204. Name:_____ (_____) (_____) (_____)
       CEREMONY   RECEPTION   R.S.V.P.
    Address:_____
    Gift: _____ (_____) (_____)
           DATE: RECEIVED   ACKNOWLEDGED

205. Name:_____ (_____) (_____) (_____)
       CEREMONY   RECEPTION   R.S.V.P.
    Address:_____
    Gift: _____ (_____) (_____)
           DATE: RECEIVED   ACKNOWLEDGED

206. Name:_____ (_____) (_____) (_____)
       CEREMONY   RECEPTION   R.S.V.P.
    Address:_____
    Gift: _____ (_____) (_____)
           DATE: RECEIVED   ACKNOWLEDGED

207. Name:_____ (_____) (_____) (_____)
       CEREMONY   RECEPTION   R.S.V.P.
    Address:_____
    Gift: _____ (_____) (_____)
           DATE: RECEIVED   ACKNOWLEDGED

208. Name:_____ (_____) (_____) (_____)
       CEREMONY   RECEPTION   R.S.V.P.
    Address:_____
    Gift: _____ (_____) (_____)
           DATE: RECEIVED   ACKNOWLEDGED

209. Name:_____ (_____) (_____) (_____)
       CEREMONY   RECEPTION   R.S.V.P.
    Address:_____
    Gift: _____ (_____) (_____)
           DATE: RECEIVED   ACKNOWLEDGED

210. Name:_____ (_____) (_____) (_____)
       CEREMONY   RECEPTION   R.S.V.P.
    Address:_____
    Gift: _____ (_____) (_____)
           DATE: RECEIVED   ACKNOWLEDGED

Wedding Guest/Gift List

211. Name:_____ (_____) (_____) (_____)
                                                 CEREMONY   RECEPTION   R.S.V.P.
     Address:_____
     Gift: _____ DATE: (_____) (_____)
                                         RECEIVED   ACKNOWLEDGED

212. Name:_____ (CEREMONY) (RECEPTION) (R.S.V.P.)
     Address:_____
     Gift: _____ DATE: (RECEIVED) (ACKNOWLEDGED)

213. Name:_____ (CEREMONY) (RECEPTION) (R.S.V.P.)
     Address:_____
     Gift: _____ DATE: (RECEIVED) (ACKNOWLEDGED)

214. Name:_____ (CEREMONY) (RECEPTION) (R.S.V.P.)
     Address:_____
     Gift: _____ DATE: (RECEIVED) (ACKNOWLEDGED)

215. Name:_____ (CEREMONY) (RECEPTION) (R.S.V.P.)
     Address:_____
     Gift: _____ DATE: (RECEIVED) (ACKNOWLEDGED)

216. Name:_____ (CEREMONY) (RECEPTION) (R.S.V.P.)
     Address:_____
     Gift: _____ DATE: (RECEIVED) (ACKNOWLEDGED)

217. Name:_____ (CEREMONY) (RECEPTION) (R.S.V.P.)
     Address:_____
     Gift: _____ DATE: (RECEIVED) (ACKNOWLEDGED)

218. Name:_____ (CEREMONY) (RECEPTION) (R.S.V.P.)
     Address:_____
     Gift: _____ DATE: (RECEIVED) (ACKNOWLEDGED)

219. Name:_____ (CEREMONY) (RECEPTION) (R.S.V.P.)
     Address:_____
     Gift: _____ DATE: (RECEIVED) (ACKNOWLEDGED)

220. Name:_____ (CEREMONY) (RECEPTION) (R.S.V.P.)
     Address:_____
     Gift: _____ DATE: (RECEIVED) (ACKNOWLEDGED)

Wedding Guest/Gift List

221. Name:_____ (_____) (_____) (_____)
                                                          CEREMONY   RECEPTION   R.S.V.P.
     Address:_____
     Gift: _____ DATE: (_____) (_____)
                                                            RECEIVED   ACKNOWLEDGED

222. Name:_____ (CEREMONY) (RECEPTION) (R.S.V.P.)
     Address:_____
     Gift: _____ DATE: (RECEIVED) (ACKNOWLEDGED)

223. Name:_____ (CEREMONY) (RECEPTION) (R.S.V.P.)
     Address:_____
     Gift: _____ DATE: (RECEIVED) (ACKNOWLEDGED)

224. Name:_____ (CEREMONY) (RECEPTION) (R.S.V.P.)
     Address:_____
     Gift: _____ DATE: (RECEIVED) (ACKNOWLEDGED)

225. Name:_____ (CEREMONY) (RECEPTION) (R.S.V.P.)
     Address:_____
     Gift: _____ DATE: (RECEIVED) (ACKNOWLEDGED)

226. Name:_____ (CEREMONY) (RECEPTION) (R.S.V.P.)
     Address:_____
     Gift: _____ DATE: (RECEIVED) (ACKNOWLEDGED)

227. Name:_____ (CEREMONY) (RECEPTION) (R.S.V.P.)
     Address:_____
     Gift: _____ DATE: (RECEIVED) (ACKNOWLEDGED)

228. Name:_____ (CEREMONY) (RECEPTION) (R.S.V.P.)
     Address:_____
     Gift: _____ DATE: (RECEIVED) (ACKNOWLEDGED)

229. Name:_____ (CEREMONY) (RECEPTION) (R.S.V.P.)
     Address:_____
     Gift: _____ DATE: (RECEIVED) (ACKNOWLEDGED)

230. Name:_____ (CEREMONY) (RECEPTION) (R.S.V.P.)
     Address:_____
     Gift: _____ DATE: (RECEIVED) (ACKNOWLEDGED)

Romance in the Tropics

Newlyweds glow In the sunset at
Aston's Polpu at Makahuena on Kauai.

WEDGINGS

Aloha Weddings & Honeymoons of Maui

Let us create your choice of weddings:
- ☐ A. Tropical Hana Wedding
- ☐ B. Park Beach Sunset Wedding
- ☐ C. Yacht Sunset Sail Wedding

WITH YOUR CHOICE OF:
- ☐ Silver Wedding Goblets
- ☐ Chauffeured Vintage Rolls Royce Service
- ☐ Minister, gratuity, rice throwing, witness
- ☐ Fine Champagne
- ☐ Video taping
- ☐ Wedding Cake
- ☐ Photographer
- ☐ Hawaiian Wedding Musicians
- ☐ Rental Car or Jeep
- ☐ Traditional Hawaiian Wedding Flowers; Haku Headlei and Bridal Bouquet with matching leis for Bride and Groom
- ☐ Accommodations— Hotel, Condo or Oceanfront Homes
- ☐ Hawaiian Luaus, Sunset Dinner Cruises, Horseback Riding, etc. Activities can be arranged for wedding couples and their guests.

We hope we can be of service to you. If you have any questions, please do not hesitate to contact us.

TOLL-FREE 1 (800) 367-8047—Ext. 540

MOLOKA'I

Preserving Hawaii At Its Best

Birthplace of the hula, vacationland for kings and queens. Molokai. For those wanting the beauty and tranquility of their Honeymoon set in the best of today's resort activities and accommodations. and coupled with the heritage and lifestyle of old Hawaii. For information and a detailed brochure. call

Toll Free
1-800-367-ISLE
1-800-367-4753.

MARRY
IN HAWAII
in a private tropical garden at the beach

Island of Oahu

DAMIEN WARING
ESTATE

All services provided
(800) 648-5040
or P.O. Box 7184 Honolulu, HI 96821

Mainland couples wishing to get married in Hawaii can make full arrangements with wedding consultants doing business on each of the major islands. Services provided usually include everything from clergy to photography.

On Oahu, the **Damien Waring Estate,** just minutes from Waikiki, is actually a private residence which makes a perfect setting for a Hawaiian garden wedding. This oceanfront estate is worlds away from the usual excitement of Waikiki, complete with tropical landscaping, waterfall, fountains and even exotic birds.

Mother of the Bride is actually an individual, Pat Kelley, who provides the rather unique service of being the substitute mother for brides, making preparations and arrangements much like the bride's mother would do. Pat's knowledge and experience in the Hawaii business community are extensive.

Celebrations, has an excellent reputation on Oahu for exquisite weddings and receptions. Owner Paul Boomer has assembled a talented staff to assist to every detail.

In the back of Manoa Valley on Oahu is the famed **Paradise Park.** Famous for its lush vegetation and tame tropical birds, this attraction makes the perfect setting for a Hawaiian wedding. Their services include choice of minister, photography, limousine service and all the usual amenities.

Aloha Weddings & Honeymoons in Lahaina has been creating custom tailored ceremonies for more than two years.

Also on Maui is **Paradise Weddings,** owned and operated by 15-year-resident Andrea Thomas. Her emphasis is on dealing with the individual needs of each of her clients. "Each couple is very special to me. If it's wonderful for them, then I'm happy."

For those couples who enjoy sailing and water recreation, Hawaii has wonderful opportunities to be married at sea on a private yacht. **Tradewind Charters, Honolulu Sailing Co.** and **Lotus Flower Sailing Adventures** offer complete wedding packages as well as neighbor island honeymoon sails.

Request No. 604

Your Wedding in
HAWAII

by
Hawaii's leading
wedding consultant.
We make your dreams
come true.

Celebrations

(808) 949-0909

Century Center, Suite 3403
Honolulu, Hawaii 96826

Request No. 605

PRIVATE WEDDINGS & HONEYMOONS AT SEA
ON ONE OF OUR BEAUTIFUL YACHTS

The ultimate romantic setting for YOUR wedding and honeymoon in paradise.

Packages and options for every taste and budget. Private ceremony performed by your captain. We can accommodate 2-250 guests.

- Videography and photography
- Hors d'oeuvres, dinner, champagne, cake, flowers, and limousine.
- Bridal suite aboard private yacht.
- Honeymoon inter-island cruises available and more!

TRADEWIND CHARTERS

1833 Kalakaua Ave.,
Suite 612
Honolulu, HI. 96815

Call Captain Ken
U.S. (800) 77-SAIL-1
HI (808) 973-0311

How to have a
Maui Wedding
with the Greatest of Ease!

- Chauffered Antique Classic Cars
- Sunsets • Sailboats
- Tropical Gardens • Champagne
- Hawaiian Flowers
- Professional Photography

**Let Andrea Thomas assist you
with a relaxing, romantic and
unforgettable experience.
Your Satisfaction is
Guaranteed!**

Paradise Weddings

P.O.Box 424
Puunene, HI 96784
(800) 657-7857
Get Started Today!

Request No. 606

Heavenly
Weddings Afloat

Your wildest dreams of a supremely romantic wedding or honeymoon in paradise will all come true aboard the world renowned, majestic 56 ft. teakwood sailing ship, Lotus Flower.

Our unique specialty is to provide every imaginable detail to make your wedding so divine, it will dazzle the angels!

Send now for complete details and free pictures.

Lotus Flower Weddings Afloat
24 Sand Island Road, Suite 27
Honolulu, Hawaii 96819
(808) 259-5429

Request No. 607

THE WEDDING
OF YOUR DREAMS
On Your Own Private Yacht

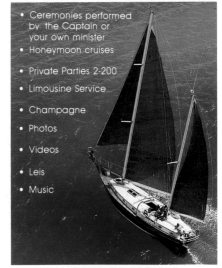

- Ceremonies performed by the Captain or your own minister
- Honeymoon cruises
- Private Parties 2-200
- Limousine Service
- Champagne
- Photos
- Videos
- Leis
- Music

RESERVATIONS:
Toll Free (800) 367-8047 ext. 264
(808) 235-8264

Honolulu Sailing Co.

45-995 Wailele Road, #49
Kaneohe, HI 96744

Request No. 608

DECISIONS, DECISIONS, DECISIONS...

HONEYMOONS

With thousands of honeymooners flocking to Hawaii each year, there have been created a wide variety of choices available from which to select the ideal package for the budget-minded as well as upscale travelers.

One of the largest tour wholesalers servicing Hawaii that offers such a diversity is **MTI Vacations** based in Chicago. Their honeymoon packages combine island options with a range of prices. Clients select their hotel preferences and neighbor island plans and MTI tailors their honeymoon to fit the couple's budget. With the MTI honeymoon package comes more than $125 in free room upgrades and special gifts.

A convenient way to book hotels or condominiums directly is through a well-established management company such as **Aston Hotels & Resorts** and **Hawaiiana Resorts**.

MTI's Hawaii is a honeymooners' paradise.

Avery Helm

Your new life together. Romantic. Intimate. These special moments deserve Hawaii, where memories that last a lifetime are made.
MTI Vacations celebrates your honeymoon with free upgrades and gifts especially for you.
All it takes is the two of you—and MTI Vacations. The rest just seems to happen.

E.T. Masterson

OVER **$125** VALUE

Honeymoon in Hawaii with MTI and receive FREE upgrades and special gifts— compliments of MTI Vacations!

- FREE Room Upgrades
- FREE Rental Car Upgrades
- FREE Champagne
- FREE $10 Gift Certificate
- FREE Gift Basket and Honeymoon Photograph
- FREE Pineapples

Free upgrades and gifts available at participating honeymoon hotels and condos.

Call your professional travel agent today!

MTI VACATIONS®

Request No. 60

Clockwise from left: a couple has some fun with authentic South Pacific costumes at the Polynesian Cultural Center. A sun worshipper catches a few rays between more strenuous activities on Maui's westside.

Make Hawaii Yours.

Enjoy the Hawaii honeymoon you've dreamed of at one of the Aston's 29 hotels or resorts and drive a free compact Budget Rent a Car every day. As honeymooners, you'll also receive hundreds of dollars in free meals, gifts, and admissions. Rates from $51 to $199 daily.

ASTON HONEYMOON

Toll Free (800) 92-ASTON (922-7866)

Budget rent a car®

ASTON Hotels & Resorts®

HAWAII'S SPECIAL HONEYMOON

A convenient way to book hotels or condominiums directly is through a well-established management company such as **Aston Hotels & Resorts** and **Hawaiiana Resorts**.

Both have excellent packages on all major islands. Aston offers a free **Budget Rent a Car** as well as free meals, gifts and admissions to honeymooners. Hawaiiana's popular "seventh night free" promotion is also practical for honeymooners who typcially want to travel around less than most travelers.

In Maui's Kaanapali Resort is the lovely **Kaanapali Beach Hotel.** Guests enjoy beach activities of every kind, two championship golf courses and a tennis ranch nearby. Fine dining, nightly entertainment and dancing under the

Budget can help make your very special visit to the islands carefree and complete with guaranteed reservations on your choice of convertibles, sedans, Jeeps, luxury cars at special low rates with unlimited mileage.

Plus valuable free admissions, free meals and free gifts.

Rent with confidence from Hawaii's leading car rental company.

See your travel agent or
PHONE TOLL FREE
800-527-7000
P.O. Box 15188
Honolulu, Hawaii 96830-5188
And for your wedding, rent Lincolns from Budget.

Budget rent a car®

Come Celebrate!

The Polynesian Cultural Center is celebrating its 25th anniversary throughout 1988. Even if you've been here before, enjoy a happy return and experience...
- **"This is Polynesia"** evening extravaganza—the world's most exciting Polynesian revue.
- **"Pageant of the Long Canoes,"** a water-borne show in the Hale Aloha amphitheater.
- **Seven authentic South Pacific villages:** Samoa, Maori New Zealand, Fiji, old Hawaii, Tahiti, the Marquesas and Tonga.
- **An all-you-can-eat dinner buffet feast.** • **And much, much more.**

25th anniversary

The PCC is open Monday–Saturday (closed Sunday) from 12:30 p.m. For information and reservations, stop by our Waikiki ticket office in the Royal Hawaiian Shopping Center, ground floor of Bldg. C; or call **293-3333** or **923-1861.** From the mainland, call tollfree: **1-800-367-7060.**

POLYNESIAN CULTURAL CENTER
There's never been a better year to see the South Pacific in a day.

Affordable, Romantic
Weddings in Hawaii
by
Mother of the Bride
4633 Aukai Ave.
Honolulu, Hawaii 96816

call **(808) 737-1818**

or toll free
1-800-367-8047

Request No. 613

stars add to the casual, fun atmosphere of this famed resort. With a booking of five nights or more, the hotel offers free car rental and other complimentary activities.

Just two miles north of Kaanapali is a fine resort condominium. The **Royal Kahana Resort** is on a good sandy beach and the units are nicely furnished with views of ocean and the West Maui mountains. Moderately priced restaurants and shops are just steps away and the Kaanapali Airport is less than a mile.

No trip to Hawaii is complete unless it includes a visit to the number one paid visitor attraction, the **Polynesian Cultural Center** in Laie on Oahu's north shore.

In its 26th year, the PCC was founded by the Church of Jesus Christ of Latter-day Saints (Mormon) as a means of providing employment to students from the South Pacific attending the nearby Brigham Young University-Hawaii campus.

The PCC succeeds in giving visitors a truly authentic glimpse into Polynesia with daytime visits to seven villages of the Pacific. Topped with the evening buffet and polynesian revue, this attraction remains a truly memorable highlight to any Hawaiian vacation.

Over the past decade other neighbor islands have spent considerable sums promoting their islands as destinations. But there is a low-profile island with a rich Hawaiian history and beauty that is virtually unknown in the visitor industry. That island is marvelous **Molokai.**

Just minutes by air from Honolulu, Molokai offers true tranquility for the honeymooning couple who wants an alternative to bright lights and city life. Nice hotels and golf courses lessen the primitive image Molokai conjures up in the mind. And for the adventuresome, the seemingly unexplored valleys and canyons offer a nice departure from the other islands.

Whatever the choices in a Hawaiian honeymoon, a couple's memories are sure to be filled with spectacular vistas, fun activities and the scent of plumeria.

Note: If you would like additional information from any advertisers in this Hawaii Honeymoon Guide, use the Reader Service Request Form (Envelope) provided herein. For faster service contact those advertisers who have provided toll free numbers.

Home, Home on the Beach.

The Royal Kahana Resort offers a condominium home on the beach just a few miles north of Maui's famed restored whaling port of Lahaina. You will enjoy all the comforts of a private home plus the service and amenities of a resort hotel.

Each spacious studio, one- or two-bedroom condominium overlooks the Pacific with incredible sunset views of neighboring Lanai and Molokai. Each features: central air-conditioning, telephones, color television, washer and dryer, private lanais and daily maid service.

For the sports or leisure buff: a large pool with cabana, two tennis courts, shuffleboard and his and her saunas. Nearby are attractions such as Lahaina and Kaanapali, an antique sugar cane train, two championship golf courses, fine restaurants, craft shops, shoreline and lush Maui countryside.

Rates from $72 per day.

For toll free reservations call:

U.S. (800) 421-0767

Or Contact:

Royal Kahana Resort
4365 Honoapiilani Highway
Lahaina, Maui, HI 96761

Phone: (808) 669-5911

ROYAL KAHANA RESORT
ON THE BEACH ON MAUI

Request No. 614

HAWAIIANA RESORTS
At Home in the Islands

Seventh night free!

Ahh, this is the life. A home of your own on the island of your choice. Nothing to do but play tennis or golf. Or sit on the beach.

At a Hawaiiana resort, you'll have all the comforts of home in Hawaii's most popular resort destinations. You'll enjoy spacious island living with the convenience of full kitchens. You'll be close to all the activities and attractions that make for a great Hawaiian vacation. And when you stay six nights, your seventh night is free.

We offer a range of beautiful accommodations that match your lifestyle and fit your budget. So call our toll-free number or see your travel agent. And make yourself at home in the islands.

KAUAI
In Poipu:
Whalers Cove and
Kiahuna
In Princeville:
Sandpiper Village and
Hanalei Bay Resort

OAHU
In Waikiki:
Discovery Bay
On the North Shore:
Kuilima Estates
HAWAII
In Kona: Kona Reef

MAUI
In Kihei: Maui Vista and
Laule'a Maui Beach Club
In Kaanapali:
Maui Kaanapali Villas
and Kaanapali Royal

 Hawaiiana Resorts

1-800-367-7040
In Canada, 1-800-423-8733, ext. 159

Request No. 615

Request No. 616

Weddings in Paradise

With "newlyweds" in mind, Paradise Park presents romantic weddings in enchanted settings. Surround yourself in our gardens filled with exotic flowers of the islands.

We are located in Manoa Valley, one of the most beautiful and historically significant sites in Hawaiian history.

Wedding packages are available, or our consultant can customize the wedding to fulfill your dreams. We can take care of every detail as well as provide all the "special" touches that will make the difference.

Paradise Park, Inc.
3737 Manoa Road
Honolulu, Hawaii 96822
(808) 988-2141

Wedding attire provided by Tuxedo Junction

A Taste of the Real Hawaii on Kaanapali Beach

Feel the magic embrace of Maui's golden days and starry nights. And be pampered by a staff who understands how special these moments are. Our perfect Hawaiian Honeymoon includes deluxe oceanview room, fruit basket with champagne and souvenir flutes, gift book and sunset cruise. **From just $500 for two, for three nights.**

Fresh Pineapple
Lei making and so much more.

KA'ANAPALI BEACH HOTEL

We're a Hawaiian hotel, not just another hotel in Hawaii.
2525 Kaanapali Parkway, Lahaina, Maui, Hawaii 96761-1987
See your Travel Agent or Phone Toll Free 1-800-367-5170

Reservations by **OUTRIGGER** Hotels Hawaii

Request No. 617